CHILDREN'S SECRETS

BOOKS BY THOMAS J. COTTLE

Time's Children: Impressions of Youth
The Abandoners: Portraits of Loss, Separation and Neglect
The Prospect of Youth: Contexts for Sociological Inquiry
The Voices of School: Educational Issues Through Personal Accounts
Out of Discontent: Visions of the Contemporary University (*with Craig R. Eisendrath and Laurence Fink*)
Black Children, White Dreams
The Present of Things Future: Explorations of Time in Human Experience (*with Stephen L. Klineberg*)
A Family Album: Portraits of Intimacy and Kinship
Perceiving Time: An Investigation with Men and Women
Busing
Children in Jail
Barred from School
Black Testimony
Psychotherapy: Current Perspectives (*with Phillip Whitten*)
College: Reward and Betrayal
Private Lives and Public Accounts
Adolescent Psychology: Contemporary Perspectives
Human Adjustment (*with Phillip Whitten*)
Children's Secrets

Children's Secrets

THOMAS J. COTTLE

ANCHOR PRESS/DOUBLEDAY
Garden City, New York 1980

To Claudia Mari Cottle, Jason Edwin Cottle, and Sonya Ruth Cottle, our children; and to the memory of Miss Leah Weinstock, our beloved aunt.

ISBN: 0-385-14457-1
Library of Congress Catalog Card Number 78-14696

Acknowledgments

I would like to first thank The Ford Foundation, The Children's Defense Fund of the Washington Research Project, and The Tavistock Clinic for their assistance and encouragement. In addition, there are many people who in all sorts of ways have contributed to the writing and production of this book. They include Richard and Ruth Rogers, Deirdre McSweeny, who as much as anyone ignited the idea for the book, Sally Makacynas, Professor William Hunt, Rosemary Daniels, Tim McGinnis, Marie Brown, Ellen Levine, Dr. George Pollock, Kay Field, Miss Anna Freud, and the staff of The Hampstead Child Therapy Clinic, Professors Robert Townsend, Robert May, and Gerald M. Platt, Professor Oliver W. Holmes, Hanna Holmes, and Barbara and Sidney Cheresh.

A special thank-you to my friends and associates at Columbia College in Chicago, notably Mirron Alexandroff and Lya Dym Rosenblum; Amherst College, notably Rose Olver; and the Harvard Medical School, notably the people in the Department of Psychiatry at the Cambridge Hospital.

Always I owe a special debt to my immediate family: My wife Kay M. Cottle; my parents, Gitta Gradova and Maurice H. Cottle; my parents in law, Bab and Ed Mikkelsen; and of course our children, to whom this book is dedicated.

Finally, perhaps the most important thank-you goes to the families whose accounts are heard in this volume. Sharing a piece of one's life with a friend is always an act of generosity and kindness. In this case, the families demonstrated rare acts of courage in addition to their generosity. I cannot thank them enough; I hope they know my feelings for them.

CONTENTS

Introduction   1

PART I   *FAMILY DISINTEGRATION*   9
"*The Myth of Stability*"

ONE
Parental Abandonment   11

TWO
Infidelity   41

PART II   *FAMILY VIOLENCE*   61
"*The Myth of Harmony*"

THREE
Physical Battering   63

FOUR
Incest   86

PART III   *FINANCIAL MATTERS*   105
"*The Myth of Affluence*"

FIVE
Debt and Bankruptcy   107

SIX
Unemployment   127

PART IV MATTERS OF DEVIANCE   153
         "The Myth of Being Straight"

         SEVEN
         Sexual Practices   155

PART V MENTAL ILLNESS   181
        "The Myth of Normalcy"

        EIGHT
        Alcoholism and Drug Taking   183

        NINE
        Breakdown, Hospitalization, and Suicide   209

PART VI CONCLUDING REMARKS   245

         TEN
         Children's Secrets, Family Myths   247
         Bibliography   267

Introduction

All of us as children and adults have kept a fair number of secrets, or at least promised to keep them. At one point in our lives the promise not to tell a living soul of a certain matter became the essence of our bond of friendship. At another point in our lives our secret keeping not only strengthened our bond of friendship but allowed others, perhaps, to lighten their burden. Secret keeping, in other words, offers protection now and again, just as it enhances human attachments. Naturally, if secrets bond some people more closely together, they also can play a divisive role in friendships. All a child has to do to cause frenzy in another child is announce that an important secret is being kept. Hell hath no fury, one might say, like a child denied access to secrets.

This is a book about children's secrets. It is, moreover, a personal book in that it presents a series of portraits, life studies of children who share one personal trait in common: They all are keeping secret some significant story about their family. It is also a personal book in the sense that my own involvement with and investment in these children cannot for a minute be disguised.

For more than twelve years I have been researching families, listening to parents and children speak about their lives, their hopes and ideals as well as their regrets and misgivings. During this time I have spoken to family members individually as well as together, since often people are influenced by the presence of others. If we do not establish our roles out of the context of our human surroundings, then we perform for others. I have heard children talk about their parents, to their parents, with their parents. I have heard various versions of the same event or experience. I have heard the parents' version, the child's version when he or she is alone, and the child's version when a parent is present. I have also heard the child's version in my presence, and read the child's version, written when the child was truly alone. From all of these experiences with various and varying versions, I have come to realize not only that family members hold different versions of particular experiences but that there are often versions of an experience that are never told at all. Well, this is not completely accurate. Some versions of experience are for members of the immediate family only, which means not for relatives, friends, teachers, and most especially psychological researchers. Other versions are meant only for parents, which means they are not to be discussed in front of the children. Still other versions are meant only for certain family members; one's age or sex may not be the basis on which a decision to tell that version, or that story, is made. Put in different terms, we begin to recognize that families not only perpetuate myths about family matters but occasionally demand that a particular experience, or version of it, be kept secret. And this demand for secrecy, as we will note in the following pages, also contributes to the production of family myths.

While some stories are rarely told on the grounds that the teller or his or her family would emerge with undue pride, most stories are kept secret because of the shame that might befall a family member, or an entire family, if that story were made public. This is another aspect of the protective feature of secret keeping. There is a catch to the point, however, one that I will elaborate on in later chapters: namely, to keep certain secrets and thereby ensure that the dreaded shadow of shame will not fall upon a family or family member often causes the secret keeper to feel shame. It seems ironic that the act of secret keeping should represent a process whereby people not only prevent shame from spreading to their family but in addition take the shame into themselves. The act almost reminds us of the servant of the King confronted with the order to taste all food before it is served to his honored master.

As the reader can deduce from these opening passages, this book not only focuses on children's secrets but also examines family myths and the shame that might accrue to a family were a particular secret made known, as well as the shame that seems to accrue to the child secret keeper. From these three concepts—family secrets, myths, and shame—we derive the outline of our exploration. To begin, we will examine secrets kept by children about family matters that might very well bring shame to that family were the secret not kept. This is an important point. As an operational definition, I have selected from a host of children's secrets those accounts wherein the fear of shame is a realistic one. The stories or versions of experiences are not superficial or capricious, but refer to utterly serious matters for the family in question. Along with the potential public effect of a secret being made known, we will also explore the effect on the child of keeping secrets. Some secrets, after all, are kept by children with no demonstrable side effects. Other secrets, however, seem to touch children's most inner recesses, or influence their thinking or feeling about an issue that looms especially relevant given their age, circumstances, or activities. Our eye, then, is on the actual secret as well as on the meaning of keeping that secret to a family and to the child sworn to secrecy.

We have organized the secrets according to the family myth ideally perpetuated by the secret. Thus, we have combined secrets involving parental abandonment and infidelity into a category called "The Myth of Stability." We have, moreover, combined secrets involving physical battering and incest into a category labeled "The Myth of Harmony." Secrets revolving around financial issues, notably debt, bankruptcy, and unemployment constitute a category called "The Myth of Affluence." A fourth category, "The Myth of Being Straight," is comprised of a discussion of secrets devoted to sexual matters. Finally, secrets involving problems of alcoholism and drug abuse as well as mental breakdown, hospitalization, and suicide, constitute "The Myth of Normalcy."

In each chapter we will consider actual accounts of children as they reveal secrets, in most cases for the first time. In all instances, the children *and* their families have granted permission to publish these accounts. This point is stressed, for given the nature of many of the following accounts, it is difficult to believe that some of the families would be willing to make such an extraordinary transformation from secrecy to public admission, or confession. In methodological terms, all the families were presented those sections of the manuscript pertinent to their accounts. They read the sections and checked for errors in content and tone. As noted in later chapters, some families asked that certain passages be deleted. All family members knew from the beginning of our friendship that I might someday write about them. Not surprisingly, then, only one family refused to allow me to publish the particular chapter about them. To maintain confidentiality, the names and in some cases places of family residence have been changed.

I have discussed rather quickly here some of the details and methods of the research. For those readers interested in the development of these so-called life studies, several references may prove worthwhile.[1] Without belaboring the method, however, a few points should be clarified.

While my research on children's secrets has been proceeding for nine years, in truth I did not articulate the topic of children's secrets until seven of these years had passed. I point out this fact because it is important to understand that in most cases when speaking with the children, I remained totally unaware that anything "peculiar" was going on in the family; specifically, that the child was keeping some secret. In most every account reported in the book, the child's confession came as a surprise to me. In most of these instances, moreover, I was the first person to hear the secret, which usually the children had been safeguarding for several years. I should also point out, as the following chapters make plain, that my relationship with the children and their families often changed markedly after the revelation of the secret. Occasionally the child's confession caused our relationship to grow much closer; sometimes the confession had just the opposite effect.

Given the nature of my work generally, and the specific focus on children's secrets, it seems relevant to note that I did not use a tape recorder. Moreover, I tried to keep all note taking until after I had left the family's home. All accounts, therefore, are reconstructed; they never represent, however, composites of more than one person or one conversation. Granted, complete accuracy is sacrificed when following this procedure. Yet the reader can understand the physical impracticalities of using tape recorders during such trying conversations. There is also a personal factor: I could not have dealt with the children during these moments of confession in the presence of mechanical devices like recording machines, even when we were sitting alone in a kitchen or living room, which we often were not. Indeed, several of the accounts took place in the street or in parks precisely because the children sought environments free of

---

[1] See for example T. J. Cottle, *Black Children, White Dreams* and *Private Lives and Public Accounts*. See also Robert Coles, *Children of Crisis*, Vols. 2 and 3 (Boston: Atlantic-Little, Brown, 1972), and *Telling Lives* (Washington, D.C.: New Republic Book Company, 1979).

eavesdroppers, be they human or mechanical. In this regard, it should be understood that in many instances, permission to publish particular accounts was granted as many as six years after the actual confession of the child's secret. It should also be made clear that whereas I was the first hearer of many of the secrets, some of the secrets referred to events occurring several years before a particular conversation took place.

Earlier I used the term "life study" and indicated that this book is comprised of a series of these life studies. I mentioned, too, that life studies, predicated on letting people describe in their own words how their lives are being led, should be differentiated from so-called clinical case studies. The children heard in this book were not patients. Nor must we think of their accounts as mere illustration of some aspect of secret keeping. We reproduce long passages precisely to reinforce the point that the children are not illustrations of some "greater" conceptual issue, and to let the reader experience these children in a more complete sense. The accounts, therefore, should not be viewed as anecdotes, but rather as the expression *and* interpretation of essential aspects of the children's lives. Accounts of the nature we are about to consider represent not only a *rendering* of material based on long-term interviewing but in addition a person's own *interpretation* of a situation or experience. That is, within the passages, we find not only the experience children wish to describe but the intellectual and emotional meaning they give to these descriptions.

In undertaking research deriving from the principle (and method) of allowing people to describe in their own words how their lives are led, one question invariably comes to mind: How does one know, really, that the truth is being recorded? How do I know that what people are telling me, in their own minds, is a truthful rendering of experience? All researchers, surely, must confront this question, but those of us doing intensive interviewing retain a special and personal investment in the problem: We wish to know whether there is something about us, as people, that keeps others from telling us the truth of their lives, or in this instance, their secrets. In a word, we must keep an eye on the method of our research, and an eye on the way we, as the friends of those we "study," transact our personal and research business.

There is a second problem about the research aspect of truth telling. As we become increasingly implicated in the lives of families, we find ourselves hearing accounts of experiences and secrets that clearly are at variance with the accounts and secrets family members share with one another. So, whereas at times we wonder whether we are learning the "real truth," at other times we find ourselves the only people in the family discovering the "real truth" of some secret. Said differently, I often find myself involved in a family's system of transacting secrets in a different way than other family members are involved, which would be all right except that it adds to my confusion about the truth of a particular experience or secret. Then again, the special role I play provides opportunities for family members to check with me about *their* readings of the way secrets are transacted in the family. Presumably, as an outsider or mere observer, I should bring some reasonable perspective to the matter of the secret.

Now, while I ponder the validity of these studies of families and their secrets, the families themselves carry their own questions, about me, and for me. They wonder whether I am capable or worthy of knowing a secret when it is told to me, and what I might do with the information made available to me. At least they worry about these issues early in our friendship. As time passes, many of the families present other concerns to me. They wish to know, for example, whether I know and appreciate the problems their children are facing. They wish to know how I perceive the development of their children. Are their children growing "properly"? They also ask me the unanswerable questions: What will happen to their child? And why has their child turned out as he or she has?

In the past, I have been accused of writing in an excessively naïve manner about families, and children in particular. I write, it is said, as though I actually understand very little about human psychology; so clearly the naïveté is misleading if not deceitful. I argue the accusation by saying this: No one trained in any school of psychology enters a human relationship free of theoretical or ideological biases. They are the price one pays for being in the profession. Occasionally the training or schooling allows one to see more, occasionally it makes one blind to many factors of human development. At times I encounter a human life that, admittedly, would seem to conform to some psychological theory, but this is hardly the typical case. More typical is the experience of believing one knows why certain behavior, say, surrounding a secret, may be prevalent in a family, only to see all one's easy interpretations and analytic conclusions dissipate as one learns more about the family. Perhaps I would rather appear naïve than constantly twist around people's personal accounts so that they will conform to my own biases and perspectives. As I say, I am more than a trifle perplexed about what honesty means in the way I conduct life study research. And as, well, naïve as it sounds, I feel I am never certain about matters that deal with social and psychological events. I try to remain tentative if only to impress upon myself the fact that no matter how much I may know about someone, even his or her secrets, there is always much I do not know. There is also the constant flow of everyday experiences which have the potential to change people, their personalities, and, equally important, the ways they describe and interpret themselves, as well as their secrets, to themselves and to others.

We cannot be certain why personalities form as they do. We cannot be certain why some children grow up to be criminals or policemen, others grow up to be judges, and still others grow up to be corrupt judges. We do not yet know why a child from a seemingly upstanding and honorable family would enter a life reeking of immorality, or why a child from the most despicable, inhuman, and violent community would grow up to be a person of exquisite taste, gentleness, honesty, and love. Correlations assist us in defining the statistical variance. Theories and hunches aid us in delineating some of the parameters of personality development. But a final accounting of what makes us what we are still rests in the hands of the gods. We must never be deceived by manifest simplicity. Singular causes for complex behavior inevitably become an approximation of causation, never a complete explanation. Manifest simplicity refers to *our* reading of an experience or piece of behavior; it never completely refers to that experience or piece of behavior. When we are certain about these matters, we deceive ourselves. Our dogmatism derives from our undying and unquestioned belief in the methods and theories that have come to dominate our perceptions and observations. Formally trained or not, each of us views the world according to preconceptions, which form the instant we learn language. Probably they begin forming even before then. When we say we are speaking objectively about human processes, it is merely a shorthand way of announcing that we try to be judicious, unimpassioned, and systematic observers. But we cannot be objective in the literal meaning of that term. The phenomena we study preclude purely objective treatment.

How, then, do we progress; how do we begin to approach something like children's secrets in a somewhat new way, free of the preconceptions I claim to be inevitable? Each of us arrives at a different answer. My own is the one I would say to a person seeking to determine how to tell something of the utmost importance. Say it in your own words, I have admonished friends. Forget theories and interpretations and the implications of what you are saying and express it in the most natural, honest way you can; I'll try to listen in accordance with the same rules. I'll try to listen to your words, attend to your account as one would listen to a bit of history. What comes up will come up, but let us allow it to arise before we hunt for answers and meaning. In this regard, I am reminded of Freud's original definition of dream interpretation. The patient, he wrote, recounts a dream, and then, for as long as it takes, recounts the associations he or she can make to the dream. When the associations have been reported, the dream is interpreted. Similarly, when a person has told us all that he or she can of a particular experience, a secret, perhaps, my assessment, or reading of the work with that experience, is completed.

I raise these points in the hope of emphasizing our need for new languages, new approaches, new ways of thinking in psychology, even knowing that the new approaches will touch on "old" truths and, ineluctably, create their own preconceptions about personality. The points seem particularly relevant to a study of children's secrets. Almost in my sleep I hear the parents asking those two fundamental questions: Why has the child turned out this way? What will become of the child? Indeed, I begin to realize that this entire introduction may be nothing more than a wordy justification for me to answer, when those questions are posed: I wish I knew.

Part I

FAMILY DISINTEGRATION

"The Myth of Stability"

ONE

Parental Abandonment

No one should make the assumption that all families keep secrets or live as if they actually believed in purely mythical ideals and circumstances. My own research is hardly of the sort that would either confirm or disconfirm the notion of the universality of family myths or secrets. Throughout this book, therefore, we must guard against a tendency to generalize too broadly from a relatively few life studies. We must also beware of an often insidious predisposition on the part of many researchers: namely, to believe that the whole world seems to turn on the very thing they happen to be researching. In my own case, by the time I had articulated children's secrets as the topic to be explored, I began discovering secrets in all the families I encountered, on a research as well as a purely social basis. Whereas the paranoid person might be said to be harboring thoughts that the world is keeping secrets from him or her, I, on the other hand, was convinced the world was prepared to share their family secrets with me. Surely a lapse in a conversation or a child's uncharacteristic silence meant that I was about to be made the recipient of more data on secrets, more ammunition, if you will, for my research.

In truth, a sufficient number of children's secrets came forth, as this and the following chapters make clear. It was also true that a good number of the families I visited on a regular basis revealed no secrets to me, or gave the slightest indication that secrets were being withheld, or that they lived according to certain mythical presuppositions. I stress this point at the outset, because our first topic is that of secrets pertaining to parental abandonment and, in the next chapter, cases of parental infidelity. Together these two phenomena constitute what we have called "The Myth of Family Stability." For obvious reasons, most families wish to give the impression to the outside world, if not to their own members, that within the home, all is calm and peaceful. Children, in the main, "appreciate" the myth since the rumblings of parental wars and the threat of separation are hardly stabilizing factors in the child's developing personality. Parents and children alike "appreciate" the knowledge that arguments need not automatically end in separation or, for that matter, death, as children often imagine. The real and fantasized stability of the family helps all its members to believe in the ultimate strength of the family and to have faith in the idea that families can wage war yet end up as allies, perhaps even closer allies than before the wars began.

Much of this is self-evident. It is also evident that families, adults and children alike, have now begun to quake under the strain of ubiquitous divorces, although divorce rates lead to a series of myths of their own. That a certain seemingly growing percentage of marriages end in divorce has just about convinced everybody that their own marriage is far more frail, precarious, and sadly, in some cases, strained than they ever recognized. Like microbes carrying illness, the threat of divorce, as they say, is in the air, and not an insignificant number of families huddle together waiting for these nasty disease carriers to reach their home. Granted, we exaggerate divorce rates, but no one can deny the increasing rates of and potential for family instability. Furthermore, no one can deny the fact that the reality and possibility of divorce are no longer topics for secrets alone. The stigma of divorce is lessening, which means that people are freer to speak about it, both to friends and to members of their own family. What was a secret between a man and woman a few decades ago is now breakfast-table conversation. Correspondingly, whether one wishes to admit to this fact or not, with the dissipation of so-called secretive material about families generally, the sacredness of marriage and more particularly the marriage bond are eroded, and marriage, in many people's eyes, becomes yet another one of life's profane monuments or institutions. Similarly the once unspoken of, shunned, and nasty idea of divorce has passed through the phase of Western history where it is no longer even especially titillating and has entered the realm of still another of life's more profane monuments or institutions.

Let me clarify these points. I am not suggesting that divorce is an innocuous event or ceremony for the people involved. Quite to the contrary. For these people, family stability may well remain a sacred concept and hope. Despite the prevalence of divorce, it may cause great pain even in the people who institute it, not to mention the people innocently victimized by it. Something else: The large majority of people who get divorced remarry, and remarry fairly soon. Divorce, in other words, is not a statement of opposition to the institution of marriage. My point is only this: as a notion, a practice, a reality, divorce no longer carries that unspeakable codicil and therefore secretive condition. Ironically though, the very "speakableness" of divorce may well be one of the matters that cause a great many people a special hurt: namely, one finds a tendency in our culture to substitute "speakability" with the successful resolution of human problems. All one has to do is speak about divorce, death, abortion, and one's psychological tensions or misgivings or fears or doubts are automatically dissipated. Letting a ghost out of a closet hardly guarantees the demise of the ghost. It doesn't even guarantee the fact that the closet safeguards other ghosts, or that it may even generate ghosts.

My own work with young people from divorced families, a topic clearly for another volume, is not easily summarized. Some children come out of the divorce psychologically scarred, and like the physiological metaphor would suggest, the scar seems to shrink over time, often a short period of time, to where it is barely noticeable. Other children do not emerge as gracefully; their scars are visible. In some instances I have found children flourishing after divorces, suggesting that while family integrity may well be one of their coveted rewards, their own family had pressure-cooked them beyond the boiling point. If not scarred, these children surely had been scalded, and divorce had brought them, manifestly, lifesaving relief.

Now, if these impressions are valid—and let us be reminded that the data derived from psychotherapeutic work with children from a divorced family necessarily produces a serious research bias—if children are emerging from divorce with all sorts of reactions, some desirable, some less so, then the act of divorce itself cannot adequately explain the various reactions. In other words, there must be myriad factors attending each divorce action that influence the child or, shall we say, produce or prevent that proverbial psychic scar. Even this is too simple, for there remains a temporal factor to be considered: Will the child now with the scar lose it in years to come, and will the child now free of scar tissue develop the scars as a function of experiences he or she *may* encounter later in life?

This is not the proper volume for a discussion of divorce. In fact, this chapter addresses only one aspect of divorce, an aspect, not so incidentally, that looms as one of those potentially damaging features in some but certainly not all divorce cases. In this and the following chapters, then, our concern is abandonment. More specifically, the two life studies in this chapter illustrate instances of parents abandoning children, children, moreover, who were obliged to keep the abandonment secret. While divorce, generally, may be perceived by the child as abandonment, my own impression is that this assumption is overworked. Many divorced parents do not abandon their children, but some still do, and if one asks these children to tell of their parents' divorce, it is abandonment that they speak about, and not necessarily family dissolution. The perceived or felt abandonment, in other words, may be heard in the child's account of divorce, but external events, and more precisely the new environment established for the child, may well dissipate these perceptions and sensations. In the cases of Janic Sutlcworth and Willie Fryer, however, there was nothing about the "new" environments in which they found themselves that could possibly counteract the literal assault *not* of divorce, but of outright human abandonment. And the fact that they were meant to keep these experiences as well as their feelings about the experiences secret only exacerbated their despair.

JANIE SUTLEWORTH

Janie Sutleworth's story is not especially unusual. What happened in her family happens in a great many families. Still, one hesitates to label her story representative of the experiences of parents abandoning their family. I never knew John Sutleworth, a man who would have been in his early forties. Indeed, I believed him to be dead; I am certain one of the children told me this. In the notes recording my early conversations with families, I found these words: "Father may have died of terminal illness; no indication of psychological stuff." Janie at the time was ten, her brother, Stevie, two years older.

Adrian and John Sutleworth had been high school sweethearts. They married immediately upon graduating from high school, as everyone expected they would do. What surprised their friends, how-ever, was the length of time they waited before having children. It was almost ten years before Stephen was born. When asked about the delay, Adrian Sutleworth would reply, "Why must there be a rush? We got married to be together, not so we could have chil-dren." There was irritation as well as anxiety in her response.

It was clear to her mother, Lucy Dexter, that Adrian's marriage was not working, although she never breathed a word of her suspi-cion to anyone. Her husband had died, presumably without any knowledge of his daughter's marital problems, although as Mrs. Dexter said, "My husband was of the old school. When children weren't born to a marriage within a couple of years, he called it a bad marriage. But being in the old school meant he wouldn't ever say anything to a living soul."

I learned quickly that in the Sutleworth and Dexter families no one told anybody much about anything even when, in that prover-bial way, everybody already knew about everything. Perhaps talk was unnecessary, as the families were only too aware of their problems. If it worked out best for them to sweep their miseries under the rug, who was I to barge into the Sutleworth home and demand some soul-baring session. Yet everyone would have resisted the idea, al-though the children let it be known that from time to time it would have been helpful to at least mention the subject of their father, if not his absence. I say absence because after several months of meet-ing with the family, it was obvious that John Sutleworth was alive. There may not have been a single reminder of him in the house, but he was not dead. Then, on a freezing afternoon a week before Christ-mas, three years after my first meeting with Mrs. Sutleworth, she walked me to the front door, reached her hand out, and gave me a slip of yellow paper. It was a laundry bill. "Other side," she remarked sternly. On the paper was the name Fred Corcoran and a telephone number. "You want to meet my husband, Fred Corcoran will intro-duce you."

"I guess I should say thank you," I mumbled. "But I must tell you this is beginning to take the form of the sort of mystery stories I adore."

"Call it a Christmas present," she answered, a deadly serious ex-pression on her face. "A present not for you; for the children."

John and Adrian Sutleworth thought of themselves as middle-class people. John was an electrician, his wife, a part-time office employee who never wanted or needed a full-time job. Early in their marriage, John tried to establish his own electrical contracting firm, but the venture failed. His talent, he learned painfully, lay in doing electrical work, not in bookkeeping, estimating, running a business. Henry Selwyn, his original boss, was happy to take the young man back. Sutleworth was the best man he had. At twenty-one, there wasn't an electrical problem he couldn't solve. If John wanted to return, he was welcome, and a raise came with the acceptance.

By the time they were twenty-seven, the Sutleworths had purchased their own home, a small two-story brick house with a small yard. And then their children were born. The Sutleworths were known as a quiet family. Their neighbors commented: "Who even knows they're alive? He leaves in the morning, comes home at night. She goes shopping. Other than that, who sees them! They must have some friends. And their children are pretty." Indeed, their children were pretty, and quiet. If they fought or fussed, no one heard them. If they caused their parents problems, no one ever knew.

As it happened, a teacher in Janie's school made a passing mention of the family to me. "Strange," she said, "how a perfectly healthy, simple, nice girl could suddenly come down with so many problems." That was the beginning. Janie was nine. She had been the perfect student, never late, never absent, never anything that would cause a teacher to look twice at her. She was not the most cheerful child, but she had energy and patience, her playful side and her serious side. Then, suddenly, the perfect little girl had begun to stutter and be absent from school. It was thought to be nothing serious, merely normal periodic illnesses. But the illnesses were not so normal, as teachers reported Janie's occasional fainting spells in class. Moreover, I learned from Mrs. Dexter that only some of Janie's periodic absences were due to normal childhood illnesses. Along with the colds and stomachaches was excessive fatigue caused by her having been up all night with terrifying dreams of screaming monsters and animals. "Can you imagine," one teacher told me, "the quiet little girl with the noisy dreams. I suppose it has to come out somewhere, sometime."

My first hunch was that her grandfather's death might have triggered some of Janie's problems. There is no telling how a child will respond even to the death of someone to whom the child was not particularly close. I often think, if Freud shocked the world with proclamations about children's sexuality, we might be shocked again to know the depth of their understanding of living and dying. It seemed, therefore, a reasonable hypothesis: Grandfather dies, granddaughter has psychological reaction, even though the psychological reaction follows the death by several years. It could happen; a delayed reaction.

Three months after meeting with the family and gently raising the problem of Janie's night terrors and sudden onset of stammering, both symptoms disappeared. I became a close friend; a hero to my teacher friends in Janie's school. I warned everybody: "I've done nothing; the symptoms will probably reappear." The stammering did. Mrs. Sutleworth was delighted to send Janie to a friend of mine, a pediatric neurologist. Evidently, no one had suggested consulting a doctor, which meant that Mrs. Sutleworth had taken the burdens, and guilts, of Janie's illness upon herself. When the medical examinations turned up nothing, she was content that she had done everything possible for her daughter. If Janie's stammering resumed, the responsibility no longer rested with her.

Janie Sutleworth was almost thirteen years old that Christmas week when her mother handed me the laundry bill with the name of Fred Corcoran on it.

Fred Corcoran had known John Sutleworth, rather well, in fact. They had gone to school together and afterward learned the electrical trade together. He attended the Sutleworths' wedding, which took place the month of his own marriage to a girl friend of Adrian's. The Corcoran marriage had ended in divorce within two years, after what Fred called World War X. In the last few years, he had seen John Sutleworth only a handful of times. "Divorced guys," he said, "don't mess around too much with these old family types." He didn't know John no longer lived at home. But he knew an electrical firm in another part of the state where he was certain John worked.

The unfolding of the Sutleworth story was becoming increasingly more like one of those mystery stories where the detective's client actually knows the information he has hired the detective to uncover. I say this not only to justify the inclusion of various details of the case, if I may use this word, but to give the reader some idea of what one occasionally goes through merely to find out the so-called simple facts of a family. Here I was, in the middle of winter, attempting to track down John Sutleworth with the nagging feeling that his wife probably knew where he was and in a way wanted me to know, too, but without having to announce it. So she gives me the name of a man who she believes will lead me to her husband, if he is still her husband.

But the route to John Sutleworth was circuitous. Four more people entered the chain of connections before a telephone call reached him at his home, ninety miles from where his wife and children lived. There had been no divorce. Furthermore, he knew about Janie's problems, which, judging by the sound of his voice, troubled him, but not enough that he had ever done anything to help her. In fact, my entire conversation with him, brief as it was, consisted of him remonstrating with me for having tracked him down and "meddling in affairs that were dead a long, long time ago."

"You aren't the children's father, then?" I barked angrily, thinking about the effort I was making to put some pieces of a family I barely knew back together.

"I don't think that's any of your damn business," he replied acrimoniously.

"Janie's fainting spells, stammering, night terrors, don't concern you?" I pursued him, showing him not the slightest respect.

"Ditto" came the answer.

"Could I ask you one question, Mr. Sutleworth?" I began slowly. "What the hell is going on with you, your wife, and your children?"

"All right, pal, you asked for it," he responded. I could sense him grinning.

"You aren't going to answer, I take it."

"Never said I would. You asked if you could ask a question and I said . . ."

"Yeah," I grumbled, "I remember the dialogue." You could cause me to stammer, have night terrors, *and* faint, I wanted to tell him. In fact, I said little else. But before hanging up I said, "You have any questions for me?"

"Why should I?" he responded with disdain.

"Just wondering." Now it was I who was grinning. I wanted him to know it. I wanted him to think that I, the Hercule Poirot of psychology, had it all figured out. And in a sense, I did have something figured out, because John Sutleworth never asked how I had tracked him down, which meant, I reasoned, that he assumed his wife had told me. And that meant, to me at least, that the two of them maintained contact, possibly even saw one another. And that meant that Janie and Stevie knew, God only knows what.

The day after the phone conversation I asked a psychiatrist friend if a child could faint from knowing things or having seen things he wasn't supposed to know or see. Or *think*. "I suppose he could," my friend allowed. Then he added: "I had a patient once, a little boy, who found out something terrifying to him and began to have night terrors, then started to stammer. It was as though he wanted to tell people, but he just couldn't get it out. And for good reason, too, as it turned out."

My friend's words could have applied to Janie Sutleworth. Her father left home suddenly and she couldn't bring herself to speak about it. The death of her grandfather, irrespective of whether it predated or followed her father's leaving, could only have exacerbated the problems caused by the departure and her inability to verbalize it. Yet again, the confusing thing was that John Sutleworth's attitude implied that the children knew everything about his leaving and in no way were prevented from speaking openly of the family's history. Indeed, he had acted as though he assumed I knew everything about the family. It must have been Mrs. Sutleworth, therefore, who was choking off her children, a phrase, incidentally, I found myself using quite regularly. Then again, perhaps it was Janie herself who, for one reason or another, censored the expression of her feelings.

At thirteen, Janie Sutleworth was a handsome girl with deep sad brown eyes, high cheekbones, thick black hair, all the features that would make her a beautiful woman. She spoke despairingly of her freckles, but clearly they were far more disagreeable to her than to anyone else. Appearance was important to her. Good grooming, cleanliness, looking as well as one can, were significant values for her. Had one ever quoted to her that line about beauty being only skin-deep, she would have concurred with the sentiment, but her valuation of good appearance would not have changed in the slightest.

On a cool April afternoon, I provoked Janie as hard as I had ever dared. Truthfully, I was tired of being drawn into her game of "everything in my life is fine; I don't understand why people think something's wrong around here." Aggressively, I played out the detective role, as increasingly I was doing with many of the children who appeared to be holding tightly to their precious secrets. Normally, I could restrain my eagerness to learn the special secret, but Janie's physical symptoms made her case somewhat special. "Who is it, Janie, you or your mother?"

She was confounded. "Who is what?"

"Who is it that says you're not supposed to talk about whatever it is you don't talk about?" I was merciless; my tone and manner were like nothing she had ever encountered in me. My intent, I suppose, was to reveal my impatience along with an unstated ultimatum: Either we get somewhere with the problem, or I leave! This part of the message she caught at once.

"Talk about what?"

"It isn't politics, my friend."

"You mean my father?"

"Yeah."

"You mean that he's supposed to be dead?"

"Supposed to be dead?" I could have gone more gently. The moisture in her eyes was a signal to go a bit more gently.

"Well, he was supposed to be dead."

"But he isn't?"

"I don't think so."

"Do you think, Janie, it's normal for people your age, living in circumstances like yours, not to know whether their father is alive or dead? I mean, is that part of the now generation?"

I report my words with neither relish nor pride. My strategy and demeanor hardly serve as a model for conducting friendship, much less what is called a therapeutic interaction. They reveal my frustration. If she was stammering, putting the brakes on, then I was exploding, flooring the accelerator and wanting something dangerous to happen.

Janie Sutleworth looked at me, tears falling down her cheeks. Her expression was one of profound sadness, but not contempt. One can fear one's dentist, but if he does something painful that ultimately dulls an ache, one cannot hold contempt for him. One can, however, pledge never to see him again, and I suspect Janie did that with me.

"It's not normal not to know whether or not your father is dead. I thought he was. My mother said he had gone away, and then died. Maybe she didn't say die, I can't remember. Maybe she said we were to think of him as being dead. As far as she was concerned he was dead. We weren't supposed to think of him or talk about him. She got rid of everything in the house that would remind us of him. For a while I thought he was dead. Before that I thought he would come home. Then when he didn't, I guess I must have believed he was dead. I used to cry at night, because I was afraid to let my mother know I was thinking about him. I must have done a good job convincing myself that he was dead, or if he wasn't, I would never see him again. Either way, it was *like* he was dead. I would start to hate him for going away, then I would think, how can I hate him if I don't know for sure if he went away? I can't hate a person if they die. I could have hated my mother just as much, if you think about it that way. *She* was the one who was confusing me.

"Then one day, I was nine I guess, I saw my father. Walking away from our house. I saw him. He didn't see me but I saw him. So I asked my mother and she said I was crazy, I didn't see my father. My father was dead, or as good as dead. That's what she said. That night I had my first bad dream. I can't remember anything about it other than it was scary. You know how children get afraid of ghosts and goblins—well, it was like I had seen a ghost, because I was sure I saw my father. Then I saw him again. This time there was no chance it wasn't him, because he was talking to my mother in a car. They weren't sitting close together, but I saw them. Then I saw her get out and walk toward the house. I hid behind a tree so she wouldn't see me. I think she did see me but she never said anything about it. She couldn't, because if she did see me, then she knew I saw her with my father.

"After that my nightmares really got bad. I would get so frightened I couldn't make myself stop crying or screaming. I had seen a ghost. A part of my mind knew my father was alive, another part kept telling me, no, he's dead. He has to be dead or your mother is a liar. It was like I kept telling myself, you mustn't tell anybody, you mustn't tell anybody. By then the way I speak was changing. I was so afraid to say anything because if I said the wrong thing my mother would get angry, and what if I told somebody at school, not even on purpose? I didn't even tell Stevie. I don't know why, but I was afraid to tell him. I wanted to tell *you* a long time ago because I thought you aren't really part of the family, I mean you're not like a close friend, so maybe you should know. But then I changed my mind because I thought that would only get me in trouble. With things like this, you don't start telling strangers, and you'll always be sort of a stranger.

"So I went to my grandmother. This was after my grandfather died. I was sorry when he died because he was a nice man. He didn't play too much with Stevie and me, but I always felt he liked us. He didn't make a fuss about us like my grandmother did, he just took us for what we were. I think I almost liked that better than people making a big fuss over children. Children need love, not a big fuss. Anyway, after he died, I talked to my grandmother. What she said really made me upset; that's when everybody thought I was sick in my head because my grandfather died and my father was gone, too. But it wasn't my grandfather. It was just what she said, which you want to know, naturally."

"I guess I do," I said quietly.

"I'm trying," Janie whispered, wiping her face with the back of her hand. "My grandmother told me the whole story, how my father and mother shouldn't have gotten married because my father always ran around with other women, even though my mother knew about it. My grandmother told her not to marry him but she did. She said she couldn't get my grandfather to say anything to my mother because he didn't think it was his business. So she told my mother, get rid of him and tell the children he died. Tell him you'll never see him again and he can't see the children again. It will be better for everybody. And she said if these things bothered me I could always come to her, not my mother, because my father had been so horrible to my mother, it wasn't fair for Stevie and me to bother her about him again. She would tell me everything I needed to know.

"I told her I saw my father. 'Of course you did,' she said. 'He comes back even though your mother and me tell him not to. It's strictly for the children. A man who runs around with all the women he has can't be a good father.' I told her I want him home, but she said that's only what I think now; I would learn when I grew up it was the best thing for me not to see him. She also said I shouldn't tell people because it would make my mother look bad. People don't get angry with men who leave their families. They only look at the woman and decide there must be something wrong with them. So I had to learn to keep my mouth closed to sort of protect my mother. The thing is, everything she said made sense to me. Children don't think things are confusing when their parents or grandparents tell them like my grandmother told me. What they do is later on think, I must have been crazy to think that. At the time everything makes sense. But each year I sort of had to rethink for myself, now just how *do* I feel about my mother, my father, my grandmother, my brother, me? Everything made sense at the time, but nothing made sense later on when I let myself think about it. I sometimes think I had my fainting spells because everything got so confusing. I didn't know who to believe. You spend your life tiptoeing around everybody. Sometimes you can't even remember who you told what to, or who you aren't supposed to say anything to. That's sort of my story."

To say that I was touched by Janie's account hardly captures the true feelings. But there was one more question: Had Janie made contact with her father?

She blushed when I asked it, as though I had asked about something sexual.

"I didn't do anything for a long while, but last year I decided I would try to find out about him. I thought it would be impossible. He could be anywhere. I called the electrical company where he worked and they told me right away where he was. I called him up, but he wasn't happy to hear from me. It was terrible really. He asked dumb questions, things he should have known about, like what grade was I in, and did I like school. The only question he asked that he seemed to care about was how I got his number.

"See, with all my trying to figure things out, I decided my father was good, and my mother and grandmother were bad. Also, since girls were bad, that meant I was bad, too. If bad things happened to me, it was because of things I did. I wanted it to be that way, too, because if it was true, it meant my father was good and he'd want to take care of me and be glad I called. That's what I pretended. But the second I talked to him I knew my plan wasn't going to work—my plan was to run away and live with him. He didn't want to know about me, or Stevie either. He was angry that I called. So I was stuck where I was, if you see what I mean. My grandmother was right after all, and so was my mother, although I think if he really wanted to come back she might say yes. I wouldn't ask her, but I asked my grandmother and she said my mother wouldn't let my father in the house if he had a million dollars in his hand. Maybe that's true, but I'm pretty sure I saw him coming out of our house that one time, so I still don't really know what's going on, do I? All I knew then was that it wasn't all my mother's fault. That was the only good part of that telephone call, even though I cried a lot after it and had horrible dreams. At least it meant not all girls and women are bad. My father wasn't any great hero either. But I thought I was getting somewhere, knowing a little more about the situation, so maybe I'd start getting better. The dreams stopped. Or anyway they don't come as often as they did. Once, you know, I thought they came because my father was coming to our house. I thought, if he'd stop coming, or my mother would let him in, my dreams would go away. But it's not that simple. And that one time with you when my talking problem left I really thought I was over it. It goes on forever like this, though, doesn't it? Every year things will make sense and I'll have to refigure out the last year, which won't make sense anymore. One year my father's good, the next year he's bad. One year my mother's bad, the next year she's good. God, pretty soon it will be Stevie I won't be sure about, not that I'll ever, *ever* be sure about Janie. You *do* remember her, don't you? Do you see now that I didn't know whether my father was alive or dead? So does that make me normal, in at least *one* way?"

The story of Janie Sutleworth has a happy ending, happier, at least, than a great many. On my urging, she consented to see a young psychiatrist. Their friendship truly stuck, and in a matter of months the stammering and night terrors disappeared. To be free of these problems lifted her spirits tremendously. My friendship with her mother also improved. It was as if the cat was out of the bag, or enough of the cat, anyway, to allow us to become closer. We never talked much about family problems with Mrs. Sutleworth. I suspect she was glad I came around if only to keep an eye on Stevie, who seemed to be managing rather well. The surprising finding for me came on my first visit with Mrs. Dexter, a woman who always eluded me. Somehow, whenever I visited the Sutleworths, she had either just left or would be arriving after my departure. Lucy Dexter was an extremely tall woman with long silver hair, Janie's dark brown eyes and thin nose, and freckles. It was the one feature she utterly disliked. She had hated freckles as a child, and she continued hating them as a sixty-year-old woman. Even her very pronounced stammering didn't seem to displease her as much as the freckles.

She could tell by my expressions the sort of connections I was making between her and her granddaughter. Mrs. Dexter, as she herself knew well, was a highly intelligent woman. "Oh yes, Tom Cottle," she would say, "you have a few of the pieces turning over in your head, but you haven't much of a sense, I suspect, of the big puzzle." She was right.

"How about Janie?" I said in response. "How much of the big puzzle does she have in her head?"

"No one can say about little Janie," she said, looking away sharply as though she had just heard a noise. "Only time will tell. Of course, if you ask me, she understands a great deal for a child. I'd say some of us are going to have to do some serious praying, and some of us serious changing of our ways."

On that point we agreed.

In work of this nature, one must be careful not to designate any one story as typical or representative. People speak only for themselves, for their own lives, and no account, no matter how telling, should be taken to be *the* typical or prototypical case. Surely the reader can see how carefully one must proceed in studies of family secrets. The temptation to jump headlong into one person's life and make claims about other families on the basis of that one life is not only questionable social science but an intellectual act I seem unable to perform. Perhaps what clinicians are attempting to do when they speak of typical cases is acknowledge their familiarity with the patterns of certain stories. Surely the theoretical issues of one life study tie many life studies neatly together.

Now, that last phrase, tying life studies together, is the potentially dangerous one, for tying issues together often makes us lose individuality, uniqueness, for the sake of integrating cases that advance our theory. It is amazing, really, what we can do with data in order to make "facts" fit into our preconceived molds. Often, to make people's stories fit our categorizations, we not only omit various pieces of the stories but also distort the material we have chosen to include. An example of this point may seem obvious, but let us consider it.

To some social scientists, the human personality is formed almost completely in the first years of life. To other social scientists, the basic formation has been concluded within the first few months. My own bias is that the personality, however one defines that word, continues to form throughout life. Aspects of personality are always changing, or existing with the potential for change. Granted, there is a continuity between infancy and old age; it is, after all, the single life, the single person, that defines personality. But continuity hardly implies a firm structure wholly formed in the first months or years of life. The earliest years, naturally, would seem to be the foundation of the personality, and the later years pile up progressively on them. The point is logical, obvious. The first floor sits on the foundation, the second floor on the first. A house is only as strong as its foundation. That's the analogy regularly offered in discussions of personality; it's a sort of engineering analogy which appeals to my sense of logic, but not totally to my sense of the way life is led by many people. Furthermore, the temporal order of years building upon one another is only that: a temporal or linear order; there is an infinite number of ways that events may build upon one another in time. If we have doubts about this, we need only inspect our dreams where the order of events may make perfect psychological sense, even though in the actual representation of linear time the order is nonsensical. Just because we cannot celebrate our sixth birthday before our fifth, or because we do not learn to read before we learn to crawl, doesn't mean that some events and experiences of our later years won't be required in order to make sense of our earlier years.

Using the engineering analogy again, the crucial problem is whether the third floor is strong enough to hold our weight and belongings: The foundation may not be affected at all. Or perhaps we devise ways of holding our weight up without putting much pressure on the foundation. The point is made: It may be deceiving to think that early childhood experiences are by definition the most profound ones, the ones ultimately determining the foundation of the personality. The earlier question remains: How much do we distort the facts of a person's life when we insist that these facts must fit our definitions of personality development? What are we losing when we push the data into our self-styled molds?

To some, this brief discussion may seem irrelevant to the topics we are addressing in this book. For me, these are crucial matters because I remain unable to define the nature of this thing called personality development. Upon hearing some people's stories, I remain convinced that the classical Freudians are correct; the personality, to all intents and purpose, is formed in the early years. When hearing other people's stories, I become convinced the personality is never formed, and I must be careful not to claim this person's problem is that his or her personality wasn't formed by age three. Again, the reader must remember that these contemplations derive from years of interviewing people, not out of psychotherapy, where most practitioners work out of some prearranged psychological theory or mold. If a therapist believes in early personality development, then sooner or later the patient or client will be asked to tell about early childhood experiences. In contrast, if a therapist believes strictly in material of the here and now, then early childhood experiences may never be fully recounted. And all the while, as patients or clients are undergoing treatment, they are learning how to think about themselves; that is, how to psychologize and account for experiences according to the theories and biases of their therapists. Similar predispositions exist in the interviewing experience, except that the interviewer isn't necessarily hunting for causes of particular problems, even though his or her biases and preconceptions will surely determine the sort of material collected.

In the case of Janie Sutleworth, the early years of personality formation were exceedingly important. By their own admission, the Sutleworths were in trouble before the birth of their son, Steve. From what one can piece together, divorce was probably mentioned, and perhaps, too, there was discussion of their marriage as a mistake. Maybe they stayed together for the sake of their children, or believed children would be the answer to their problems. No one knows for certain. My assessment of the Sutleworth situation is that Janie "inherited" some of the problems embedded in the relationship between her mother and grandmother. What these two women were unable to resolve somehow found its way into the psychology of a little girl. The notion is metaphorical, of course, but I was continually struck by Janie's need to look at her life in terms of what girls and women become; what they did to each other, and what men did to them. But a momentous consideration for Janie was the developmental one: What will I become given what has happened to my grandmother and mother?

Secrets kept from us are like the future in that we know or imagine someone knows their content but keeps the content from us. Frustrated, even angered, by not knowing the content, we reconcile ourselves to living with unknown content, or make ourselves believe we know the content. All civilizations have developed means for convincing people that the future could be known, or foretold. For some people, knowing the future's secrets is a paramount concern. For other people, it is the past that holds secrets. This was true for Janie Sutleworth. What she would *become* was for her a contemplation of the *past*; it was an attempt to "foresee the past," as paradoxical as that may sound. Answers to her questions regarding the facts of her life were offered by her grandmother, but it was evident to Janie, even at age ten, that her grandmother's reading of the past and present were influenced by her involvement with her daughter, Adrian, and not her granddaughter. The secrets that Janie revealed to me were only the tip of the iceberg. There were many more secrets that affected Janie Sutleworth, although I knew only a few of them.

The point to be made concerns not this one child exactly, but the conceptual matter of personality development generally. We may believe that time passes only in a linear, objective form, each second succeeding the one before it. But in *subjective* terms, it is evident that in our minds we play with the passage of time. We lift one experience out of its actual temporal order and put it before or after another experience. Indeed, our recollections and anticipations are filled with these subjective temporal manipulations. We do something else with time when we reinterpret our private histories. With each new experience, we "look back" upon ourselves in a slightly new way. We may smile at the thought of how we have changed, or in anticipation of how our future self will make our present self outmoded. Similarly, our future psychological self will make our present psychological self seem outmoded.

For children who receive the brunt of a serious revelation, their family's history, as well as their own private and psychological past, will be profoundly altered. No matter how we determine the logic, form, or substance of our personal development, all of our calculating must change as a result of the secret being revealed. Our entire set of hypotheses about ourselves and life generally will be rearranged. Still, the analogy here to scientific experimentation must not be drawn too precisely. Living is hardly a scientific experiment; life hypotheses are not laboratory hypotheses. The discovery that a supposedly dead father is not dead at all is not hardly akin to having an experiment go awry. Janie Sutleworth's discovery that her father was alive not only caused her to reconsider the relationships within her family, as she had been lied to, but awakened in her primitive beliefs regarding living and dying. It is generally assumed that when children ask about the facts of life their interest lies solely in the conception and birth of children. In the main, this assumption is warranted, but too often our own as well as our children's preoccupation with sexuality leads us to this conclusion. Children also are fascinated with the literal facts of life: What does being alive mean? What does being dead mean? And in the Sutleworth instance, how can a person be dead and alive at the same time? If John Sutleworth was simultaneously dead and alive, then everybody in the world is dead and alive simultaneously. The past is the future; the future is the past. Being awake, furthermore, is really being asleep, for sleeping and waking are symbolic representations of death and life. Carrying the metaphor one step further, if one is dead and alive at the same time, then separation or abandonment equals togetherness or presence. Hence people are together and apart at the same time. Seeing is not seeing, hearing is not hearing, knowing is not knowing, speaking is not speaking.

The metaphor is complex, and filled with significant psychological antinomies. Yet it is the picture I found myself drawing of Janie Sutleworth, despite my desire not to analyze her, and my sense of satisfaction knowing how well her own clinical investigations were proceeding. The being awake when asleep, alive when dead, could well have been the basis of her night terrors and most especially the fainting spells. Possibly, as the dreams came forth when the terror increased to intolerable limits, the fainting was caused by a wish to have the past be gone and to awake, as they say, to a new dawn. Magical thinking, after all, is no stranger to someone confronted with the bizarre problem of having one's father alive and dead simultaneously. What Janie wished, I cannot say. One obvious guess is that she wished to have her father home, her parents reunited. Yet perhaps at some level, she also wished to have him dead if only to resolve the problems caused her mother by his being alive. If a society can legitimately debate abortion and euthanasia, an individual psychology can reconcile the terrors and potential humanity of having a parent die.

Janie Sutleworth may well have allied herself with her mother, or grandmother, in wishing for her father's death. Perhaps, too, the wish had the power to overwhelm her. John Sutleworth's rejection of his daughter, indeed his refusal to recognize her on the telephone, might also have convinced Janie that *she* was not alive. Yet none of this could be spoken about; as old secrets were revealed, new secrets took their place. Knowing and not knowing, telling and not telling, are the ideal ingredients, I believed, for the production of a stammer. I wondered, too, how does one know one is alive? By dreaming? Not necessarily, since people dream of death and believe they are dead. Their realization that it has been a dream comes when they awake. Absence of communication seems to be a better indicator of death for a child. If one can talk, one can think; one is alive. For Janie Sutleworth, the stammering stationed her on the magical but terrifying border of life and death: talking and not talking. The double irony was her grandmother's stammering, and the fact that she could never adequately determine whether or not her parents were speaking to one another. One might say that Janie identified with, or in her mind became part of, all three people.

In any discussion of the secrets held by family members, one must acknowledge the dynamics of the ultimate secret, the secret of life, whatever that means to a child. All human beings deal with these ultimate secrets. Even if the issues of origins and destinies, birth and death, sexuality, are discussed at great length in families, the very nature of the issues makes a satisfactory resolution of them impossible for a child. But I still want to know, the child says, what is being born, what is being alive, what is dying. Or, what will happen to me? Thus, any secret has a mystical, almost mythic quality about it.

Over time, people become fascinated in these ultimate life secrets; they safeguard them, almost as if they alone knew the answers. Or they believe, as children often will, that there are people somewhere, possessing knowledge of all secrets, if only one could get these people to reveal their knowledge. While this may sound irrelevant to the lives of children like Janie Sutleworth, it must not be forgotten that children's considerations of origins, birth, begin at fundamental levels: Where did I come from? The answer typically offered goes, "From Mommy's stomach." The child eventually sees pregnant women, and the answer, presumably rather strange at first hearing, seems more reasonable. But in light of her particular family history, Janie asked a second question regarding origins: Who are my parents? And if my father is gone, how do I know he truly is my father?

When Janie told me of the unfriendly phone conversation with her father, I could not help but think that the conversation, and her own detective work, had been undertaken to make contact with him and learn through the quality of the contact whether or not John

Sutleworth was her real father. How would she know this? By his tone. If he was loving, accepting, he was her father. If, as it turned out, he was rejecting and cold, then it was evident he was not her father. The emotional response would confirm or disconfirm his biological fatherhood. It was a logical deduction: How else can one know if a man is one's father? Legal records can be forged. A man proclaiming "I'm your father" could be lying. The best way is to have him live with you or be loving even when he no longer lives with you. John Sutleworth's rejection of his daughter gave her an answer to one of the so-called ultimate secrets: He was not her father. Her mother and grandmother were correct: Janie was born from and to women only. Their destiny was her own, their psychology was hers. The secrets of life were held by women, in their bodies, in their minds.

But it hadn't always been this way. Not so many years ago, Janie and Steve Sutleworth had had a father. They remembered him— Janie was nine when he left. They had known years of normal family life, normal in the respect that a father came home every night after work, ate dinner with his family, slept under the same roof. The Sutleworth home, in the eyes of the two children, was identical to the homes of their friends. Then everything changed, but with a strange lack of finality, as Janie never understood for certain whether her father left for a short while or forever. Was he alive or dead? This part of her childhood I did appreciate, as she spoke occasionally of the differences between the times her father was around, and after he had gone. Indeed, her portraits of these two periods of time, though not necessarily filled with brilliant detail, nonetheless had the quality of two completely different lives. Strands of experience, clearly, created continuities between these two periods. But in her descriptions and expressions, I heard the severing of some of these experiential strands, although I could not quite articulate the problem until Janie had recounted the story I have just reported. Then one day she casually remarked, "Sometimes I feel like I'm two people."

To be sure, one could argue that Janie, like many of us, seemed to feel as though a myriad personalities lived in her soul simultaneously. For one reason or another, certain situations or experiences made one of these personalities more salient or publicly prominent than the others. One of the ultimate secrets held by many of us is the reality of our numerous selves. Still, in Janie's case, I felt it more appropriate to respond to her remark about being two people by saying, "Maybe you don't *feel* you're two people as much as it *seems* like you were one person before your father went away, and a somewhat different person after he left." In part, my words were meant to quiet any fears that she had about going crazy, a fear she appeared to entertain now and again. She looked relieved. "That's better," she said kindly. "That's much more like it really is."

It is this observation that brings us full circle. I began this discussion by saying that unquestionably, early and later childhood experiences were important in the shaping of Janie Sutleworth's personality. But there was that one significant event, followed by a period of secrets, mystery, and genuine ignorance of the facts of her family's life. Then came not only the gradual reduction in pain, a lessening of the psychological hurt as will happen in cases of classical traumatic injury, but in addition, the revelation of the secrets. Not so incidentally, this is an important distinction to make. If one may argue that John Sutleworth's abandonment of his family caused a traumatic reaction in his child, a reaction replete with Janie unconsciously forcing out of conscious awareness memories of the events, one also might allege that information was being *withheld* from Janie as much as she was *repressing* it. The night terrors might have been related to the repressed thoughts, but the terrors subsided when the truth of her family's history was made known to her. While Janie's experiences do not represent the classical return of the repressed, one could say she experienced a catharsis of a sort when the secrets were revealed. Importantly, much of the so-called psychological dynamics at work in this child took place on a conscious level. Yet, more significant, I think, than whether or not these sorts of dynamics are conscious or unconscious is Janie's notion of having lived two lives: the life before Mr. Sutleworth disappeared, and the life that began after the questions of his disappearance and possible death were resolved. Although I dread putting words into her mouth, I felt Janie was symbolically reborn when the secrets were revealed. Life, in a sense, began anew; she was more than what she had been. Although not original, it is worth repeating the notion that personalities may be seen as developing in the form of an endless series of birth-death-rebirth experiences, each one bringing the so-called prior self into a slightly new psychological context. In this framework, it makes sense to speak of developmental discontinuities, periods of time that appear to an individual to represent a psychological hiatus. Certain special events or experiences, possibly even traumatic ones, may be necessary to cause these birth-death-rebirth moments, these developmental discontinuities in which any number of personality rearrangements may evolve. But I should think that profoundly painful or unpredictable events are inevitably the major stimulant to these rearrangements and personality alterations. If one examines, for example, the lives of artists, or creative people generally, one finds them almost working to produce in themselves, through adjustments in their work or life-styles, dramatic stopping and starting moments. One finds in the accounts of artists expressions of dying out and rebirth, periods of time in which a person seeks *renewal,* even if renewal means the end of something once highly cherished. The experience, then, of rebirth will probably be painful, though it need not always be initiated by some externally painful experience, as happened with Janie Sutleworth.

One last point about the notion of personality developing as a series of birth-death-rebirth experiences. Early childhood experiences must be important in the development of the personality. From the psychoanalytic point of view, early childhood experiences in fact have given shape to the very personality that will seek to create or know birth-death-rebirth moments throughout life. No one can know about this with certainty, for at present all these notions exist merely as metaphors, no matter how well they are organized into a theory. Proof of the notions rests partly in experimentation, partly in personal description, partly in dispassionate if not objective observation. Yet one point that intrigues me when I hear the accounts like those of Janie Sutleworth and Willie Fryer, which follows, is that secrets play a powerful role in the patterns of personality development. The moments of birth-death-rebirth rely heavily on the revelation of secrets, or more precisely, on the revelation providing energy and legitimation to the feeling of starting anew. Holding on to secret material may be translated by the child as a need to hold back. Thus one cannot move forward in one's life until the secret is shared, or the burden of secrecy lessened.

One thing more. If a life becomes a series of birth-death-rebirth experiences, no one but the person going through the experiences will know about them; they will be the new secrets people safeguard until the moment when their revelation brings forth an imagined new development, a new wrinkle, as it were, of the personality. So, while we may derive these notions from the accounts of the young people heard in this book, the ultimate secrets of life, and especially those related to personality change and development, will not be heard directly in these accounts. They will have to be implied from the life work of any given individual. We learn something about these experiences in writing, art and design, still more from the words of a person confronted with the social and psychological dilemmas posed by the existence of real secrets. From this reality we then make our interpretive leaps into the realm of the symbolic value and meaning to a person, and his or her personality, of secrets.

WILLIE FRYER

Willie Fryer, seventeen years old, the second-born of a well-to-do family. Willie Fryer, with the long blond curls, the shaggy appearance, the soft blue eyes and broad hands. Willie Fryer's father was a professor of law, his mother a journalist. Both were talented, hardworking people. They loved their three children, but they wanted successful careers, too. Their children grew up with the knowledge that adults lead two lives, their work life and their family life, and there was no sense for children to scream for their parents between the hours of eight and six, Monday through Friday. They just wouldn't be there. Nor did the children think of the summer as a time when families vacationed together. The family typically stayed home; the children were sent to day camp. So everybody left the house at eight in the morning and returned at six in the evening. Still, it was a close family, even if its five members grew up leading separate lives.

Indeed, that was another virtue the Fryers taught their children: Dependence is a dangerous stance. After the child reaches a certain age, there is no reason for him or her to be dependent on anyone, especially parents. People must learn to be independent, self-sufficient, self-possessing. That way, the shock of life's vicissitudes, as Martin Fryer repeatedly reminded his son, will be reduced. Love people, he would tell his children, but never need them to the point of dependency. Shirley Fryer preached the same lesson, particularly to her daughters. Needing and loving are two foods, she would say. Too many people, and especially girls, confuse them. Don't let one substitute for the other. To Willie, she would add, "There is no man who can be happy, ultimately happy, when he's married to a woman who *needs* him rather than *loves* him. If she loves him, she'll enrich his life. If she only needs him and pretends to love him to satisfy her need, she'll bring him down. She may be loyal, but if you want loyalty, marry a German shepherd!"

Willie Fryer was told many things by his parents, but his mother's remark about distinguishing between love and need remained the most prominent. The message made sense to him, although it carried a bit of fright as well, not that he could define this feeling. The idea that people who needed him would drag him down could not have been more dramatic. He could see it with his school friends. As a young teenager, he had close friends. But there was also a group who pretended to be his friends. In their way they expressed a need for him, but his mother was right. They were driven by their *need* for him, not by their concern for him. They were precisely the people to look out for.

If further proof of his mother's statement was needed, Sylvie Jenner provided it. Willie began dating her when they were in the eighth grade, and at seventeen they were still together. Sylvie clearly needed Willie, but it was love that held them together. Never did he feel brought down by her needs. He once asked her, "Do you love me 'cause you need me, or need me 'cause you love me?" Sylvie looked confused. "If I know what you're talking about," she answered, "I think I don't love you *or* need you. Or is that a song?" Willie remembers thinking how the idea was right, it was just too soon to tell. When he told his mother of the exchange with Sylvie, Shirley Fryer laughed. Willie could see she approved of what he had tried to do. She, too, agreed it was too soon to tell. It had been Willie's phrase, too. He would use the same words several years later when he told me the story of his mother's decision to leave the family.

Willie Fryer did indeed have broad hands. When we went for beers at the Silver Parrot one afternoon, his hand practically wrapped around the entire tall glass. I often remarked to myself on the contrast of that broad hand ready to crush the glass and the delicate manner with which Willie sipped his beer. He seemed somewhat self-conscious about sitting in college hangouts when he was a high school senior. Or perhaps the self-consciousness grew out of our conversations. The hand of a man, I would think, the drinking style of a little boy.

In Willie's case, it was not important how we met, or what exactly he felt the nature of our friendship to be. As he himself told Sylvie, the point was that if he didn't speak to someone soon, he was going to explode. He needed what he called an outsider. So we met on and off for several months, talking mostly about books, politics, and, as it was the autumn of his senior year, college applications and the sorts of things he might want to study in university. The subject of his mother's leaving, something I knew nothing about, arose with Willie saying: "I've got a little problem I thought you might be able to help me out with. I don't know exactly what you can do about it, but maybe you know somebody." This last phrase, so common among young people holding tightly to precious secrets, always sounds so poignant. "Maybe you know somebody." Somebody to do what, I always want to say. Listen? Fix it? Kiss the hurt? And in Willie Fryer's case, love him but not need him?

Willie's hands were hidden by the table, his face was only a few inches from its top. The noise in the Silver Parrot was so great I could barely hear him.

"About a year and a half ago my mom came to me with this little problem. Well, problem isn't the right word . . . listen, you got to stop me if you've heard this one before. I mean, I'm sure a lot of kids have stories like this one, so don't let me cry into your beer, okay? What I was saying, it wasn't really a problem, it was just a message. She had grown a little tired, that's the way she said it, of being a mother and a wife and a journalist. She couldn't do everything at once and be happy. So she had to give something up. It wasn't going to be journalism since that meant a lot to her, and we were all pretty much grown up so we didn't need a mother, like children need a mother, and besides, you know my mother and needing. So she had decided she was going to leave my father, and us. I tell you, when she said it, I felt like I was living in the middle of that expression "pulling the plug out." I mean, it was like somebody pulling the floor out, not the rug. I mean the floor, so you fall down, down, down, like into endless space.

"But here's the interesting thing: I must not have had any expression on my face. Just a look, like, go on, Mother, keep talking, I'm still listening. I couldn't even get the feeling I was feeling. It was just boom, except for one thing. She said it in a way that sort of made it impossible for me to say anything, or feel anything. Like, I had to keep anything I was thinking from her. So she said a little bit more, like how her leaving everybody didn't mean she didn't love us and that it was her work that was making her do it. She talked about how in the old days when people weren't meant to live as long as they do now it was all right for a man and woman to get married for life, but in modern times it's probably too long to stay together forever. It's nice to say it in a marriage vow and all that, but death, if you're lucky, doesn't come for a long, long time, so you could probably have a couple of families and still not be that old. She's talking on and on and I'm feeling like someone's choking the air out of my lungs but I'm not to let on I'm being choked. I didn't want to bother her. She'd obviously prepared her little speech, and I wasn't about to let it all come to nothing because this nice big fifteen-year-old kid—this was two years ago—was breaking down on the floor sobbing. And this was no big male thing on my part. I would have gladly cried if I thought I could have with her standing there. But if *she* could be calm, *I* could be calm. So I kept giving her the look, 'Keep going, Ma, I'm still listening.'

"Now comes the end of the speech: Don't tell Dad. The girls have known for a couple of weeks. They were told not to tell anybody, not even me, and now the three of us know but the old man doesn't. I mean the four of us know. Great game! And when does he find out? She's not sure. In time. She knows she has to make a break, but she's just not sure when, and she doesn't want to worry him because he's in the middle of a big project at work. So we get to keep a little secret. I'll tell you how I felt then, especially when she said, 'You want to tell me anything?' and all I could say was 'Not really. Maybe I'll think of something.' I felt like all the clocks in the world stopped and time went back to the beginning. All of us had to start all over again. It was like I was a new me. After all, no more mother; that makes me different from what I was when she came into my room. She went out the door and all the clocks stopped. I remember that night my younger sister looked at me and she didn't have anything written on her face. I couldn't tell what she was thinking. Then all of a sudden she has this big grin and she says, 'Merry Christmas, Lone Ranger.' I said, 'Merry Christmas, Tonto.' It was April then.

"So now the Fryers are leading a wonderful life. There's a little time bomb in the house, ticking away under my father's nose, maybe I should say in his bed, but he doesn't know it. At least he lets us *think* he doesn't know it. But he couldn't have known it and pretended like that. But none of us, not even my mother, knew when the time bomb was going off. Every night in bed, I'd say to myself, well, it wasn't today, maybe it won't happen. Then, as the time goes on, you begin to forget about it. Like, all secrets are fantastic, upsetting, whatever, in the beginning, but then the excitement wears off. Still, that feeling of, well, starting life all over again, and this time without a mother, I mean being born all over again without a mother, that didn't leave me. I was starting a second time, really a third time, and it was going to be a fourth time before it was over. This boring you?"

"Hardly," I whispered. It was the first breath I was conscious of taking in minutes.

"When my mother gave me that speech, years before, about loving and needing, I think that's the first time I started to live life all over again. She was warning me, even if she wasn't aware of it. But knowing her, she probably was. I didn't know what was coming off, but I was being told, stop the old clocks and start the new ones, pal, your old lady's going away one of these days. In a sense, that was like the first secret she was telling me. Be prepared; there's a time bomb being manufactured. Then the time bomb becomes real, which was when she told me she was leaving. The next time the clock stops and starts all over again is six months after she made her little speech. Now both my parents come to me one night. My sister Patty is with me this time. They're both so straightfaced they look like they're going to ask me for the toothpaste. My father by now knows everything. The bomb went off and nothing. No one heard a noise. If it hit him, no one could have guessed by the way he was looking at us. So what can I think? They made their plans and they're neither delighted nor upset, and we're waiting around for the next step. Do they sell the house? Do we go with *her?* Do we go with *him?* Do they quit their jobs? No, that much I knew. Jobs come first after children reach six years old. So the clocks are going off again and I'm sitting on my bed feeling like a goddamn refugee. Just tell me when to pack and which country I'm supposed to walk to. And can I take my security blanket? This is all happening on Thanksgiving vacation. They waited until Thanksgiving vacation in case we got a little upset we could take it easy a couple of days and not miss school. Thoughtful. Thoughtful people.

"Here's a funny thing. For a minute there, while the two of them like a couple of football coaches were giving us their half-time speech, how we're going to have to play a little better the second half, the second half of our life is more like it, I was actually feeling relieved. She waited so damn long she had me believing she wouldn't go through with it. It might have been better had she just said she was going and go. But now I didn't have to keep the secret anymore. At least it was out in the open and we could talk about it. And don't think they didn't try to get us to talk about it. Probably because all the books said when you knife your kids in the back be sure they get a chance to talk about it with you; it makes them feel better. Except that Patty and I looked at each other and didn't have a thing to say. I don't think we talked about it for weeks. Fact, I don't *ever* remember talking about it. Patty said, 'Where do we go?' My mother said, 'You'll stay here with your father. I'll see you regularly.' But get this, she tacked on the trailer, 'Willie, you must have some questions. You're never this quiet.' Oh yeah, man, I got a question. Do you think you could take your foot off my chest long enough so I could take a breath of air?

"It was really terrific. If anybody had made a movie of us, they could have sold it to television for one of these afternoon specials which are supposed to help children learn about *real* family problems, except we didn't have any problems because our family was breaking up amicably. That's my father's word. My mother called it *peaceably*, in case Patty or me didn't know the word amicably. Anyway, I felt relieved because no more secrets. I couldn't have said anything if they tortured me. But the more she kept saying, 'Willie, you must have something to say,' the more I could have killed her. She has a great way of not letting anybody express any emotion and she thinks they're purposely holding back. But she strangles us. That, maybe, is the biggest secret I was asked to keep in my entire life: my emotions. I *had* to keep them secret because she didn't have a way to deal with them, or the time. In fact, that may be why I keep saying that thing about time stopping and starting all over again. There never was time for our feelings. Our feelings were the big secret, *our* big time bombs which weren't allowed to go off because Mommy and Daddy's work schedules would have been messed up. Can you imagine the three of us, the most wordy children in America, not saying a thing about what was going on? I mean, that has to go beyond a pledge of secrecy. She never said we couldn't talk to one another about it. Although she did in her way. She kept us from raising anything with her, or with each other, or with anybody, that would keep her from getting where she wanted to go. This time she wanted to get out of the house. Can you see Patty and me exchanging Christmas greetings in the middle of the *spring*? Merry Christmas, Lone Ranger? What the hell were we doing?

"You want to hear the kicker? They take one secret off the agenda for us, now they got another one. This time it's my father who's breaking the big news. He'd just been told by my mother a couple of days before how she had decided to walk out. So what's on my father's mind? We shouldn't breathe a word of this to anyone. It was the right word for him to use, too, because I couldn't breathe anymore at all. For his business and reputation, and her business and reputation, divorce wouldn't look good. My mother pointed out that when men leave women it doesn't look so bad as when women leave men. Either way, though, it ends up looking like there's something wrong with the woman. Either she's not good enough to keep her husband, or she's unstable and leaves him. So there we were, pledged to secrecy all over again. And there was the clock stopping and starting again. I was beginning to feel like a car bumping along a dirt road without any gas.

"As you can see, I'm not doing all that well with my parents, but I've got to be among the world's top secret keepers. I didn't tell Sylvie for a long, long time. When she'd come over she wouldn't ask where my mother was because she knew my parents worked. She didn't see anything different because the three little Fryers were such good secret keepers, or is the word good liars! I didn't tell a soul; I led my life like a good little boy, and let myself choke on the whole scene. The secrets were still going strong in the Fryer home. If the split bothered anybody at 18 Willow Road, nobody could have told. But that's not really amazing. The amazing thing is that my parents kept up the secret, thanks to the sealed lips of their beloved children, one of whom's birthday was forgotten this year, and last year, too. They arranged to go to certain important social events together, the whole works, just to let people think they were together. People still wrote to her at home thinking she lived at home. Great, huh? No one at their jobs knew, and the people they work with are the biggest gossips I've ever met. The fact is, the greatest family project the Fryers ever undertook was the keeping of that secret. My father must have known better than anyone how good we were at it, because we kept the one before it from him pretty darn well.

"That's my story. I still feel strangled to death, like I can't get air, and like every time I turn around I hear clocks stopping and starting and stopping and starting. I guess I feel, too, that I can't be young anymore, which isn't all that bad, not that I have any idea anymore who I am. Who I really am, I mean. No, that's a lie. I do know who I am, up to a point. I just can't put it into words; but I can sort of feel who I am. It's my parents I don't know. Talk about people you live with, or used to live with, or are *supposed* to live with, being strangers. Jesus, I don't know who they are, who they were, *what* they are. The big secret is the charade. The all-night, all-day drama playing over at Willow Road. The people are real, the events are real, only the emotions are fictitious to protect the innocent, as if anybody could be innocent after what's been going on.

"I think my parents are asking us to keep a far more important and dangerous secret than they think. Sometimes I think my mother's worse than my father, then I think he's worse. Both of them, in my eyes, are really sick people. They both need a team of psychiatrists working on them. But they don't see it, and nobody who is friends with them thinks there's anything wrong. Not telling anybody they're separated is a little matter next to the fact that their whole life is a lie. It's a lie when they were together, and when they're apart. That's what I can't tell anybody. Not even Sylvie. I have to be loyal to them. They think I'm loyal by not talking about their separation. They probably think I'm afraid to jeopardize their jobs because I may not have enough money for college, but that's a lot of crap! I couldn't care less about that. I'm sorry to say that since you took a lot of time talking about college with me. But it's *them* I think about; not money for clothes and cars and college. And both my sisters are the same.

"I'm being loyal, acting the way I am, but the act is taking it out of me. It's changing me, which is all right, but it's making me think there are things I once thought I could do that I don't think I can do anymore. It's cutting into my confidence. You can't grow up worrying about your parents or putting them out of your mind. It's normal for kids to grow up and find out that well, your dad and mom weren't as great as you thought when you were small. Sure. But I have another problem. I have to grow up and put them behind me, or try to convince them that one of us is crazy, and I know it isn't me because *I'm* not going around asking people to keep secrets about *my* life. Believe me, I have a much healthier relationship with Sylvie than they ever had, and certainly better than that crazy business they have going between them now. Nobody goes through life with the strength they *could* have when their parents run around like that. This secret business is absolutely foolish, crazy. I say it's both. I also say I'm going to crack.

"You want the last straw? The secret makers have just come up with their latest dandy. For the last six months they *have* been telling some people they're separated, although we're still not supposed to talk about it. But here's the latest: My mother is going to write a book about it. It, that means about us, the little counterspies of Willow Road. So now she really doesn't want me to talk about any of these things until I tell her how I've lived through the last few years. You want to see a grown man or almost grown man cry?"

"It wouldn't bother me."

"I'd love to. But they've taken the tears out of me. I'd love to have a good old-fashioned cry, or laugh, or anything over this. But all that secret-keeping business, all that holding things in, I don't have a damn thing to let out. Maybe that's what I've been trying to say. The secrets took it all out of me. I told nothing in exchange for giving up every feeling I've had. Wow. I feel I've been talking a whole day. Tell me, after hearing this you think I'm crazy? Or maybe I should ask, you think I *need* my parents, or *love* my parents?"

TWO

Infidelity

Accounts of infidelity abound. Indeed, they are among the most often quoted "evidence" for the disintegration of the culture. The very substance of morality, it seems, rests on family stability and fidelity. These facts are well known to the families I have been visiting over the last years, many of whom could recount their own particular versions of infidelity. Stories of infidelity, moreover, like cases of divorce, typically focus only on the main characters involved. One inevitably locates the "agent" of infidelity, yet one must remember, too, the victim, the person who, knowing or unknowing of the affair, leads his or her life with the weight of a partner's sin or transgression. Hearing these accounts, I invariably ask myself that fateful question: If you committed adultery, would you tell your spouse? Talk about significant secrets!

There are other people, however, involved in the infidelity drama, or melodrama. Granted, we the listeners might consider these other people lesser characters, but the people themselves hardly consider the repercussions of a friend's or relative's infidelity insignificant. In some cases, because of prior or ongoing attachments, the accounts of these so-called lesser characters assume paramount importance. The secrets held by the lesser characters, furthermore, may even represent the final "lifeline" of the so-called major personages.

Years ago I became implicated in the life of a woman who smiled broadly when she read this introductory statement and found herself being referred to as a "lesser character" in a melodrama. Fortunately, she was not insulted by my words; she understood the point. At the time, no one thought much about her role in the incident I am about to report. In fact, and here again lies that quintessential irony of secret keeping, there was no story, no drama or melodrama as long as she remained constant, faithful, and above all silent.

JACQUELINE FREEMONT

Jacqueline Freemont was the sort of young woman one calls innocent, at least this was the impression she made on most people. A tall lovely-looking fifteen-year-old with curly brown hair and smooth white skin, Jacqueline had grown up to become what her parents unself-consciously called the perfect child. The youngest of four children, Jacqueline received much love from what seemed, even to her, a great many people. Surely her sisters, Susan and Jennifer, had lavished attention on her, but as she was quick to point out, "that's what older sisters are for." Besides, she had paid the price of following behind her sisters in school. As both had done well, a more difficult burden fell on her. It was expected that Jacqueline Freemont would be the outstanding student that Susan and Jennifer had been.

Being the sister of William, however, yielded a different set of circumstances. Bill Freemont, nine years older than Jacqueline, had taken a special interest in his sister. When she was a baby, he found her irresistible. In time she became his pet, while he became the family's most solicitous baby-sitter. When Jacqueline was four, Bill liked nothing better than to read to her or take her for walks and make up stories about things they had seen. Clare Freemont, a woman who supervised her children closely, was perfectly at ease when putting her oldest in charge of her youngest. No one doubted Bill's sense of responsibility, and no one observing the children together could have missed the love Jacqueline had for her brother.

Not surprisingly, the close relationship between Jacqueline and Bill continued over the years. Every day, it seemed, the elder Freemonts had to make peace between brother and sisters, but rarely did Jacqueline and Bill need separating. Nor for that matter did their involvement seem excessive. Both led their own lives, but found each other's company, when they could be together, pleasant. It went on like this until Bill Freemont telephoned his family one night from college to announce that he was getting married. To say the least, the family could not have been more delighted. Perhaps at twenty-one Bill was a trifle too young for marriage, but then again, as Clare Freemont reminded her husband, despite all the talk about young people's "modern behavior," people still got married at twenty-one. Besides, both Bill and his fiancée were committed to completing college. If Bill was in love, that was sufficient. Why stop trusting him now!

Fred and Clare Freemont had themselves gotten married in their early twenties. Practically next-door neighbors as children, they had grown up together in a small Connecticut town abiding almost religiously to the values of their parents and grandparents. Both were the first children in their respective families to attend college, although they felt uneasy about the fact that college might launch them into high-pressured, competitive life-styles. Unable to imagine themselves residing in a large city, they agreed that jobs with small-town businesses would suit them best. So, upon graduating college and getting married, they settled in a small town fifty miles from where they had grown up. Fred took a job with an insurance company, while Clare worked in a local school as a special reading teacher. Within a few years they had purchased a small house and soon after the children were born.

I suppose that my initial description of the Freemonts might well have contained that word "innocent." They were, simply put, a good and decent family. They neither put on special performances for me nor sought to convince me of anything. Our early discussions, to be sure, contained references to certain values and principles they held in respect, but there was nothing dogmatic about their notions. Nor were their perspectives puritanical. They had fun together as a family; they argued, fought, held grudges and forgot them ten minutes later. Admittedly, when meeting some families I find myself reacting negatively to their somewhat candy-coated life-style and manners. I'll groan to myself that they belong on the cover of *The Saturday Evening Post*. It is an unfair and condescending response, but truthfully, it does erupt now and again. I had none of these feelings, however, with the Freemonts. I enjoyed being in their home, and they seemed to accept me, particularly Jacqueline, who had little to do with her sisters and missed her brother, who was away at college.

No one knows whether all family members hold the sort of por-

tentous secrets we are examining in this volume. Surely no one can
know with certainty on first meeting whether the person sitting
across the kitchen table or standing in front of the living room
bookshelf selecting a school album to show is harboring some momentous secret. When I came to know the Freemonts, as is true
with most of the families in this book, I had no idea that so-called
family secrets would emerge as a research interest. I would drive
home from the Freemonts more often than not recalling what one of
my aunts used to answer when I would ask, "What's new with you?"
"Nothing special," she would reply in a way that made one think,
It's all right, you know, for nothing special to have happened. I felt
this same way about my visits with the Freemonts: nothing special; a
pleasant visit with a lovely family.

Then, several years after William had married, Jacqueline revealed
to me a secret she had been keeping. She had decided that I was one
of the few people she dared tell, primarily because she did not consider me *that* close to the family. I barely knew her brother, and had
never met his wife, Lauren. Like the elder Freemonts, Bill and
Lauren had chosen to live in a town about fifty miles away from
Bill's birthplace. They had rented a small apartment in a large
house, and in many respects represented the ideal married couple.
Fate had smiled on Mr. and Mrs. William Freemont. Within a year
and a half of their wedding, Lauren was pregnant. I rarely asked
Jacqueline about them, only because it appeared that their life plans
were proceeding without hitch.

"You *ought* to ask about them," Jacqueline admonished me one
day in my car. "Not about *her*, but about my brother. Better still
you ought to ask *him*. I'd love to know whether Mr. Smarty Perfect
would let on about anything: Isn't it all amazing! I grew up thinking
my big brother was so perfect; when I think about it I could laugh.
You know how children idealize their parents? Well, I did it, too, a
little with my parents, but I went all the way with my brother. I really believed he was Mr. Terrific. You generalize about people from
your own family. If your mother's horrible, you grow up thinking *all*
women are horrible. I grew up thinking that boys, no matter how
bad they acted, *had* to turn out all right because of my brother,
whose name I can barely say. William the Great!

"Everybody thinks they have the perfect relationship. It's so pitiful; Lauren does, too. She doesn't know how my charming brother
has taken a *lover!* An eighteen-year-old *lover*. He was her camp counselor a few years ago when he was in high school. She's almost *my*
age. Maybe that's why he always took good care of me; he was born

to like younger women. What a horrible mess. This is the kind of news, you know, that could really destroy our family; not my sisters, they couldn't care, but my parents would drop dead if they knew. It's not that they don't know that affairs go on, they just don't believe it's possible for them to happen so close to home, if you see what I mean. It shouldn't either. They brought him up as well as any boy could be brought up. He was a prince in the family. It was like a fairy story with him. He got it all his way, and he used to be nice. And look what happened to him with everybody practically *waiting* on him. They spoiled him, and *he* spoiled *me*. Now he's turned around and spoiled everything. And that poor wife of his doesn't know anything about it. Nobody does, except me.

"I don't know why, but I feel the whole thing really *is* like a fairy tale. The naughty sisters, the good sister, and the supposedly good brother. Maybe I thought when I was a child I could marry my brother. Maybe lots of girls, when they're little I mean, think they can marry their brothers. The naughty sisters want the prince but only Cinderella gets him. Only *this* story has a dirty ending because another girl gets the prince and if you ask me, he's no prince at all! It was all supposed to come out with everybody living happily ever after. Maybe our family never really knew what a real problem was. Families have to have *some* sadness, but I think death would have been better than this. I really could kill him for doing it. He should be whipped, or forced to lose something, but he'll probably get off perfectly clean; he's always been the perfect person, so why not. *I'm* the only one who could ruin it for him; I'd like to do it, too. I feel angry and sort of let down. It's like I was expecting some present and I didn't get it, but I can't really tell anybody what I wanted, or the fact that I'm sad because I didn't get it.

"When I think about my brother, it makes me feel like I'm a little girl. I never feel I'm my age when he's around. Even when I talk about him, I feel like I could be six or seven. It's our relationship that makes me feel this way. Now I feel like we're not even related anymore, like we've been cut apart. I mean, I know he's married and all that and going to be having a baby pretty soon, but suddenly it's like he's not my brother anymore. He's just another guy, doing what all guys do: cheat on their wives. I'm *sure* he thinks he's in love with this girl. And I'm *sure* she's in love with him. He makes you feel this way about him, the coward. Or maybe he's a love bully, forcing people to care for him because he's so nice all the time. I really could kill him!

"I knew I was going to tell you when I saw you. It's not that I wanted to get it off my chest. I think it's 'cause I wanted you to do something. You're the outsider, so I guess I wanted you to punish him. He deserves it. It isn't fair him doing this while nobody knows. A girl couldn't get away with it. And you know why? Because no boy would keep a secret for her. They'd tell the first person they saw. I don't even know which part is the most unfair: that he's doing it or that he doesn't know I'm like the fairy princess who has to keep the knight's honor clean? He should be punished.

"He doesn't know how much he needs me, but he does. He needs me to keep my little mouth shut more than he needs anything else in his life. I'm the little secret portion of his life, and I *hate* that feeling. I hate the position he's put me in, and Lauren in, for that matter. I'm compromised, too, whether he knows it or not. I'm caught up in his affair. It's like a quadrangle instead of the usual triangle. He's guilty of infidelity and I'm involved. I'll bet he comes to me sometime and confesses everything. He wouldn't tell my other sisters, and he doesn't go to church. He might tell some man, brag to him, probably, but I'll bet he'll come to me sometime. You know what I'll do? I'll listen and act a little shocked, a little unhappy, a little of everything so it seems real. 'Oh, is that so. My, my, my; that isn't a nice thing to do, is it, William dear, you bastard. You want me to tell Mother first or Father? Oh, wouldn't I? *Try* me. What do I want to keep my mouth shut? Nothing you could give me, William dear. There was something once, but you don't have it anymore. It's called honesty, the kind that's supposed to go along with real love, even if the love is only between a brother and a sister. So, William dear, you don't have a *damn* thing to give me anymore!'

"I wouldn't give him kindness, not anymore. Of course I'm more loyal to him than I am to Lauren, but that's not the point. The point is I'm just as betrayed as she is. I'm also locked in by everything.

"I can't be totally honest about anything anymore because I'm bound to keep his secret. So a good part of my life is a big fat lie now. It's not what I do, but it's certainly a lie every time I'm with them, or when I talk to anybody about them, especially my parents. I might want to say something, to sort of get revenge, but I won't. In fact, the whole thing makes *me* feel guilty, if you can believe that. When I heard about it, I thought I didn't want to be close to him anymore. Or because I *can't* be close to him, which I don't want to be, maybe I'll be free of him. He *is* a rather important part of my life. So I thought, all right, now's my chance to escape from him and all the other things that tie me to the family. But that was foolish, because if anything, I'm more caught up in his marriage now than I ever was. The net suddenly got thicker and deeper, and if I was ever feeling guilty about things before—because I don't know how healthy my relationship with him really was—I'm weighed down with guilt now. I carry my life on my back; his life, too.

"You know, when I was young, I used to think, he spends so much time with me, much,. much more than either of my parents do, so how will I ever be able to pay him back? I'll never be able to pay him back for all the wonderful things he's done for me. So look what fate has delivered at my doorstep: a nice juicy scandal that breaks wide open the second I breathe a word of this to anyone. *You're* anyone. Maybe I'd like you to start some scandal. Go punish him. I guess that's what I want you to do with this information. Go make things horrible for him. And if he wants to know how you found out, tell him. Tell him baby Jacqueline broke the news. Broke a lot of things at the same time, the bastard!"

ROSCOE ETTINGER

Roscoe Ettinger carries the same name as his father, grandfather, and great-grandfather. The firstborn sons of four generations were called Roscoe, and each was strongly urged to enter the family business, which, to young Roscoe Ettinger when he was nine, seemed to be the business of making money. When people asked Coe, as he was called, what his father did for a living, he would answer, "He makes money like his father taught him how to do."

Coe's impressions weren't too misguided. In fact, the Ettinger family had been in the investment counseling business and, to say the least, were highly successful. Coe wasn't too old when he realized that his family was rich, which meant that he would be rich as well. If a person could honestly say they had all they wanted, Coe Ettinger, at age thirteen, could announce to his parents he had more than he knew there was in the world. In their summer home, his family kept horses, in the winter home their stable contained cars, foreign and domestic, new and old. Coe's father scoured newspapers looking for announcements of old cars for sale. He never had enough. His passion was cars. Nothing pleased him more than repairing and refurbishing old cars and have them standing in the garage looking as if they were manufactured that very day.

Coe Ettinger, Sr., worked hard at the family business. The work required him to travel much of the time, but when he returned from trips, or after a long day in the office thirty miles away in the bowels of the city, as he called the banking district, he knew how to relax. He poured himself and his wife a drink, watched the evening news on television, and went out to the garage to putter about on the cars. According to his son, putter was the proper term, for the senior Ettinger never took the time to dismantle automobiles. Nor did he repair upholstery or paint exteriors. He puttered. He might spend a whole evening in the garage removing spark plugs, cleaning them, replacing them. Or he would start a car's engine and just sit in the driver's seat listening to the motor. It was all in the sound, he told his son, who, from the day he was born, it seemed, had an aversion to cars. Young Coe hated the sight, smell, sound of cars, his father's, all the cars in the world. Had the garage burned down and all the cars ruined, Coe might have rejoiced. He never went near the garage unless his father urged him to join him on one of the weekly inspections, a ritual the boy despised.

"Now, this is a 1946 Mercedes, very rare," his father would say. "Found it in a scrap heap in Pennsylvania. Now, you tell me, could anyone guess what we had done to . . ."

The words trailed right out of Coe's mind. All cars belonged on scrap heaps. Besides, why did his father continually have to say *we* put it back together, *we* restored it, *we* salvaged it. The boys did the work, the seemingly hundreds of teenage mechanic types who hung around the Ettinger home. His father merely puttered with spark plugs, cigarette lighters, and windshield washers. Eleven o'clock at night, Coe would find them in the garage, filthy with grease, the floor littered with thousands of dollars' worth of tools. They must have loved it: a garage in the condition of a house, the opportunity to work on gorgeous automobiles at salaries four times what they would have earned in a service station. Roscoe Ettinger was a decent man with lots of money who needed the talent the young men possessed and was willing to pay for it. The arrangement was ideal. When the boss, as they called him, acquired a new car, there was always manpower ready to begin restoration the instant it was delivered to the garage. Each car was a new challenge, a new sculpture. When a boy had to quit, Mr. Ettinger had fifty to take his place. When he prepared cars for automobile club rallies, the boys worked through the night, and no one complained. Young Coe wouldn't have known about complaints, as he stayed away from the garage, especially when the boys were working.

Roscoe Ettinger was disappointed that his son showed little interest in the cars, but he took comfort in the fact that in recent years, his wife, Helen, had become as addicted to them as he. While she didn't putter about the garage, she took great interest in the work being done on the automobiles. She also took an interest in photographing the cars when they first arrived, again during the period of their restoration, and finally when they reached their completed form. Helen Ettinger's photographs lined the walls of the garage. Above the sink was the old Italian car with Billy at the wheel, the kid whose brains were in his hands. Near the garage door was the photograph of the Mercedes coupe and the three boys, two of them brothers, who had taken it apart bolt by bolt and rebuilt it to where the Mercedes people themselves were dazzled.

Then there was the color photograph of young Coe standing next to a little Ford pickup truck that Roscoe had purchased for fun. Several of the boys had taken on its restoration almost as a joke, but Roscoe took the task seriously as he felt it might have been the only car in which his son enjoyed playing. The look on Coe's face in the photograph suggested that the little Ford truck with the wooden siding might have afforded him some pleasure after all. After being restored, the truck was housed in a shed away from the garage. Although rough inside, it was so spacious, Coe could play house in the back of it, even sleep in it. When children stayed overnight, they frequently slept in the Ford. Mrs. Ettinger would fix up blankets and pillows on the floor, and Coe and his friends would take food and off they'd go to the old truck. Invariably, Mr. Ettinger offered to take the boys for a ride, but Coe preferred to have it remain a little toy playhouse.

When I first met the Ettinger family, Coe was thirteen. Our early visits were nondescript, except that he made certain to let me know two things. First, he disliked his father's cars and if I was interested in them I'd probably not find much of anything to talk about with him. Second, even if I wasn't interested in cars, there probably wasn't much we had to talk about together. When, on the first visit, he saw me striding along with his father to the garage, he must have thought, the guy's a little old to be a mechanic, but why not? Years later, he said his first impression was that I must have been rich, and that probably I had come to make an offer for one of his father's cars.

After two years of friendship, Coe and I had become rather close. One of his many interests was American literature, and so we spent hours together talking Hemingway, Bellow, Faulkner, Agee, Melville,

Hawthorne. He liked the poems of Hart Crane immensely, but Wallace Stevens did not please him. Nor did T. S. Eliot. "One of us isn't ready for this," he remarked, referring to Eliot. We spoke often about his parents, which he could hardly do without getting into the subject of cars. He gave me his own special tour of the garage, and on one occasion pointed out the shed where the Ford truck had been kept. It was no longer there, he explained. His father had sold it, so there was no sense visiting the shed, the scene of boyish pranks and jubilant evenings. Just as well, I thought. The shed was overgrown with grapevines.

If the shed and the truck had significance for Coe, he revealed nothing. The impression I retain from that first tour was that our friendship probably meant something to him, but his antipathy toward the cars was not warranted by his father's interest in them. The senior Ettinger loved his cars but he hardly spoke about them every waking hour. He had other interests, and importantly, was willing to involve himself in any activity if it meant getting closer to his son. This was not the case, however, with Mrs. Ettinger. As far as she was concerned, her role as mother had long ago expired. She continued to feel needed by her son, but it hardly seemed appropriate for her to pursue interests that might bring her closer to him. If he wanted to go riding with her, or swimming or sailing, that was fine. But if he chose not to spend summers with his parents, that, too, was acceptable. "Fifteen-year-old boys are not babies," she would say. "They're men. Both our homes are always open to him. He knows where we are and what we have." There wasn't bitterness in her message; resignation was more like it, with that certain trace of sadness, I imagined, all parents experience upon realizing their children no longer need them.

Coe Ettinger was an excellent student, though not an overly popular one for reasons I never completely understood. Perhaps it was because he chose to be a loner. What troubled me more than his lack of popularity, however, was one visit to the garage when he revealed an almost venomous rage in describing his father's cars and the young men who "brought them to life." It was Coe's expression: "They're old ugly wrecks when my father brings them in, then these guys make their magic and the cars are young and beautiful again. It's like giving youth hormones to old ladies."

It was a disturbing simile. "How about saying youth hormones to old *men* and women?" I suggested good-naturedly.

"Just women," he muttered.

The story that Coe Ettinger told me when he was sixteen might have been predicted, or reconstructed, from the clues he had laid out. One never knows, of course, whether a person one is close to in fact preserves some story he wishes to tell. Sometimes, even we the secret keepers are not fully aware of what it is we carry in our heads. Or if we know we're sitting on some bombshell, we cannot decide who is the best person to hear about it. As is often the case, it was Coe's intense reaction to the cars, coupled with his father's willingness to drop the car business if Coe wished, that indicated a problem. The energy with which the boy spurned car restoration, the garage scene, the young men who refurbished the automobiles, was almost sexual in tone, or so I felt. Indeed, I guessed the story to be one of sexual adventures in the garage, possibly a homosexual affair, even a suicide. Perhaps there had been a sister, I conjectured, and perhaps she had killed herself. Coe never knew of my suspicions, of course, but I would have been remiss had I not remarked to him that I sensed something urgent on the tip of his tongue, and wondered whether I might someday hear it. I would always follow this up with some disclaimer like, "You know us psychological types. We're like a bunch of dogs in heat." Coe would say, "That's a pretty good image: dogs in heat."

"*Is* there something, Coe?" I asked him one afternoon.

"I don't know for sure," he answered almost grimly. "There could be."

During an August vacation, I received a postcard from him. It was the only written communication I ever received from him. Like most young people with whom I speak, he never wrote, rarely telephoned. If there was to be a meeting, I made the arrangements. But now the card. The picture on it was of an old man lying on a beach gazing at his wife but imagining a beautiful young woman in a scanty swimsuit. The message on the back read: "Scenery's here; wish you were beautiful. You were closer than you thought with dogs in heat. I'll tell you the novel I'm writing when I see you."

Surely with this as a tease, his story had to do with some sexual adventures. Or perhaps he was in love. Evidently he was more sexually active than he let on. For when our talks touched on the topic of girls, Coe practically went blank. A fifteen-year-old boy, an exceedingly rich one at that, discovering the pleasures of young women, could his mother have had any doubts why he preferred his newfound entertainment to horses and sailboats. But of course Mrs. Ettinger knew what her son was about. Hadn't she been the one to say that Coe couldn't be bothered with his parents anymore, that he had a new set of friends? How explicit did she have to be!

In early September, just before he resumed school, Coe and I had our briefest, but most powerful talk. He had revved himself up to tell me his "plot for a novel," as he derisively alluded to it. He had decided to speak his piece and have me leave. I was to say nothing; offer no solace, comfort, advice. The "contract" he sought, moreover, apparently stipulated that I never raise the issue again.

"I feel like an absolute fool telling you this," he began, "although you've probably guessed it already. Your sniffers had to tell you something. So stop me if you've heard this one.

"Once upon a time there was this very rich boy with a nice mommy and a nice daddy. He grew up having all the things in the world any little boy would like. He didn't even have a brother or sister to get in the way. He had his mommy and his daddy all to himself, although there were quite a few nursemaids along the way. So the little boy grew up loving his mommy and his daddy and thought they loved him, too, which they did and they didn't, but all that comes later. When the boy got a little older, he learned that his father liked cars a little too much for a man his age; maybe he loved them more than anything else in his life, or should I say any *one*. And his mother, well, she's a bit more difficult to understand, tragic hero, and all that. It's quite complicated because the little boy, he felt sorry for his mother because she loved the little boy's father but he seemed to love his business and his cars more than he loved her. There was nothing she could do but love the little boy, but that didn't make up for her husband not loving her as much as she loved him. So she got interested in cars, because all she cared about his business was his money. So there was the little boy who loved his mommy and daddy but they both seemed to love the cars and the garage and all the boys who took care of the cars more than they loved the nice little rich boy. Now, you see, the plot gets ugly because we begin to see that the boys who looked after the cars are really more manly than the little boy who didn't like cars, but likes books instead. Because there's nothing less manly than a boy who would rather be by himself than with other boys, and on top of that, not like cars.

"But the little boy *did* like cars, or some of them, like the little Ford wagon in the shed. And he did have friends when he was little. They played together just like you're supposed to play with your friends. And while all that was going on the family seemed happy because the little boy's mommy and daddy could spend more time with their cars while the little boy played with his friends. And just maybe, they hoped, he would grow up to love cars, and the family business as well.

"Then one day, the little boy came home from school early with a very bad earache. He knew his mommy would be home because she was always home on Tuesdays, but when he got home she wasn't there. So he went to look for her because his teacher said she might have to take him to a doctor. He went to the garage and nobody was there, which was very strange since somebody worked on the cars all the time. But somebody *was* there because the radio was on. The little boy thought, now where could they be? So he went looking in the room off the garage and nobody was there. He went back to the house and still nobody was there. Now, there's something funny about this part of the story, because the little boy never called for his mommy, he only went looking for her, as if he knew he would find her, but didn't want her to know he was coming to look for her. It was like a game, only it wasn't really.

"Then the little boy thought, I'll go out in the shed and play in my truck and maybe my ear will feel better. So he went out to the shed and opened the door and went up to the little truck and guess what he saw? He saw his mommy in the back of the truck, lying on his sleeping bag with all her clothes off, and with her were the two brothers who worked on the cars. They had their clothes off, too, and what they were doing is a story for another novel, except the little boy was so surprised he barely knew *what* they were doing. But he knew enough. And you can be sure he got out of there as soon as his head went clear again. Nobody knows, you see, how long he actually stood there, although he saw enough to make him think his brain was going to pop out. And here's the funny part, the little boy didn't know, and doesn't know till this day, whether his mother or the boys saw him, although the way they were going at each other, he doubts any of them knew he was there. He went out quietly and he didn't tell anybody what he saw. Ever. Now, you could say this was a horrible thing to happen to the little boy, but as he was running back to his bedroom where he stayed the rest of the day, he realized his earache had stopped.

"So that's the story of the little boy who by nature of a little accident realized that everything he thought about his mommy and daddy, everything he thought about life and living, since children don't know all that much besides their family, was totally wrong. What was right he didn't know, but what he did know was wrong. Because now he thought his mommy didn't like cars at all, it was the boys who fixed them that she liked. They refurbish *her*, too; make her feel young, and new. And his father, well maybe his father did and maybe his father didn't know about her. Maybe his father discovered her like he did and couldn't say anything to anybody either. Maybe his father kept the cars going to keep his wife in hormones because maybe she would have left him otherwise since she could get all the money she'd ever want in a divorce case, and maybe the father didn't want this because it would have made him unhappy, and made his little boy even more unhappy. Maybe the father and the mother and the little boy had to lie to each other, or not say anything about anything if they wanted to stay together. And maybe his mother was protecting his father, because a divorce wouldn't have done the family business any good, or the little boy.

"It's a wonderful novel, isn't it? The reader can make up a million reasons for everybody acting the way they did. Except there's no ending that makes the little boy happy. Every direction he goes he falls in the quicksand, and there's never anybody to pull him out. At least he can't be certain there will be someone to pull him out. Or maybe the whole family's in the quicksand, except that's not going to be his business anymore because he's got to look out for himself, except that's not working either because the more he looks out for himself the more a loner he gets to be, and he knows better than anyone that books don't substitute for living. And besides, if you're running away from life at age fifteen, what good can happen to you when you grow up.

"I say looking out. Those are rather strange words, wouldn't you say? If I hadn't been looking, but instead had been yelling for my mother that day, a whole lot of things would have been very, very different. Or would they? If I'm not in the forest, how do I know the tree falling makes a noise? I suppose I would have known one way or another. But maybe not. Who can say what would have happened to the little boy. After all, he could blame his teacher for sending him home with an earache, too. But the peculiar part of the novel is that all I know for certain was what I saw, that raw scene in the back of the truck I never played in again. My father must have found out something; he sold the truck right after that and no one went in the shed again. But I don't know any of this for sure. It could be he doesn't know a thing about my mother. And did she do it all the time? She must have, but I don't know. And I'm not about to ask her. Does she know I know? I think not, but then again, she asks me so little about what I do in my life, I have to believe she doesn't ask because she's afraid I might ask her about *her* life. My father? He must know. But does he do the same as she does? Did she find him with a woman once, and that's why she did it with those boys? Maybe she was interested in his cars until she found out about his goings-on with women, if there were some. Then there's me, which is the sequel to the novel, although my life figures to be even worse, if this is what's supposed to be the foundation for it.

"You want to know the strange part about all of this? All three of us have been keeping our secrets, right? No one knows what the other person knows they know. Or maybe my parents know about each other but they haven't told me. But there *are* secrets going on here. Yet in my little heart of hearts, I really don't think families can keep secrets like these from one another. One way or another everybody knows what the other people know. Even when there are ten children involved, or a hundred children. You either suspect it, or guess it, or wonder too much about it, but there have to be clues. So with all the secrets, there aren't any secrets at all. But what a way for me to discover the birds and the bees, huh? Me, the guy who'd rather be with Hemingway than with girls. That has to tell you something. People at school tell me I'll be a playboy someday; fast cars and fast women. It's a joke. A big horrible, dirty joke!"

Like many of the young people who have shared some of their secrets with me, Roscoe Ettinger had a way of telling his story as though he were recounting a novel he had written. Granted, presenting the story in the third person allowed him to step out of the terror and hurt of the tale, but his novelistic approach evoked something else in me about the nature of secrets: namely, that which is revealed, Mrs. Ettinger's sexual exploits in this instance, somehow masks a series of experiences or events that were seen by Coe to be even more potent secrets. As devastating as the experience of finding his mother with the young boys was for him, it seemed that this one hideous event opened doors to other experiences that apparently constituted the foundation of his entire life. And these so-called foundation experiences could be labeled the truly important secrets he was barely able to confront.

Throughout our conversations, Coe offered clues to these foundation experiences. He spoke of the limited times he spent with his mother and father. Inevitably the cars and nursemaids came between him and his parents. It must have seemed, too, as if the cars had intervened between his mother and father. Clearly, Coe recognized that the way to his father's heart was through the cars. One of the foundation secrets held that love was attained only through negotiation. To be loved by his father meant that he must love automobiles.

If the boy's impressions were accurate, moreover, his mother, too, "bought into" this arrangement. The contingency nature of love, therefore, was a centerpiece of the Ettinger family secrets.

If the cars were the conduit to love, if not the symbol of love, then they were also perceived by Coe as grotesque and illicit sexual objects. Perhaps Coe perceived his father's interest in cars as sexual, perhaps as infantile. Whatever he believed, it is obvious that a great many feelings, expressed and unexpressed, revolved around the Ettinger automobiles. Along with the cars went the boys who serviced them, boys with whom Coe would have no part.

A classical Oedipal interpretation of the Ettinger family would suggest that with business and automobiles occupying so much of her husband's time, Mrs. Ettinger was left alone and, in her son's eyes, available to him. Whether a possibility for intimacy with his mother scared or pleased Coe is something else we know little about, except that as it happened, Mrs. Ettinger chose to become involved more with the cars than with her son. In a sense, then, the cars were viewed as more appealing and lovable than the boy, or so Coe might have concluded and kept as still another secret.

If one examines closely the words of Coe Ettinger, one finds him playing with the notion—still another secret—that his father appeared to be offering his mother as a reward for becoming involved with automobiles. Granted, one has to reason backward, as it were, even recontextualize his entire life, as Coe did, to reach this conclusion. But there is little doubt that the boy reconstructed the situation and arrived at this position. He reasoned something else as well: If the boys who serviced the cars were rewarded with his mother, then, in symbolic terms, the notion of becoming involved with the cars was abhorrent. The idea seems preposterous, but for Coe it remained plausible. Furthermore, as Coe himself suggested, Mr. Ettinger may have had nothing sexual to offer his wife except the cars, which meant the boys who restored them. And if this was true, then to work on the cars was tantamount to having sexual relations with the woman of the house. In many ways, then, the young mechanics represented the unstated ideal of what Coe Ettinger was meant to become. One might conjecture, moreover, that Coe would grow up believing the definition of manhood or manliness involved the possession of objects, human and material, that boys normally are *not* meant to possess—namely, cars, wealth, and women, and most especially one's mother. To succeed one's father, to literally follow in his footsteps, as the Ettinger family tradition demanded, meant that Coe should possess his father's cars *and* his woman.

Through Coe's account, we observe a young man growing up with his mind filled with secret messages and directions. Not only is he trying to discover a definition of self divorced from his family's wishes and fantasies for him, but he is seeking as well to prove to himself that he is healthy, normal. If the cars in fact are associated with a host of complicated wishes and fears, then Coe's repudiation of them may represent his search for normalcy, or at least a release from the anguish the cars invariably caused in him. Granted, he had done his best to prove to his family that he was psychologically normal, and hence a worthy successor to the family name and fortune, not that he craved wealth. Nonetheless, the secret ritual of passage, the involvement with cars, remained the obstacle to family integrity, the confirmation of his maleness, his right to become heir to his grandfather's business, and finally the opportunity to know a form of intimacy (with his mother) that few boys ever experience. Yet again, all of this was held in secret trust. For the test of Coe Ettinger's childhood was to earn a position in two exclusive clubs, one public, the other secret. The public club was represented by the family's position and status; the secret club involved Oedipal fantasies, wishes, and most assuredly, a degree of terror and dread.

What continued to bother Coe, as I gathered from subsequent conversations, was how his parents rarely allowed him to be a child. I offer no claim that "normal development" requires that people be permitted the caprice of childhood, although I suspect a premature rush into "miniature adulthood" must take some psychic toll. Still, it is evident from listening to Coe Ettinger that he was not meant to mature like most boys, even though his parents made him feel uneasy when he failed to act in the manner of other children. How Mr. and Mrs. Ettinger defined normal boyhood is one matter; how Coe defined it is something else. For one thing, he made it clear that he was not to sound like a little boy. To call for his mommy or daddy, as if they were even around to respond, was deemed inappropriate. (I would stress that being denied the privilege of calling for one's parent when one feels upset, frightened, or in pain is a quintessential aspect of the very denial of one's childhood.) Becoming an adult meant for Coe becoming totally independent, whatever secret wishes one suppresses in the process. One does not call one's mother because one assumes she won't be around to hear, and because one has been taught to be self-sufficient. Now, while this matter may seem somewhat metaphorical, the secret aspect of it bears additional discussion.

Coe Ettinger never forgot what he saw, although he dared not recount the event. The secret to be safeguarded, therefore, balanced precariously on the acts of telling and hearing. If one cannot tell others, one tells oneself; one literally hears one's own voice in one's head. Surely in his mind, Coe went over and over the events of that fatal day when he returned home unexpectedly from school with an earache. But the notion of having a secret becomes even more complicated when we consider that the concept of repression implies that a person is unable to tell even himself or herself a particular message. The sound of the secret, as it were, is drowned out in one's own mind. (Coe recounted to himself all too many times the "novel" of his life, almost as if he were rehearsing scenes, before screwing up his courage to tell me something.) One hears, in other words, a particular message first in one's own mind, then again in the telling of the secret. Perhaps, too, one hopes that in the first public "hearing" of the secret, time will flow backward, and the event one is recounting will magically recede and disappear, and there will be nothing left in the atmosphere but the sounds of one's voice.

Once again, we are dealing with tantalizing metaphors, but recall Coe Ettinger's preoccupation with the *telling* of his story. Not only did he assume the voice of the third person, the storyteller's voice, but he consciously endeavored to enhance the "tale" with an elaborate, even contrived narration, something to which he admitted. One tries to hide, perhaps, in the telling of a secret, for if one's story is artistically told, then one can temporarily "forget" that the story actually represents one's own life story.

One final point about Coe Ettinger's account, an impression really, that has stayed with me ever since he revealed his "grotesque novel." Listening to his account, I believed him to be leading up to the confession of some sexual event, perhaps even the disclosure of his father's homosexuality, or his own, or, as I once imagined, the existence of a sister. The possibility that incestuous behavior was no stranger to this family had also crossed my mind. Heaven only knows what secrets young men like Coe Ettinger might create after safeguarding the one "real" secret they have protected so long.

Then a peculiar notion struck me. The event he had witnessed as well as the way he contextualized and interpreted it seemed to evoke in him a variety of infantile and childlike attitudes toward sexuality generally. Whatever he might have believed, or chose not to believe, about sexuality, was suddenly shattered by the sight of his mother with the young mechanics. I came to think of the episode, therefore, as the "explosion" of Coe's "infantile wonderment." A dreadful prank, seemingly, had been played on him, and the most devastating sexual experiences that he might have allowed himself to imagine were born on a single afternoon. He had discovered his mother in the back of the truck he had taken to be his own special play space. The truck represented, in other words, the one acceptable attachment to his father, or to his father's interest in automobiles. And the boys, in his father's eyes, substitutes perhaps for him, were now enjoying the intimacy of his own mother. If it was not a fatal practical joke, then surely Coe Ettinger had walked headlong into a terrifying dream, one that he secretly shared with both his parents. Of all things to keep the Ettingers precariously close—does one dare say intimately close—was a secret whose entire contents I never learned. Coe's so-called novel concluded, and I never heard the chapters that Mr. and Mrs. Ettinger must have composed, if only for themselves. "Stop me if you've heard this before," Coe had said as he was about to recount the magical secret. He, too, must have sensed the jokelike quality of the experience.

For a long while Coe Ettinger abided by the proviso that he never reveal his secret, living uncomfortably, to say the least, with the hurt of that one afternoon. He never needed to stoke the memory of the event, for the mere presence of his parents, the cars, and the young mechanics, even the old shed covered almost symbolically by a grape arbor, were constant reminders of that one festering secret. As it will sometimes happen in the lives of these special secret holders, the reverberations of that one event spread backward and forward into the time of his life, outward into his public experience, and inward into the core of his personality, until his sense of being and identity were shrouded in it.

It is best, perhaps, to ensure the safety of "infantile wonderment," I would think leaving the Ettingers' home. Eventually it disappears, or breaks, or falls away. Like the precious membranes protecting the embryo, it must be held in trust for a certain period of time if the next stage of life is to be properly prepared for, and the health of the young human maintained. Alas, another metaphor; surely a metaphor derived from still another one of life's mysterious secrets.

Part II

FAMILY VIOLENCE

"The Myth of Harmony"

THREE

Physical Battering

Probably the most publicized issue in the spectrum of children's rights is physical battering. Invariably, when one even mentions the topic of children's rights, most of us think of child beating. It is indeed a serious problem, although strangely, experts cannot seem to agree on its causes. The arguments typically go that child beaters are people who themselves were beaten as children, people with gross personality disorders, people expressing their anger and frustration with unlivable housing, unemployment, poverty.

I don't know *the* reason for child beating, but I lean toward the sociological argument; that is, wretched living and work conditions lower people's thresholds of tolerance and frustration. The baby who will not stop crying is the last straw in a day or week or lifetime of bitter unhappiness, despair, and an overriding knowledge that one is utterly powerless to do anything to improve one's lot. So the innocent baby gets hit, but not because the parents hate it. One thing I do know about families where child beating has been reported is that none of the parents live without guilt and shame. Typically, they are a pitiable group of people, often overcome by the horror they have instigated. Never have I spoken with such a parent and not come away with this feeling. I start off despising them for what they have done, but end up admitting to myself that I have had the same urge as they, and given the circumstances of their lives and that crescendo of frustration, confusion, powerlessness, I might have done the same thing. No, I *would* have done the same thing. Had I lived my life as they led theirs, I wouldn't be who I am, an observer writing of their anger and unhappiness.

I offer this introductory statement because of the special nature of child battering. Many of us are guilty of committing the same acts that the children in this book have kept as secrets in their own families. Not all of us have battered our children, especially when they were infants. Yet one must not leave the impression of standing above these people, in some higher moral plane, and judging their acts to be incorrigible. Besides, as I have said, almost anything one says to a child-beating parent is superfluous. They know the words, and they feel the feelings, which is far more painful.

Physical battering refers also to adults, typically men beating women. Like child beating, adult beating is far more common than we suspect, or admit, although accurate statistics on this behavior are impossible to collect. As is true in child beating, cases of adult beating are liable to be hushed up when the families involved are wealthy. In poor neighborhoods, police are regularly called in to keep warring husbands and wives from killing one another. Often they arrive too late. In richer neighborhoods, police are called more typically for burglary. It's the psychiatrists, psychologists, and social workers who hear of cases of wife battering. Not ironically, they usually hear of the cases from the battered ones. In Western society, while it is hardly legitimate for a man to beat his wife, the act is looked upon as far less grievous than that of battering a child.

It would be inaccurate to say that in my conversations with affluent families the problem of wife beating is common. The young people with whom I speak do not report the act of parents slapping one another as being a common occurrence. But again, who is to know what truly happens in these homes, for a person hardly announces to the world that his mother was beaten by his father. Indeed, a person might not even talk about it to his sister, or even to his mother, who sits across a table from him, her face covered with bandages. But why don't these people talk about it? Why would a woman "take it," as the expression goes? How can a man who leads what to everyone seems a calm and successful life not admit to himself that he has some serious problem if, on occasion, he beats his wife to the point of causing serious injury? Wouldn't the fact of her lying at his feet, unconscious, blood pouring out of a broken nose, be a hint that perhaps something somewhere is wrong? Is he afraid of a divorce case, public embarrassment, the loss of his job, even felony charges?

The more I speak with families where battering of children and wives, some of them pregnant, takes place, the less I understand the behavior. I give in to the urge to label someone in the family sick, and offer therapeutic assistance of some sort, but something tells me this may not be the best tack. More important, one must keep an eye out for the reverberations in the family system. A family, after all, is hardly a collection of people. Bonds hold family members together and at times, I fear, apart as well. A bond may be a metaphor, but it is a real enough phenomenon in the psychology of families. The metaphor of the stone hitting the water and the ripples going out seemingly forever in their endless concentric rings is well known, and overworked. But it has relevance to a family's reaction to something like wife beating. The word "ripples" may be a bit too gentle for describing the reaction of children to wife beaters, but ripples is meant to imply a prolonged period of reverberations. Thus we say, something happened years ago but it still continues to take its toll on a child.

All people forget experiences, or make themselves forget experiences, especially ones that are particularly frightening. In psychoanalytic terms, traumatic events are somehow repressed. I say somehow repressed because there must be a mechanism of repression, a psychological or biochemical mechanism, that makes us manifestly unable to recall the dreaded event. The event itself, moreover, must be horrendous if we cannot recall it when in fact we saw it and heard it.

Again, my own bias is revealed in favoring concepts like repression and trauma. Surely there is much tucked away, however precariously, in our minds that may come back to us. It is material, traces of experiences, apparently not lost to us forever. Because it is not lost forever, and because bits of this so-called unconscious material do return to us in terms of what Freud properly called the psychopathology of everyday life, as, for example, dreams and slips of the tongue, we have no idea of the degree to which we remember events and experiences.

Still, while my intellectual bias (and training) tells me this is so, my experience with the families I visit tells me something else. Too many of us throw too many psychological terms at too many people, and at ourselves, and then proceed to diagnose and label people on the basis of these words and the concepts and theories that underwrite them. More specifically, one of the unsettling discoveries I made in listening to the family secrets of young people is the number of cases in which I thought something had been genuinely repressed which in truth had not been repressed at all. How is it, I would ask myself, that this boy doesn't know a thing about his father hitting his mother? How can he deny, repress, disregard, go blind and deaf to what happens in his own house? Surely what this boy has done goes beyond repression into the realm of self-ablation of the brain matter. But the boy, as it turned out, did know, everything. He might have stared blankly, innocently, he might have mumbled when a topic was brought up for discussion, but he was acting. He was acting like the espionage agent who would lead his interrogators to believe he knew nothing of his country's secret plans. I don't know what you're talking about, his face says, while in his mind a voice screams, I know far too much, far too much.

The prose, admittedly, becomes melodramatic, but then again, many young people feel the lives they lead to be melodramatic. They *are* secret agents with information that must be kept secret. And while some young people reveal what might be considered classical repression of traumatic events, other young people reveal the identical behavioral patterns when in truth nothing of the so-called traumatic event has been repressed. The young person, knowing the consequences of revelations, may *act* as though events have been repressed. The story of Jacqueline Provo, which follows, represents an instance of genuine repression. Here was a young woman with a magnificent gift of recall unable to remember anything of a set of events that occurred in her childhood until an experience when she was sixteen evoked these earlier recollections. Her story fits rather nicely into that cluster of cases psychoanalysts call the return of the repressed.

The story of Peter Malone, however, is not explained by repression, as I had once thought it might be. What Peter saw and heard as a little boy never left him, the ripples never ceased. Unlike Jacqueline, Peter never forgot a moment of the experience. The details remained fresh in his mind as if they would not disappear until he could tell someone of them. Even then, he knew they would not disappear, but would continue to haunt him. While the event may stop, the ripples continue. Furthermore, while the major characters of these accounts may have settled their disputes, some family members may not have found solutions to their problems. In listening to stories of young people like Peter Malone and Jacqueline Provo, I often imagine myself in the audience of a deeply disturbing play. We trudge out of the theater shaken to our very core, while the actors mechanically remove their makeup, having totally put out of their minds their business of the night.

At the end of this section, I shall say more about the psychological implications of being a witness to child and wife beatings. For the moment, let me stress the issue of a young person dealing with the experience of having witnessed what must be construed as a murder —a murder, more exactly, of one family member by another.

JACQUELINE PROVO

Jacqueline Provo's father was born in West Africa, her mother in Barbados. Soon after their marriage, they moved to New York, where Jacqueline and her three brothers were born. Edward Provo had known days of unemployment. His wife, LuAnne, worked when she had to, although she always preferred to stay at home with the children. She felt being near the children was a mother's place. That is putting it mildly, for according to Jacqueline, who is seventeen, her mother abhorred the idea of having to work, and grew furious with Edward when he would announce in that capricious style of his, "Well, guess who's out of work again!"

The oldest child, Jacqueline has vivid memories of that scene, her father stepping gaily into the room, her mother sensing the announcement, and LuAnne's tight lips, her stare, and the silence as she just shook her head. Damn you, she seemed to be saying. God damn you! Edward would look to little Jacqueline and she would put her arms around him, not without some fear, and somewhere in the small apartment a baby cried, or was it two babies, or were all three boys, born in consecutive years, crying at once?

That scene, Edward having broken the news for the hundredth time, LuAnne shaking her head, Jacqueline's body quivering with fury, and the crying children, captures all of Jacqueline Provo's childhood. Whatever else there was, school, meals, the happy times, a few trips, life in a poor neighborhood, visits with people, all of it is drowned in time; only that scene survives.

And tell someone about those few seconds of a one-sided conversation between her parents? What for? Who would want to hear about it anyway? Every family had their little scenes, the father telling of one more bout with unemployment, the mother furious because it meant she had to go out and find work, leave the children, face the fact that when things were supposed to be going a little easier, they were going a great deal harder. Maybe in other families a daughter didn't embrace her father, or maybe she did but could do it without that fear Jacqueline always felt with her father's arms around her. What was the difference. Every family had its problems. Poor ones, rich ones. "Don't let anybody kid you," Jacqueline would tell me again and again. "Every family has its problems; no one is perfect. And the family that laughs a lot, maybe they got the biggest problems of all. You never know. Only the people in the family know."

If Jacqueline Provo is to be believed, absolutely nothing of any consequence took place in her life from the time she was born until she was sixteen years old. "I couldn't tell you what any of us did on any day," she has said. "They're all the same. It's not my memory either. I can tell you what I had for lunch six years ago last Tuesday, but there's nothing to remember, just Daddy's little unfavorite announcement, and Mamma's look, and the embrace, if I did it all the time, which I don't think I did, and then the fear part, and the baby crying. There's nothing else." At sixteen, however, a few memories of those putatively empty days returned.

I met the Provo family on the eve of Jacqueline's eleventh birthday. I remember going with Edward to a little store looking for gifts for the children who would be coming to the Provos' to celebrate. Edward had purchased his presents for his daughter weeks before. I bought Jacqueline a book, as Edward said she read every free minute and never had enough books. I recall inscribing a sentimental line in the book about how much I hoped we would be friends. Two days later I received a lovely note from Jacqueline in which she said anybody who gave her books had to be her friend. A year later her father and I gave her a present of a parakeet. Edward feared his wife might not take to it but LuAnne said it was the finest gift she'd ever seen. The children adored it; Edward and I were heroes.

The gifts, surely, enhanced my friendship with Jacqueline, but something else, too, brought us together. She needed to have a friend outside the family, and to get out of her family once in a while. So we took trips around the city, and she met a number of the other young people I see from time to time.

It wasn't long in our friendship that Jacqueline told me about the single scene she recalled from childhood. I would tell her, "Jacqueline, I'm not here as a psychotherapist; we're just friends." Her reaction to my words was pleasure mixed with confusion. She would look as if she had just choked on a piece of food and she was waiting to see if it would pass. It always did pass, and we would be on our way with me wondering about the memoryless child with the capacity for perfect recall.

At sixteen, Jacqueline took a job with a family in a suburban community. She was hired to work Saturdays, cleaning up around the home but mainly looking after the family's four-month-old baby. Nordell and Theresa Wishner, in their middle forties, had decided to have a third child. The baby, Belinda, presented quite a challenge to her parents, her thirteen-year-old sister, and an eleven-year-old brother. Saturdays especially presented a problem, as everyone always had scheduled numerous obligations. Jacqueline was the ideal solution. In fact, she was so good for the Wishners, they doubled her salary after the first day and made arrangements for her to travel by taxi. Then they offered her a room in the house, inviting her to stay with them whenever she wanted. They later would decide Jacqueline had to live with them and attend high school with their oldest child, Sara.

Jacqueline was overwhelmed, her family deeply touched by the Wishners' kindness and their invitation to a Sunday barbecue. The day was a great success, despite the slight tension that existed between the families, the one so rich, the other having to contend with unemployment, an inadequate apartment, and other problems. But it was a good day, and Jacqueline, who had slept at the Wishners that weekend, was jubilant. There was good food, a great deal of talk about sports, promises to attend baseball games together, and the added bonus of Ted Wishner becoming completely entranced by Stevie Provo. The star attraction of the day, naturally, was Belinda, who was held and cuddled by exactly ten pairs of hands. Everybody fought to touch her, even Jacqueline's youngest brothers, who nobody would have guessed had such a fascination for infants.

Jacqueline Provo's sixteenth year would be nothing like the previous ones. The Wishners had changed her life, as she had changed theirs, something LuAnne frequently pointed out. While Edward enjoyed his friendship with the suburban family, LuAnne talked of "people with all the good intentions in the world, trying to take children away from families like ours. We don't need reminders of who we are and who they are," she would say. "I understand they mean well, but I'm more interested in *doing* than *meaning*, and before they're through, they're going to turn our daughter into a white child. Schools here are good enough for Jacqueline, and this home is good enough for her, too. It was good enough before she met them, it'll be good enough now!"

Jacqueline was surprised by her mother's reactions. The Wishners had been generous, and they sorely needed her services. They were neither patronizing nor condescending. They made her work hard, but respected her and showed their affection in numerous ways. That they trusted her to care for Belinda said what they felt about her. One evening, Jacqueline overheard Theresa Wishner speaking on the phone. "We have a gold mine," she was saying. "Jacqueline's a gold mine. She's saved us. If she leaves, I die."

Then suddenly everything stopped. It stopped so quickly the Wishners never understood what caused it, nor at first did the Provos. It stopped as quickly as it had started, exactly two weeks after Jacqueline arrived at the Wishners' one Saturday morning to learn that Belinda had fallen off a washing machine and broken her cheekbone. Mrs. Wishner had looked away for no more than a second, but it was enough for Belinda to fall on the tile floor. Her face was a mass of abrasions, and the discoloration made Jacqueline feel queasy. She could barely look at the child, who surprisingly was delighted to see her. The sight of the smile forming on the injured face made Jacqueline cry. The tears came softly at first, but then she began to sob uncontrollably. Mrs. Wishner couldn't comfort her, and she was sent home in a taxi. "Tell your mother you felt ill," Mrs. Wishner said kindly. She gave Jacqueline a full day's pay.

A week later LuAnne Provo called Theresa Wishner to say that Jacqueline would not be working there anymore. No excuses or explanations were given, although everything was said in kindness. Nobody was blamed. The Wishners were shocked. Their letters to Jacqueline went unanswered. Ted Wishner tried telephoning Stevie Provo, but LuAnne intercepted the calls. She didn't want him calling her boy anymore, she told Ted politely, but firmly. Edward took no role in the matter, and Jacqueline, in a most uncharacteristic way for her, let the issue slide. She neither called nor wrote the Wishners, which was peculiar for a girl who wrote me, an unknown person, a thank-you note for an innocuous gift. It was a full rich note, too, that had taken time to compose. For the first time in my friendship with Jacqueline, it was I who was having difficulty swallowing the imaginary piece of food. I didn't tell her the Wishners' assumed reason for her sudden departure, which was that they thought Jacqueline had become pregnant. The thought might have crossed my mind, too. Still, when I raised the issue, she said only, "The piece still stuck there, Tom?"

"Very definitely. Is it with you, too?"

"Probably," she answered, and looked away.

It was a year before she spoke to me of the Wishners and what had caused the wholly inexplicable departure. Throughout the conversation, Jacqueline's tone was calm, free of emotion, her words carefully selected. It was important that she not use a word that would evoke too many feelings.

"You remember how I told you I saw the baby Belinda all black and blue? That was true. And it was true that she fell when she was with Mrs. Wishner. At first it didn't hit me. I just saw the baby and felt terrible. It was like somebody had hit *me*. She really looked bad, too, but I couldn't stop looking at her. I found myself staring, like I was looking at a corpse or something. Around her one eye the skin was yellow and purple. She looked horrible, but Mrs. Wishner didn't seem to care so much. I mean, she cared, but she kept trying to make *me* feel better because I was, like, in worse shape than Belinda. Belinda was smiling like nothing happened. It was so foolish, the whole thing. The baby looks terrible, and the mother is doing her best to make *me* feel good. I *was* in worse shape than Belinda.

"Then later that morning when I was still looking at Belinda and thinking about how good Mrs. Wishner was with me, I realized how I had been having some strange thoughts. Like first, I wasn't even aware of Mrs. Wishner holding me in her arms. I was just looking at the baby, who was moving around in her little crib. I didn't even know she was holding me. And I felt afraid. Then I started to think, why is this baby's skin so white? Is that part of the accident, too? Maybe when they have an accident their face, where they didn't get hurt, turns real white, like white paste. But she was white all over. Her hands and her legs were white, too, and they weren't anywhere near where the accident was. Then I thought, you know what Jacqueline, you're going crazy. This baby didn't *turn* white, this baby *is* white. White babies are white, they don't *turn* white. Sounds like a crazy thought, but it was the only thing that made me feel a little bit better, as crazy as *that* sounds.

"I could have stayed. I could have controlled myself, I think, but something sort of exploded in my head, although I didn't think of it until that night when I was in bed. I don't even know how I explained coming home so early to my mother. I probably told her I was sick. My mother didn't like me working out there, no matter how much she was glad to have me making some pin money. So my quitting wasn't all that bad, although she didn't give me a hug like Mrs. Wishner did. She just said, 'If you want to lie down, I'll try to keep the boys quiet for you.'

"That scene, I tried to tell you about, with my father saying he lost his job, and embracing me, and my mother getting angry and me feeling afraid? Well, I had some of the parts right, but I had them mixed up. He did come home and make his announcement, and my mother did get that look on her face like she could have killed him for what he just said and the way he said it, although he was just as upset as she was. He didn't want to scare us, that's all. But the part with the baby crying and my father putting his arms around me, that's not exactly the way it was. What happened was, that when he didn't have work, those were the worst times for us, and my mother took them worse than he did. She'd get really angry sometimes, and I'd get scared. I was much more scared of that, of course, than I was of my father not working. Little kids don't even understand about that, anyway. So she'd be upset, moping around, and real angry. You could see it the way she kept her mouth real tight, and dry. She wouldn't talk much in those times. She *hated* the idea she might have to go out and find work. She hated having to go out of the house and tell people, 'Guess who ain't working again. Our life's going nowhere but to hell, and it's going there the fastest way it can!' When she was like that, the thing that really got to her was the boys making noise, specially their crying. I tried to be the good little girl, so she had no complaints about me. But the boys, she couldn't take their crying, and babies cry. You can't do nothing about that. You should have heard Belinda. Rich babies cry, too. Maybe they don't know they're rich."

At this point Jacqueline broke out in a wide grin. She clearly enjoyed what she had said about rich babies. Then, just as suddenly as the smile had formed, the edges of her mouth dropped downward, and she resembled an infant about to cry. And Jacqueline Provo unashamedly did cry. The pieces were still stuck in her throat.

"Mamma beat our boys," she said between sobs. "She beat all three of them. I saw them. I saw how they looked when she got done. She made them be quiet, all right. Walter wasn't even eight months old when she was doing it. But she hit him. Hard. I saw her. He cried even harder so she hit him harder. She hit him until he stopped breathing, and she left him lying there. I thought he was dead. I went over to him but she pulled my arm and said, 'You stay away. I didn't kill him if that's what you're thinking.' But Walter was lying there bleeding. Both his eyes were closed, and there was blood coming out of his nose, and I thought out of one of his ears, too. She just left him. Maybe there was nothing she could do. If she took him to the hospital we for sure would have had a visit from a social worker and they would have looked around, put two and two together, and decided we weren't a fit family, to have these children, I mean. So they might take Walter away. That would have been worse than him lying there beat up like he was. She knew it. But then I'd get upset, I suppose—I don't remember everything—and that's when my father would hug me, because she never would. Maybe I was afraid I'd be next, but I don't think so.

"I think I had the memory right but I didn't have things in the right order. First he would lose his job, then he would tell us. I barely understood everything that was going on. But what I did understand was how those might be the times when my mother hit the babies. That's what I was afraid of. His coming in and standing near the door like he did, wearing his brown hat, that was the sign there was trouble. I remember Walter with all the ugly colors on his face. My mother never hugged me neither. I remember that, too. She didn't hug nobody when she got mad enough to beat her own children. Nobody touched her. Maybe they should have. Probably we should have talked about it. But if they weren't going to bring up the subject I wasn't either.

"Once, just once in all those years, I talked to Stevie about it. After that thing with Belinda I suddenly remembered a lot from when I was small. I didn't even know what he knew about any of this. I thought probably he didn't know anything. We were talking like it was some make-believe woman instead of it being our own mother. 'Say, Stevie. I was just thinking. Pretend there was a woman, and you knew she was beating up on her babies when they were, like, eight months old.' I mean, that's the way I was talking to him. 'What would you do, Stevie?' You know what he says to me? He says, 'I wouldn't do nothing. Ain't my business what she does. If she's so upset about her husband not working and she's gotta go out and find herself a job that she goes and hits a baby only eight months old, I'd say, let's be thankful she didn't start hitting her children when they were just born. Then she really might have killed them.' Stevie knew. He knew as much as I knew. But nobody said a word about it."

By now, Jacqueline had composed herself. The tears had stopped and she was holding her head up straight as she always tried to do. Her eyes were clear. "When I decided I might tell you about this," she resumed, "I decided I had to tell you about how I'm going to be when I get old enough to have children. Old enough in my head, I mean. It'd be easy for me to say I never want to be like my mother. But that wouldn't be nice. I didn't like what she did, but she didn't like it either. She just did it. You don't *promise* never to do things like that, they just happen. My promise to myself is not to be poor when I marry. There must be some money around, because without it, people like my mother, they get so worried something horrible is going to happen, they begin to do horrible things themselves. She can't stand the idea of being on welfare and not having enough money. I don't blame her. She also didn't like the idea of her daughter working. It was like I was going out to the Wishners' claiming I was poor, the same way my father would stand in the door and tell us he didn't have a job again. She's not mean, my mother. All she wants is a simple kind of life but she knows she's never going to get it. So I made a promise that I have to be sure there's enough money before I have children. People like my mother who are afraid something horrible's going to happen have a reason for thinking that. She saw too many horrible things in her life. I want to be as sure as I can nothing horrible's going to happen, as sure as anybody can be. I mean, babies like Belinda can always fall and almost die, but that's not what I'm talking about. I'm talking about when a man comes in the door and makes an announcement that from now until nobody knows when, things are going to be horrible because that's the only way they can be."

PETER MALONE

I had known Peter Malone almost five years. I watched him grow up from a thin, weak boy with pale skin drawn tight across his bones to a tall, strong, well-built fifteen-year-old with the same pale white skin now rather puffy around his eyes. Peter wasn't so little anymore, and he also wasn't as happy as he once seemed. Strangely, at eleven, he was a boy with meager energy, often tired, but happy, with bright, shining eyes. At fifteen, he had accumulated more energy than he knew what to do with, but the eyes no longer had that same gleam, and the excited eager look was gone. At fifteen, Peter was the sort of person who looked as if a minute before you met him, he had just heard something horrible, something serious enough to make him cry. I never saw him cry. Neither did his parents, neither did his older sister, Nan.

If Richard and Celia Malone noticed a change in their son, they never mentioned it to me or their closest friends. Peter was a perfectly normal boy in their eyes, and in mine as well. He was a good student, popular with his classmates, a boy who did what boys his age did, which meant, I suppose, that the Malones, like many parents in their neighborhood, had little idea of what their son did after school and on weekends. The telephone was always ringing; someone anxious to speak with Peter the same way years before they had been eager to speak with Nan, who was now at university a thousand miles away. "Life and death. It's always life and death," Celia Malone would say with a smile, referring to the phone calls from Peter's friends. " 'Sorry to bother you, Mrs. Malone, but I *really* need to speak to Peter. He's home, isn't he?' No, he's in surgery. He's always home when the phone rings. It never rings when he's not here, which means he's always with the kids who call him. Two seconds after they leave each other they remember the life and death message. Isn't normal adolescent life a bore!" Then she will look at me, as she has almost every time I visit the Malone home, with that same expression: "After all these years, I still can't figure out just what it is you're studying us for."

It was a good question. I suppose I visited the Malones because I liked them. Nan was a marvelous young woman, an outstanding student, linguist, horsewoman. Peter, besides his good school record, was a superb athlete, when he felt like it. Soccer in the fall, skiing in the winter, baseball and track in the spring, swimming and diving in the summer, and he was more than good at all of them. Celia Malone, a woman in her late forties, was a self-effacing woman but not without charm and wit. One had the sense she understood a great many more things than she ever talked about. Her side of the bed was always surrounded by books, and when her children let her near the stereo system, she chose records of solo piano, Chopin, Beethoven, Mozart, and occasionally some modern jazz, although Gershwin seemed to be the outer limit of her popular interest. Celia also was involved with interior design and advertising. Since college, she had managed to keep a hand in both businesses, but never on a full-time basis. It wasn't the children that kept her from a full-time career commitment. In truth it was a lack of interest. She wanted her free time; two days a week at a job was enough. If a particular business demanded that she work more, she simply offered her resignation, and invariably they rescinded and let her set her own hours. She was too valuable an employee, too valuable a person. The combination of her thoughtfulness, intelligence, and charm was uncommon, and her employers knew it. They would not so easily replace a Celia Malone "The woman could have gone to the top," one of her employers once told me. "She had it. Has it. But something held her back. Not her husband. I know that for a fact!"

On several occasions Celia Malone told me she had life set up exactly as she wanted it. The kids, the husband, the work, the eight-year-old Volkswagen to drive around in, no pets to care for, no summer house to worry about: "Give me a wish, and I'd wish for exactly what you see."

Except for your illness, I would think. I never said anything about it, but there was that slight hitch in the ideal life. For periodically, and with no warning, Celia disappeared into a hospital somewhere. It was never for a long time, four days at the most. I say hospital somewhere because I would never be told which hospital. Peter would say, "They told me the name but I forgot it." I never pressed him, as it was evident the family, or Celia, wanted no visitors. I respected their wishes but could not stop wondering about the illness. At first I guessed it to be alcoholism, then, for reasons I don't understand, I decided it was cancer. Life was too perfect for Celia Malone; her attitudes were idealized. She was dying, although she hardly looked sick at all. Indeed, she grew more robust as the years went on. She looked much younger than forty-eight, but isn't that what people said about cancer? People can look beautiful, but they're dying.

If Richard Malone worried about his wife, he gave no indication of it. For the husband of a dying woman, he maintained a stoic approach to life. A highly successful bank executive, Richard Malone had worked his way up in the world beyond any expectation his own father, an electrical supplier, had ever imagined. At fifty-two, Richard was economically set for the rest of his life. Tough in business, and by his own admission, slightly aggressive in friendships, he was a fiercely competitive man who matched his need to go to the top with an unyielding set of ethics. He was to everyone who knew him a principled, scrupulous, responsible but driven person.

If you knew Richard Malone, you knew in a few minutes his present position in the bank, and the position he craved. A certain chairmanship was right up there, just slightly out of reach for now, but certainly not out of the realm of possibility within a few years. His competition for the job was Roland Lendell, a man his age, with an educational history not unlike his own, but with the unfortunate problem of being thrice divorced. If the chairmanship was to be decided now, it was Malone all the way. Celia Malone made him an even more attractive candidate, which they both knew, and her illness would certainly not jeopardize his case. There was only one flaw in Richard Malone's character, it was said, and he knew it, too. On occasion, for it was not a steady habit, he could drink too much. Hardly an alcoholic, it was a problem of infrequent drinking and letting the aggression explode all at once. He could become foul-mouthed, and he often threatened physical violence. But it was occasional, and I never thought about it, except to wonder what children think when they see their parents in the throes of a temper tantrum. "I'll tell you what *I* think," Peter remarked when I jokingly brought up the subject, although not in the context of his father's occasional problem. "I think, just hold on, Daddy, I'll change your diapers and warm up a bottle."

"Well said," I agreed. "I'm sure that's what my kids think when I get mad like that."

Peter was stunned by my words. "You get mad?" he asked incredulously. "*That* mad."

"Is the Pope a Catholic?"

"You, a psychologist who's always so calm around here? Like, a tantrum?"

"Not *like* a tantrum," I answered. "A *tantrum*. A one hundred percent watch-Tommy-go-crazy-like-a-two-year-old."

"Amazing."

"Not if you see it, it isn't." I watched Peter's face closely. He looked dumb struck. Granted, I, too, am always surprised to learn that a calm, soft-spoken person yells, even screams at their child, but Peter's reaction exceeded surprise and incredulity. Then his look changed, the expression softened, and now he did appear to be close to tears, closer than I had ever seen him. "Peter," I began, "you look frightened and relieved of something at the same time."

His eyes grew moist and he asked me, in the voice of a small child, "You ever get so mad you hit your wife?"

"No," I replied with great seriousness, "but a lot of men have that desire from time to time. How does it go in this home?" My question barely made grammatical sense, but the key word was go. It was like in that instant he had agreed to tell me what had been troubling him for years. Months later he would say he had felt as if he were an airplane pilot being cleared for takeoff. He would say, too, that he believed if he hadn't let out the secret in that instant, he might never have said anything about it.

"My dad drinks once in a while," he began with a tone that let it be known he was going to finish the story, no matter where it led him. "Not a lot of the time, but once in a while. He's not a bad guy, my father, it's just that when he drinks, he can get mean. Not to us, but to my mother. I mean, he pounds her. The first time it happened I didn't think about it, because I saw her in the morning, you know, and they both told me they'd been in an automobile accident the night before. He had to stop suddenly and she crashed into the dashboard. So I believed them. Why not? It happens. But she looked terrible. I was, like, ten. Then it happened again, the same way, everybody comes down to breakfast, where's mother, because she's always with us. Well, she fell in the garage and hurt her cheek so she's sleeping late. Fell in the garage. My mother never goes in the garage. Her car sits outside. She doesn't go in at night because she's always convinced three million burglars are waiting for her. We kid her about it. But she fell. When I saw her that afternoon after school, she didn't look too bad. She had a black eye, that's all. She stepped on a rake and it sprung up and hit her in the eye.

"Now, what came over me then, I don't know. But I went to the garage to look for the rake. Like a detective, you know, looking for clues. What rake? I wanted to know, like I was going to arrest the rake. You know what I found? Nothing. We don't have one tool in the garage that you could step on and it would pop up and hit you in the face. I went back to her. 'What rake, Mom?' She looked surprised. 'What do you mean what rake?' 'The rake you stepped on. I went into the garage, there's nothing there.' 'Oh,' she says, 'that's because your father threw it out this morning. He said he didn't want anything that dangerous in our house.' Make sense? It makes sense. And you know, sometimes you can tell when your parents are lying, and sometimes you can't. I believed her. But this was the last one because now I really was like a detective.

"Time three, or four, breakfast, school day, no mother. Where's mother? Mother fell down the stairs and Dad had to take her to the hospital for X rays. He's concerned maybe she fainted and the doctors want to examine her. I was worried, so was my sister. She started to cry. We said we'd rather go to the hospital than to school but my father laughed and said, no problems, she'll be home tonight. We went to school. He went to work. My mother came home that night with a small cut on the side of her nose, and again a black eye. Same eye as before.

"A lot of guys, you know, they might have the same reaction to all of this I did. Your mother, what does she know from anything. She slips, falls, faints. Women can do all that. You don't think about men doing that. Women aren't so coordinated. You push it out of your head. But every time I'd visit her when she'd be recovering, she'd start to cry. She tried to keep it from me but I saw. She has a terrific personality. She never cries. 'Don't worry,' she'd say to me all the time. 'Nothing's going to happen.' It was an accident, three times? And how come with my room near the stairs I didn't hear her fall? A woman can't fall halfway down a flight of stairs without there being a lot of noise. You see how they made me become a detective? Case was solved a couple of weeks after my twelfth birthday. I heard them fighting and I knew my father was drunk and boy did he hit her. I mean, I didn't see it, but I heard it, and she went down, like out for the count. Foom. I couldn't see them but I had my door open and I heard them. He hit her. I'm telling you he whammed her in the face and she went out. So what did brave Peter do? I ran across to my sister's room and opened her door. It was so dark in her room I couldn't even see where the bed was. But she wasn't sleeping. She was crying with her head in the pillow to make it quiet but you couldn't make it quiet the way she was crying. Then she saw me and stopped and she said, and I mean she was terrified, 'Daddy?' 'Of course not,' I told her. 'It's me.' I was twelve years old then, how could she think it was my father. Because she was terrified, maybe, that she'd be next. 'It's me.' 'Get out.' That's what she yells. 'Get out! Now.' She's sort of whispering-yelling it. 'Get out, Peter. Now!' So I ran back to my own room and flew into the bed, like kids do, you know.

"The next day nobody said a word. Not my mother, not Nan, not nobody. What happened last night? Nobody made a peep. I said to myself, maybe you dreamed it. Maybe Mom is really sleeping like Dad says. I dreamed it. So I finished eating like a good little boy and I went upstairs and my father says, 'Where you going?' like he doesn't want me to know something. I answer, little Prince Charming that I was, 'Me? I'm just going to the toilet, Daddy.' 'Make it quick,' he says. 'I'll make it quick.' All I want to do is see my mother's face. So there I am twelve years old, and I remember my parents gave me the most fantastic presents for that birthday. Like it was a special birthday. Fantastic. But now I'm creeping into my mother's room and she's sleeping on her back and I walk up to the bed and there's that eye again, purple, red, blue, gray, black, silver. I must have wakened her and she looks at me with the good eye, it was just barely open. I remember she wasn't wearing a nightgown, but the same sweater she had on the night before. She says, 'It was just an accident.' You know what I told her? I said, 'You must be accident-prone.' She smiled. I didn't even know I knew the word. So that was that.

"But then something strange happened. Because now, you see, I knew exactly what was going on. We had the nicest family in the world. I had a successful mother, a successful brother, a brilliant sister, only my father had a funny little habit of beating the hell out of his wife every once in a while, and it wasn't all the time, and he didn't say anything, and she didn't, and my sister had let me know that *she* wasn't going to say anything, so I wasn't going to say anything. The big family secret, pulling us all together in the most healthy, happy way, right! So what does little Peter do? Peter decides that he really *did* dream the whole thing. How do you like that little bit of logic? I said to myself, since nobody's mentioning a word of it, I must have been dreaming the whole thing. And the fact that my mother's eye is closed like some boxer took her on in a dark alley, no, I decided, I dreamed that, too. I mean, it's easy to see what I'd done. I didn't want to know the truth. They didn't want me to know. My sister didn't want to talk about it. So I told myself, don't be an idiot, you're not supposed to think about this. You're certainly not supposed to tell anybody, so let's just pretend it didn't happen. All right, you guys, I would think at the breakfast table, how's the happy little family today? Everybody here and accounted for, or is the little woman lying under the coffee table somewhere with the old eye turning blue, black, purple, and silver?

"It happened again, and again. Not that often, like usual, but several times a year. Once I thought I'd like to call up the bank and talk to this man Roland Lendell, you know, and tell him about my father. An anonymous phone call from a good citizen. Then I thought, my God, that's really sick. I have to help my mother. Maybe what I should do is call up this boss of hers and tell her. Mrs. Rankling, maybe she'd help. I never did that either. There was nothing to do. I knew I was never supposed to talk to my sister about it. I mean, that's when you know you really have something horrible happening in your family when brothers and sisters don't even talk about it and it doesn't even concern them, directly, I mean. It was like there was a sworn pact in our family. When I got older I decided my father really was sick. Only sick guys do that. Like you see on television. Oh, which reminds me. Do you know that one night we watched a television show, some police thing, about a man who beat up his wife and killed her. We watched it, together, the happy little family, and nobody said a word. When it was over my mother, my *mother*, calmly gets up, turns the tube off, and says, 'It's past bedtime.' Do you believe? I watched half the show. The rest of the time I watched their faces, the little detective still hunting for clues. Maybe the murderer would show a little facial tic or something. Nothing. Not a move, not a squeak. The happy little family watched their happy little TV show in living color. Just another night of sordid entertainment. But relate to *us*? Are you serious? What's that got to do with us? That's for poor people and sick people. Not for the rich, happy, healthy Malones."

Tears were streaming down Peter's face. I made a gesture, an utterance that said perhaps you've told enough. Peter held up his hand. "It's now or never," he whispered.

"I told myself after that TV show, my father's sick. He needs help. But I can't tell him and I can't get anybody else to without telling them the great secret. And if I tell the great secret my mother, father, and sister will shoot me. In turn, using the same gun probably. Because my father doesn't hit my mother. I dream it. Five, six times a year I dream it. I dream the noise, the crying, the yelling, the screaming, the black eye, the purple eye, the blood on the pillow. I dream it. It's in my head. Has to be, otherwise we'd be talking about it around here, right? So I decided my father is sick. A man who does that with no excuses is sick, and then he goes on pretending everything is great. Sick. But my mother? She's beyond redemption. A woman who takes that, as a regular dose, or even once, a woman who takes that is weak, and totally without character. She's the worst. I hated her for not saying anything. Getting him help. Her help. Letting us talk about it even. I hated her for that. She just kept up that lie, that's what it was, too, a lie: 'It was an accident, darling.' If she told me that once, she told it to me a million times. An accident, darling. I hated her for that. I still hate her. All right, maybe you don't want to go all the way with it, maybe you don't want divorce courts, even though you know you'll be set financially, *and* you'll get custody of the children. Maybe you still love your husband. Maybe you hit him once in a while yourself. Maybe you're as sick as he is. I don't know. I don't know anything. How can anybody know anything around here when nobody has ever said one word about *any* of this.

"Maybe it's because I'm a male that I sort of side with my father, not that I agree with what he did, does, will always do. Although I side with her, too. No, that's all wrong. I hate them both for all this. For what they do, for what they did to Nan and me, making us not talk about it, which somehow meant we couldn't talk about anything serious at all since it happened. And we haven't. I don't know a thing about Nan's life. Nothing. I don't even know what courses she's taking. And she doesn't know a thing about what I do, or think. And my parents know less than nothing, and they'll never know a thing until they open up on their little secret. They don't

talk, they'll never know their children again, certainly their sweet little Peter. My mother thinks I go out on weekends with kids? That
I'm popular? That I date all these cute little girls who are the daughters of all their friends? They don't know their little Peter anymore,
little Peter the detective who solved his first and only case and can't
go to the police or anybody with his *evidence*. You know what little
Peter does on weekends, Tom? He hangs around with *boys* and he
takes all the LSD he can get his hands on. That's what he does.
That's *Peter's* little secret. His little eye for an eye, tooth for a tooth.
You think the people at my father's bank would like to hear about
that? You think I'm not protecting him in ways he'll never know?
You think I don't worry about whether my friends may not be the
sons of all those big shots he goes around with? Or my mother, too,
for that matter? The little detective is now the little protector. The
little spaced-out queen detective. And if they'd like me to change,
come clean, like they say on every television show in this country,
then I'd like them to come clean, because right now the delightful
charming little Malone family has to be the dirtiest family in town!
Ten men couldn't take the garbage out of this house as fast as we
produce it. We're choking on it!"

The accounts of Jacqueline Provo and Peter Malone illustrate several of the more serious aspects of keeping family secrets. Besides the
matter that both cases involve physical battering of family members,
a second and more obvious feature unites the cases: Both young people were holding a family secret that presumably every member of
their family already knew. Only naturally, then, I asked myself,
from whom are these two people keeping the truth of their experiences?

The answer to this question has as much to do with the nature of
psychological denial as it does with keeping families united. Whereas
Jacqueline tried valiantly—if one can speak in these terms—to forget
the scenes of her brothers being beaten, Peter forgot nothing, repressed nothing, but chose to trick himself into believing that everything he had witnessed had been a dream. Actually, Jacqueline, too,
alluded to the dreamlike quality of her faulty memory, noting, as in
a dream, how the individual segments of her recollections had returned to memory in improper order.

That something as grotesque and frightening as the *sight* of one
family member beating another must be *silenced* (the mixed metaphor is intended) points to the phenomenon of denial. But denial, as
we know from personal experience, works only up to a point. Clearly,

certain experiences evoke the memory of an event we try mightily to pretend (or wish) had never occurred. More precisely, denial rests on that treacherous "as if" premise. We live our lives *as if* something had not occurred. We dislike the timbre or texture of the experience, but we attempt to swallow it, incorporate it as quickly as possible in the hope that it will pass (away). The anatomical and physiological aspects of this metaphor, incidentally, should not be discounted. Probably because certain experiences loom so intense and real, we are unable to taste them, then spit them out when we sense their bitter quality. Instead, we are driven to incorporate them, even if this means that symbolically we continue to choke on pieces of the experience.

In abstract terms, we note in the accounts of Jacqueline Provo and Peter Malone two forms of denial, one seemingly motivated by psychological factors, the other by so-called sociological factors. We remember that the children themselves accorded either psychological or sociological reasons for feeling obliged to keep their secrets. Jacqueline blamed society, poverty, and unemployment for the distress experienced by her mother, distress that ultimately led to the beating of her brothers. She alleged, moreover, that impulse control alone would not account for the recurrence of inhuman behavior. No one living in the sort of conditions she had known, she allowed, could ever be certain they would be able to control themselves: "You don't promise never to do things like that, they just happen." Peter, in contrast, seeing no relevant sociological issues, merely labeled his father ill.

The point to be stressed involves the degree to which people are capable of controlling their feelings generally, and in particular, their urge to hurt, even kill. The capacity to control one's drives, much less curtail the destructive motives of another person, is only part of what are referred to as issues of personal and social control. We may also point to the controlling and constraining aspects of keeping a secret. Both Peter's and Jacqueline's accounts suggest that when one is bound to secrecy, one is genuinely bound. People have control over secret keepers, their behavior as well as their private feelings. Perhaps, too, this control extends to the secret keepers' ability to recall those events that ultimately have placed them in psychological bondage. I remember Peter telling me: "I couldn't talk about *anything* serious to anybody else." How frightened a person must be to believe that the slightest inopportune word might cause the very harm that he or she once witnessed. We might add that the fear of not telling one's secret may give rise to a fear of discovering *anything* of a personal nature in someone else.

Once again, we have responded in metaphorical terms to a social psychological principle of great importance. Both Peter and Jacqueline, and other young people in similar circumstances, tend to show a confusion between so-called real events and images of the mind. Confusion, perhaps, is the wrong word, for surely these sensitive and sophisticated children recognize the difference between wishing or fearing destruction, on the one hand, and actually witnessing it, on the other. Yet both expressed the feeling that having witnessed physical abuses, they were no longer the people they had been. The sight of violence had altered, somehow, the natural flow of their lives. One cannot be the same (internal) person with all these (external) events transpiring. Surely Peter's drug taking supports this interpretation. What he could not change in the past, or the present for that matter, he attempted to change in his mind. At the very least, he sought a change in (or of) consciousness. One might conjecture that Peter's drug taking was merely old-fashioned "escape from reality," as the common expression goes. I felt it meant something else; namely, the desire to obliterate the recollection of the events he so despised, or at least effect a transformation of consciousness that would yield the internal or psychological change he had experienced while keeping secret his mother's battering.

To repeat, preserving their secrets, and the measure of control secret keeping has over people, obliged both Jacqueline and Peter to change. Part of their denial and "forgetting" symbolized a desire to be rid of portions of themselves, portions they could neither confront nor confess. While the notion may seem preposterous, Jacqueline's momentary confusion about the injured baby's skin color may relate to the feeling that she, Jacqueline, had changed, or would have to change. She would have to rid herself, in other words, of those aspects of her being that she had associated (psychologically) with the events she had witnessed as a child.

When speaking with many of the children whose accounts are heard in this book, I came to believe that holding tightly to secrets puts people in a state of psychological isolation. How often I left the Provo and Malone homes imagining the children locked in glass-walled soundproof booths. There they stood, albeit in *my* imagination, isolated, frightened, unreachable. One stands alone with one's secret; there is no one to hug, as Jacqueline made clear to me. And if there is no contact, no touching or "freedom of speech," as it were, there can be no sense of one person caring for another. If no one touches me, I am not loved. If I cannot express my feelings, I am unlovable, lifeless.

The circle appears to close in cases like these, with personal or psychic destruction, obliteration, repression resulting not only from the witnessing of a dreadful act but from the additional fact that one is denied the right to reveal the act, or even express one's reactions to it. Cases of secret keeping differ markedly from cases of trauma, especially when one examines the way psychological pain following trauma is reduced. When a child is seemingly traumatized by some event, we usually seek to encourage the child to talk about the event and his or her feelings. We discover how much "resistance" is offered by the child to the suggestion merely of returning to the scene of the traumatic event. Nothing like this, however, occurs in secret keeping where children quickly learn that they must not discuss the event, even when they know full well that others already know of the event. Surely these experiences represent the epitome of dramatic irony; that brothers and sisters should be prevented from speaking of matters each knows the other longs to divulge. But let us remind ourselves of the real contingencies underlying these secrets. Sufficient evidence exists in all these cases to reinforce the children's silence. Had Peter Malone spoken of his mother's beatings, his father's job might well have been jeopardized. Had Jacqueline Provo permitted social service authorities to learn her secret, her brothers might well have been assigned to foster homes. Still, while a degree of so-called magical thinking might have influenced both children's readings of their situations, I would argue nonetheless that very real consequences underwrote the need for absolute secrecy.

As we turn now in the next and subsequent chapters to other children's secrets, and the powerful effect secrets have on individual psyches and entire family systems as well, let us be reminded that keeping a secret, as the familiar expression goes, is much like sitting on a time bomb. Powerful events initiate the need to keep a secret, but once kept the secret itself becomes an explosive device. Not surprisingly, therefore, many young people in the position of a Peter Malone or Jacqueline Provo ask the inevitable questions: When and where will the explosion take place? Will it happen in my home with all my family present, or will it happen in my mind? Can I escape the explosion, move perhaps to some other place in the world, or into some other place (or space) in my mind? And will I survive the explosion?

How deafening the noise of silent secrets!

FOUR

Incest

If children keep secret events they have witnessed, then they also keep secret events they have merely imagined. The literature of psychotherapy, and especially psychoanalysis, contains accounts of just such imagined events that children feel they must never reveal, or fantasized events they cannot remember. The expression "The mind plays tricks on us" speaks to the truth, but reality plays its tricks on us as well, as the accounts in previous chapters have shown.

As a person trained in psychology, I confess to undertaking my work predisposed to believe that the mind plays more tricks on us than reality. Thus, when I hear alarming or tawdry accounts, I instinctively interpret these accounts in terms of some grandiose psychological mechanism. Whatever the source of that child's tale, I will think it signals a supremely creative imagination, if not a symptom of some grave disturbance or psychopathology. This may seem a peculiar admission, particularly coming at this point in our exploration. Surely I have belabored the point that many children's secrets and fears of disclosing them are often founded on real events and human contingencies. Yet, in the beginning of my work, I too regularly took a rather hard-lined psychological stance: Something serious is eating away at this child if he can recount such an obviously fabricated story and believe so intensely in its validity. As I say, my psychological training predisposed me to discredit certain accounts, but so did the topics of these accounts make me (want to) resist their veracity.

In one of the first (research) families I met, a thirteen-year-old boy, after knowing me only two weeks, began describing in vivid detail the sexual activities between his father and twin sister. He told the story in an utterly sober fashion, his tone vacillating between excitement and boredom. I remember thinking, he sounds first like a person describing the sights he sees from a train, then like a stationmaster tediously reciting that day's schedule of trains. I recount below the story of that boy, as I think it contains particularly poignant and significant aspects of secrets kept about incestuous relations. Before turning to the account, however, let me offer one point.

A common belief holds that poor and especially poor minority families tend to practice incest more frequently and more openly than more affluent families. To my knowledge, no sociological study has conclusively confirmed this belief. Indeed, it is difficult to imagine how valid statistics would be obtained on such a delicate matter, not that the subject precludes sensitive research inquiries. In this case, I have chosen for this chapter two life studies, two young people who have revealed instances of incest in their families. One of these families is poor, the other rich. I have made a special point to bring these two disparate histories forward so that no one will be led to deduce from the portraits that incest remains a common practice among the poor, an anomaly among the rich.

I present no hard scientific findings on the subject of incest, but the "soft" impression I offer may surprise some readers. I have heard direct and indirect references to and actual accounts of incest in innumerable households. It appears to be a far more common family matter than I, for one, had ever dreamed when I began researching family life. After hearing myriad accounts of incest over a relatively short period of time, I once reached the misguided conclusion that *every* family must practice incest in one form or another, and my own family was the rarity. Of course this is not the case. Yet, like many issues affecting family life or human sexual behavior, incest, like homosexuality, will in time be a more "acceptable" topic And, as the acceptability spreads, we will hear increasingly more accounts of it. Books will be written— many of them of the confessional variety—and the issue, as it is said, will be let out of the closet With greater awareness of the issue, we will be obliged to alter our estimate of its frequency, and possibly, too, revise our approaches to the study of incest. But if it is more commonly practiced than we normally imagine, then how people cope with it psychologically and sociologically is barely known.

In the end, some might argue that the publicizing of incest will have negative effects on families and emerge as one more fact confirming the demise of the culture. Others will contend that just as sexual accounts found in all varieties of literature do not directly affect sexual behavior, so will the frequency of incest not increase with public awareness. Presumably, researchers will applaud open discussion of the topic as this will indicate that incest is becoming more accessible to their methods of inquiry.

Having made this qualifying point, let us turn first to the account of Tony Majors, my friend, at the time, of two weeks, and thereafter, to an account of incest told by eighteen-year-old Brenda Kelleher.

TONY MAJORS

Tony Majors was what many would call a follower, a boy who never stood out in any group to which he pledged his loyalty. When he walked with other young people, he walked near the edge; when they ran, he straggled in the rear. He offered few suggestions for action, went along with just about anything they said. Tony himself admitted all this. He would be lost, he remarked to a friend, if his gang abandoned him. Alone, he found little to do.

Like most young boys in the neighborhood where the Majorses lived, Tony preferred to "mess about" in the streets. School was hardly bearable; earning a little pocket money was a preoccupation, and getting into trouble the sort of thing one expected. While Tony spoke little about his neighborhood, I knew that the rate of unemployment among young people in his community often ran as high as 50 percent. I knew, too, that adult unemployment rates, while never as extreme, ran considerably higher than the national average of 6.5 percent (see Chapter 9). The Majorses had always known poverty. Eddie Majors, Tony's father, one of the kindest men I ever encountered, was in and out of work so often one could barely keep track of him. None of his five children—not Tony, his twin sister, Laurie, or the three younger ones—could ever agree on whether their father was working or unemployed. One child would be convinced Eddie was at his job, another child reported their father hadn't been home in three days. I once asked Laurie when was the last time all seven Majorses had sat down to dinner together. "You gotta be *kidding*," she retorted with dismay. But she went on to say that being together as a family wasn't necessarily the Majorses' main goal in life; the main goal was employment. Besides, sitting down for dinner wasn't the be-all and end-all of life. I remember her walking away from me, muttering, "Sitting down together at *dinner? Laying* down is more like it." I assumed her reference was to Eddie and Tara Majors' constant state of exhaustion. Work or no work, one could hardly miss seeing how pitifully tired these two people were. If only they could have borrowed some of their children's energy.

After I had known the family for four years, Tony, now fourteen, had gradually become more willing to speak about his life, his activities and plans. I did not sense there was anything special on his mind; he merely seemed more accessible. So we talked, about baseball, school, clothes, the boys he hung around with, one of whom he greatly feared. "Why don't you get away from him, then?" I asked, as if young people could break off social couplings with impunity.

"Hey, you don't break off so easily, man," he admonished me. "All kinds of friendships in this world. All kinds of wild-ass ways people got figured out to stay together, or get even closer. You get my meaning? I mean, can you let your mind *run*, man, have it take in what I'm trying to tell you?"

I confessed that I did not follow his line of thought. He had gone too fast.

"Now lookit," he began. "I got a father right? And I got a sister, twin sister, right? Well, now, you just use your little imagination and figure out what they been doing which they ain't supposed to, at least according to the rules *I* know. You think you got it now?"

I nodded.

"My sister told me once you asked her if we sit down at dinner, all together like? We got a dining table, but we don't *eat* there all that much. Folks too busy to be eating together. We usually run in and out of the kitchen, grabbing a little of this or that. 'Cept lots of the time my ma will make a real dinner for my father. He sits in the kitchen to eat it. Fact is, I don't know why we even keep that dining table; never do seem to use it. It's like lots of things in our house; it's just there, nobody asks no questions as to why it's there, it's just there. It's like, nobody asks no questions to nobody in our house, about nothing. Everybody's going in and out, minding their own business. We let folks alone, you know what I'm saying. You want to go there, you go there, you don't want to, nobody much care. Only rule we got is about the doors. You see a door closed, you either leave it closed, or you knock, 'cept, of course, if it's your room. Same goes with the people. You don't ask them no questions, like what they been doing. I come home, ain't nobody 'round going to say, Where you been, Tony? How come you did this or didn't do that?

"But my sister Laurie and me, we're like twins. We don't have to talk much to know what the other one's doing. You sort of sense it. I mean, we're like one person split in two. Came from one person, if you know what I mean, so we're kind of wired together. I get into trouble, you know, come home with the straightest-looking face on you could ever see, my ma, she don't know nothing's wrong, but Laurie, she can tell. Never misses. Only she forgets sometimes it works the same with me, too. She goes weird someway or acts strange, she might cover it up all right with some folks, but I can tell second I lay my eyes on her. Okay. So, like six months ago, we're watching television, and I'm looking at her thinking, what the hell she do today, sitting there looking *weird*, man? I say, 'What you do today?' She say nothing. I say, 'I don't believe it. You sure look weird to me,' I tell her. Can't be wrong, not with no twin sister. Never been wrong before. Sure can't keep no secrets from *her*. I say to her, 'You got a new boyfriend?' She look at me, I mean she gives me the *weirdest* look, man, and she say, 'Might. But he ain't no boy.' 'What the hell you talking 'bout?' She say again, 'Ain't talking about nothing.' That's all. Ain't going to get it out of her, and anyway, I didn't care too much 'cause all I wanted to do was make sure it didn't have nothing to do with me. She want a boyfriend, hey, she got a right; that ain't none of my business.

"Then a few weeks later I walk in on them. You know what I'm telling you, man? I come home, I must have been more quiet than I thought, and there they are, Laurie and my father, man, and they are humping on the dining table. I mean, she's kind of sitting and lying and he's pushing himself right at her. They ain't kissing, and he was dressed, 'cept for his fly. Broad daylight. Lightest room in the house. Only room over the street. People 'cross the street could have been looking right in on them. And she ain't got no clothes on but one stocking. Had one leg on the table, one leg hanging down real relaxed, that's the leg had a stocking on it. My dad got frightened, never saw him look like that. I ain't saying what my face had on it 'cause I don't know what was going on in my mind. Man turned so quick you could barely see him, and out he walks to his room. My sister, she just sat there. Turned 'round to look at me, just like she knew all the time I'd be walking in on them. Girl wasn't surprised.

Hell, *I* was the only one with my clothes on and *I* was surprised. You should have seen her, man. She didn't jump 'round to get no clothes on or nothing. She looked 'round like nothing in the world bothered her, man; like I caught her washing the dishes. I was staring at her tits and pussy, man, and she wasn't making no effort to hide nothing. This is my *sister*, man. I never saw her without no clothes on. And there she is, letting me stare at her pussy till finally she say, 'What the hell you think, I didn't *have* one or something? I ain't the same way as you, you know. Make you sick to see it? Here take a *good* look.' And she sticks it out right at me, man. Saw it so close I could have jumped her myself. Told myself, what the hell kind of shit's going on around here? This ain't happening to me, man. Got to be a dream. I'm standing here and my own sister's getting out of the sack with my old man, *her* old man, and I'm looking down my nose at my own sister's pussy. *Got* to be a story, man.

"You know what I told her? I say, 'Who else is home?' Believe *that*? Makes me laugh to hear me tell you. Who's home? Hey, maybe if Ma's around I'll take her on, 'specially if she got a nice-looking pussy like yours. What the hell is going on here? Had so many feelings, man, didn't know which the hell way to go. Thought I might leave, but I didn't; just stood there looking at her, and *damn* if she didn't take forever to put her clothes on. Didn't wear no bra, either. Told myself, all she's doing is waiting around till I leave so's she can get herself ready for him again. She'll put on as little as she can 'cause they ain't finished. *I* might think it's the weirdest scene in town, but they don't. They're hot to go again. Girl has itching powder in her pussy. Sitting and watching the television talking how she got a new boyfriend. My ass. I'm talking 'bout my sister, man. Talking 'bout my father, too, 'cepting he split so fast it made me forget he was part of the action.

"Like I say, I wanted to get out of there fast, but I didn't, did I? Then I thought, oh my God, I'm for sure going to throw up all over my clothes. Going to heave it all right on top of the table and my shoes. Thought if I got it on her she'd sort of deserve it. Wanted to see her, too, covered up in shit and vomit. I didn't think that till that night but I thought it. Shouldn't be able to get away with it without me throwing up on her, when she's naked, too, man. Like to see her clean the shit out of her pussy. And she wasn't cleaning up herself at all. She wasn't feeling dirty, that was *me* feeling dirty. And I didn't do nothing but catch 'em at it. I wasn't part of it, though she sure made me feel like I'd been eating her out myself.

"All of this wasn't really what I'd call having a secret. Like, I

wasn't going to say nothing to no one 'bout it—go up to Mamma
and say, Got a little evening news for you, Mamma—no one *to* tell.
They embarrassed me. Then I asked myself, I say, Majors, say you
walked in on *any* two people going at it. Say you was doing it and all
these dudes walked in on *you*, then what you going to feel? Told myself, all my charge would just up and run away somewhere. Probably
crawl under the bed somewhere, 'less I was doing it on a table like
you know who. Girls don't mind nothing like that, far as I can see.
Ain't got nothing so strange about 'em like no man. They'd all just
do like my sister, shove their tits right up at the person, make him
feel more embarrassed about himself, the way you are when you
can't hide nothing.

"Anyway, I left my sister sitting on the dining table, with her one
stocking on, thinking, going to run out of here, man, or I'm going to
hit her in the face, or I'm going to throw up. Wasn't going to tell
nobody, of course. Fact is, told myself that same story over and over
again for weeks after it. Dream 'bout it, too, when I ain't telling myself 'bout it. But the secret part, and she know it, too, cause like I
told you, she always know what I'm thinking, she looked all right to
me. I thought, hey, what the hell, my daddy's getting it on, she'd
probably rather do it with me anyhow. She built all right, too. And
man, I could see every inch of her. She wasn't in no hurry to put her
clothes back on case I changed my mind. She was waiting. Least she
wasn't going nowhere with her one leg hanging down off the table
and her pussy turned toward me, like I say. Then I thought, ain't
heard a damn word from my father. Man goes off to his room zip-
ping hisself up, but he ain't yelling at us to get out. And she sure
didn't see *me* go nowhere. Girl's waiting. I'm waiting. My father's
not telling us to do nothing or not do nothing, so he's probably
thinking, let the kid have the sloppy seconds.

"She was looking at me, too, man, looking to see if I was going to
get the charge on or not. Must have been that I wanted to, but a
man don't let hisself think of things like that, least I never did. Then
you see your father doin' it and you figure, if *he's* getting it, what's
wrong, man, you the oldest son, next in line for the position, ain't
that right? What the hell, girl's sitting there all warmed up like some
hot sports car. Like I say, why not? You know what they say about
doing it with ugly girls, put a pillow on her head. And here, where
the girl's not ugly at all, you just put things out of your mind, same
things, I s'pose, you been putting out of your mind since you was old
enough to know what you can do and what you can't do. But I
thought, ain't what you *can't* do, it's only what you ain't *s'posed* to

do. But *he* did, and *she's* willing, so what's wrong with me? We were waiting there, man, at that dining table, seemed like a lifetime 'fore I made my move to get the fuck out of there 'fore I didn't know what kind of all-time hell was going to pop loose. Two more seconds, I thought, and I'm going to be ready for the weird home. Can't be happening. *My* tongue hanging out, getting so excited to get it on with my twin sister? Two minutes before that I might have said no to the whole idea. Now I was letting it pass so slow through my mind, thinking it over, what the hell's the word my mother uses: contemplating. But something stopped me. I didn't, but something in me did. I walked away, charged up, too, man, and did I get the hell out of there. Somebody else, seemed like, was pushing me out of there. Barely got to the door, you know what I mean, and goddamn if I don't hear my sister say, and she still got that one leg with the stocking on it hanging down, which I was really beginning to hate by now, she say, 'Hey, what the hell, baby, you can always get a second chance. This ain't the first time at all this *fun*.' Just like that she say it, all this *fun*. Secret part of it is the only part that'll make shit like that fun.

"There's another secret part, too, which is wondering, like, if there really *is* going to be another chance like she say there would. They're going to be going at it any old time, so I gotta wonder, my going to catch 'em again? My going to stop 'em when I catch 'em again? 'Cause that's important, too, ain't it? Hell, maybe they'll keep going at it, no matter if I'm standing there or not. 'There's old sloppy seconds waiting 'round for old Tony.' Pretty generous of the old man and the twin sister. Family sharing. Sitting there like that with her one stocking on, shoving her pussy at me. We was one person once, she and me. I don't know about him, what he was to any of us. You think maybe all this don't make him no father to me no more? Hey, nobody knows about this. Maybe they do, but I'll be damned if I'm going to ask nobody about it. 'Bout none of it, you can be goddamn sure."

Let me again assert that Tony Majors' account is not to be taken as a prototypical model of incest. I doubt that anyone has sufficient information on this topic to even know what the "prototypical" case of incest might look like. So let us briefly refer back to this account, and anticipate the account that concludes this chapter, in order to examine the more salient issues of these moments of incest.

Surprise, shock, a feeling of being hit between the eyes with a bullet, how does one best describe the reaction of Tony Majors to the scene of his father and twin sister? He was always quick to tell me of the family's respect for individuality, or individual life-styles, which might have been his way of indicating that the family was never wholly united. Still, it was hardly a splintered family, a collection of persons having no sense of the cultural or atavistic bonds holding them together. Tony Majors, after all, had a twin sister, and was only too aware of the anatomic as well as mysterious attachments constituting this twinning. To hear him speak was to believe he had reflected on the exotic implications of twinning, or perhaps this was only my mind at work. But that is not completely honest, for he did ponder his sexual involvement with his sister, deemed it utterly pathologic, and sought to dismiss it. He did not, however, repress it, and this fact is significant. Surely a host of unconscious material flooded his mind upon discovering his father with Laurie, but a host of very conscious material also welled up within him. He was, in many ways, implicated in the scene into which he had accidentally fallen.

His response, as we note in the account, is complex, filled as it is with myriad feelings and explanations of his own as well as his father's and sister's behavior. Of the many themes one might underscore, I am struck by the interconnections of nausea, punishment, humiliation, and anger. How one best displays this variegated quartet of emotion is anybody's guess, but on a primitive, even physiological level, the desire to (or fear that one might) defecate or vomit could hardly be seen as surprising. To vomit is to throw up one's feelings, reject the unacceptable or undigestible. It is for most children, moreover, a disgusting biological act, one that is often associated with early thoughts about sexuality. The word heard most often today in this context: "gross." Also in this context, we are reminded that visions of the grotesque, the freak, the extraordinarily ugly evoke in us the sensation of nausea. Merely thinking of these sights will produce the same effect.

Along with the nausea was Tony's sense of humiliation. How poignantly he described his desire for people to cover themselves up, protect themselves from, of all things, his own eyes. Listening to him talk made me wonder whether, in the classical image of the primal scene, children might believe that mothers and fathers having sexual relations in fact constitutes an act of incest. Surely many young children "come to believe"—how, we don't fully know—that sex is bad, perhaps even that all sex is bad precisely because (psychologically) it has incestuous qualities. It makes one feel dirty, or it "dirties" another person, as Tony suggested. It may also appear, as some have suggested, as an act of anger. To do something sexual is to do something aggressive, possibly, the child may reason, out of a need for revenge. As I say, I heard these themes in Tony Majors' account. I heard, too, his sense of shyness, his feeling that it was he caught in the act; caught, as they say, without his pants on. Still, whatever motivated his feelings, one hears in the account his exquisite self-consciousness, and this term, too, should be considered in all of its meanings.

As shyness or even embarrassment may be associated with self-consciousness, so, too, is self-awareness, or more precisely, the knowledge that one is differentiated from others (like a twin sister). Self-consciousness also connotes the letting into conscious of facts about oneself, or the willingness to *see* oneself, *look* at oneself, *recognize* oneself. Each of these italicized words contains special relevance for Tony Majors' account. As I listened to him tell his story, I could not help but think of that phrase heard often during childhood, usually about the issue of food being prepared or items in a store: "Look but don't touch." Presumably, Tony wished to look at what was going on before him, as well as what might have been circulating in his mind. But to see everything, in a sense, is to condone everything, and this thought troubled him. One detects his envy along with his sense of shame, just as one detects his belief in the simultaneously natural and wholly unnatural act taking place in his home. As he worries whether he will be able to control himself, he begins to believe that his father is no longer his father. Is this because by magically "unmaking" his father, the act he witnessed is no longer incest? Or is it, rather, because he wishes to replace his father? He did, after all, joke to me, and to Laurie, about making the incestuous move symmetrical by "taking on" his mother. Then again, perhaps his wish to disassociate himself from the people in his family, as well as extricate people generally from their family roles, reflects his utter inability to arrive at satisfactory answers and feelings. Like Brenda Kelleher, in the account that follows, Tony Majors practically begged for someone to *teach* him how to think about incest. How to think, in other words, about the unthinkable.

We all know the experience of feeling physically assaulted by some vision or piece of information. We respond with nausea, hurt, something literally physical. Our response, moreover, seems to be involuntary; we do not try to conceal it, nor do we deny it. We hunt for commiseration, nurturance, but in the primitive sensation of being assaulted, in Tony's case by the vision of incest, we seek protection. We turn to the safety of large numbers, groups, hordes, gangs. We turn away from intimacy, gentleness, and seem to crave rough ways of ridding ourselves of the images. All of this happens secretively, of course. Indeed, we are delighted that we need not tell people the details of agony or unrest; they see our pain and that remains sufficient communication. Said differently, we rely on silence, and secrets. But for many young people, as we will note in later chapters, keeping this mental ruckus inside must lead one to believe he or she is going crazy. Or is this notion nothing more than the old superstition (and mental representation of social control) claiming that performing an incestuous act causes one to go mad?

Whatever Tony Majors carries now, his vulnerability, his sense of men as strange creatures, his sense of shame for himself as well as his father and sister were much in evidence when I left him the afternoon he revealed his secret to me. We spoke little of the event in the weeks that followed, but the few words he did offer indicated he was still wrestling with the animal versus human aspects of incest, and the fear that, like an oozing oil slick, his experience with incest was slowly covering his entire personality. I heard him make references to himself that suggested his need to isolate or compartmentalize the experience; keep it, as it were, in quarantine. Not so strangely, I heard this same mechanism in the words of Brenda Kelleher. Both young people sought a solution to their secret, a healthy antidote to a feeling that their unique "dramas" had rendered them larger than life. Their justifications for incest abounded. Brenda even argued once for the "therapeutic" nature of incest. But justifications aside, both Brenda and Tony sought ways to neutralize the experience, for forgetting, repressing, ablating were implausible eventualities. Their involvement with incestuous relations was easy to conceal, impossible to forget. The space between themselves and their families was now replete with secrets. As Tony said, the point was not forgetting, it was covering up. The reader will recall his reference to covering the face of an unattractive woman and see how this might be associated with his desire to conceal his own desires, memory, and vision.

Still, whatever his response to the sight of his father and sister together, be it a "wish" for women or men to be sexless and thereby utterly innocent, or his confusion over his being implicated in their act, Tony Majors came away from the experience holding tightly to a need to maintain respect for his family, and respect for the concept of family. Envious, nauseated, infuriated, terrified, he wanted, as the expression goes, to put the pieces of his family and his own sense of self together, so that he might keep his secret embedded in a respect for the people from whom he would never fully differentiate himself. I think of Tony Majors often, Brenda Kelleher, too. Because their stories have a tinge of terror for me as well, I joke to myself about phrases like "being a family man," or "making a house call," or "being an angel of mercy," or "families getting together and becoming inseparable." I joke, too, because I feel the young people's concerns about that fateful question: Can you keep a secret?

BRENDA KELLEHER

If Tony Majors was witness to an incestuous experience, Brenda Kelleher, a lovely eighteen-year-old woman from what would be called an upper-middle-class home, was a direct participant in such an experience. But I find myself pausing at my own description of her home and family, and human beings generally, being classified so succinctly as upper middle class. The novelist would offer us a richer description of this precious unit called family, the social scientist fights the urge to employ the mere shorthand term: upper middle class. It's a shockingly brief classification, and somehow, too, "diagnosis," of an entire life situation, yet it does convey something.

What really does upper middle class mean? I asked myself driving to the Kellehers' comfortable ranch-style home in an affluent suburban community. It probably refers to families that call themselves middle class, know they aren't, yet still deny they are rich, which really they are. Like citizens of most Western nations, Americans tend to describe themselves as middle class; it remains a cautious designation. It saves face, and suggests that no one will ask those "further" questions, which researchers like I invariably do. The Kellehers were wealthy people according to one set of standards, well-to-do according to another set. "Up-to-my-eyes-in-hock-well-off" is how Bernard Kelleher described himself. He uttered the phrase with a large grin. He knew better than to cry poor standing before a two-car garage, on the roof of which rose a complicated-looking television antenna. Moreover, he knew better than to bemoan his fate while his eighteen-year-old daughter, Brenda, and sixteen-year-old son, Bernard, Jr., fought over the right to walk behind the power lawn mower which bumped along fifty yards from where he and I were standing. Yet it was also clear that Bernard Kelleher, who had worked hard to reach this position in life, was inundated with debts. While he rarely complained to me of his finances, he felt the pressure that results from barely being able to afford such a lovely home and grounds.

Bernard and Maggie Kelleher, married almost twenty-five years, were marvelous talkers. In response to the most innocuous question they would go on incessantly, each of them verbally trying to nudge the other out of the way, "off the airways" as Bernard laughingly called it. At the time I met the Kellehers, I had no idea I would ever be researching children's secrets. Had I foreseen this work, however, I surely would not have pinpointed the Kellehers as a family where secrets were being kept. It always seemed that Bernard and Maggie told anyone willing to listen to them every event, episode, excursion, adventure, and intimate scene they had ever experienced or heard about. Openly gregarious people, they made it a habit to tell their friends whatever was on their minds.

Their children, in contrast, were not at all this way. Not exactly shy like her brother, Brenda Kelleher was a quiet child whose expressions revealed that she missed nothing, and held tightly to many feelings. A tall girl with flowing red hair, she looked not unlike her mother did at her age. One noticed immediately the resemblance between mother and daughter. Age had taken Maggie Kelleher's looks, she readily admitted to this. But if someone in the family was to be attractive, it was God's blessing, she said, that Brenda was the one. And being attractive meant having boys telephoning her and stopping by the house.

"Brenda has her gentlemen callers," Bernard remarked angrily one afternoon, as two young men drove off in a refurbished convertible. If any two human beings least deserved the title gentlemen callers, it was these two. Both Bernard and Maggie were reconciled to the fact that their daughter was in great social demand. Bernard, however, loathed the idea that his daughter would select even to host in their home the "mangy dogs that go sniffing around here every time you look up."

A high school senior with excellent grades and her sight set on college, Brenda Kelleher could rightly have been called her own woman. Fortunately, for her parents that is, she rarely dated the "mangy dogs," but she did let them visit, despite her father's insistence that they meet at the road and not be allowed to set foot on the property. "But Daddy . . ." Brenda would purr. Bernard would relent. Maggie would shake her head. Most men would have relented, for Brenda's way had a seductive quality as well as a forcefulness. It was as if she were saying two things simultaneously: "Do you really think I'd *do* anything with those boys?" and "You wouldn't dare stop me."

I was often party to these father-daughter exchanges, exchanges that caused me to wonder how it might go when my own daughters reached adolescence and "the boys" started coming around our house. I mused, too, on the fact that while one often hears that special seductive purr young girls seem able to muster at will, Brenda Kelleher's purr had a more, well, pernicious quality about it. Daughters, it is said, have their fathers wrapped around their little fingers. It's an apt expression, ringing as it does with tones of sexuality and coerciveness. A lovely face and figure, as nineteenth-century novelists were wont to tell, all too often threw stolid figures of authority into a swoon. But Brenda Kelleher had her father more than wrapped around her little finger. If she didn't outrightly own him, she had him caught in a spell.

Although merely an expression, it turned out that Bernard Kelleher did indeed live under his daughter's spell. While he never gave the slightest hint of what constituted this spell, his daughter was only too willing to share it with me, when, after several years of friendship, the burden of it became unmanageable.

"The word for it is incest, and if you want me to spell it for you, I'd be only too happy to. Surprised? I think it would make this whole neighborhood collapse. For God's sakes, you mustn't tell. For Bernard and Maggie's sake you'd better keep our little secret. A lot of this is going to surprise you because anybody who talks with my parents thinks they've heard every story the family has to tell. Actually, they haven't heard anything because my father only loves to talk so he doesn't have to *say* anything. He pretends he's letting people in on all the family secrets, but there are no family secrets, since the core of this family is one rather rotten secret which nobody ever hears about. I doubt that my brother knows it.

"It all begins when my mother finds out that my father isn't what you'd call a sexual person. It also begins when my father finds out that my mother isn't either. Some people, the parents of a lot of kids I know, have lovers all over the place. There's practically a chain of people having affairs with one another. But that wasn't *my* parents' problem. *Their* problem was they wanted children—they always did —but didn't like the dirty little ritual you have to go through to get them. What everybody else thinks is great fun, *my* parents thought was a trifle disgusting. But they must have worked it out because you see before you *un*adopted children. At least they knew *what* to do. They both wanted more children but they stopped. I know my mother could have had more children, so that wasn't what was holding them back. I have to interrupt myself to tell you how I know this. When my father and I began our little, whatever you'd call it—what do I mean whatever you call it, you call it *incest*—he just plain old told me. We're like lovers, so we share everything. Oh, it's all plenty sordid, believe me. Everybody believes these things only happen next door, right? But I used to believe the people they happened to would be in mental hospitals. Suddenly, you know, they'd just go off the deep end and wouldn't be able to tell the psychiatrist anything. They'd just babble on and on until maybe someone would *guess* that the thing that made them sick was incest. But here I am, speaking clearly, coherently, wouldn't you say? I refuse to call the whole thing unbelievable. Sadly, it is only *too* believable.

"About three years ago I found that, well, I sort of began to realize my father and I had a close relationship. I saw other girls were close with their fathers, but you can't tell how other people are since they're different when they're alone. Okay? So I sort of thought it was normal, regular. It didn't feel right, but it seemed right, if you know what I mean. Like, every once in a while he'd kiss me on the neck or shoulder, or put his hand on my behind. It never seemed like all that much because it never lasted that long. Just little things, here and there. Like I said, it wasn't easy to find out whether it was normal, 'cause in front of my friends we never did anything. If you ask them, they'd say Daddy is sort of cold and stern. He's terrible when boys are around. He's like an old cow; I begin to see why he's like an old bull trying to protect his little property. It *is* animalistic in its way. It doesn't seem completely like human beings do these things, or that they're acting like human beings when they do it. Of course, people aren't acting wholly human when they go out and make war and kill people, so who can say what really *is* human and what isn't?

"Anyway, it starts with these little nothing sort of kisses and touches and then one day, in the morning, he comes into my bedroom when I'm barely dressed. He didn't knock or anything and when I went to put on some clothes he sort of didn't let me. Not physically. He just said, why did I have to be shy with him? After all, he *was* my father, so I could act natural, which was difficult since I wasn't dressed. That was sort of all that happened. I didn't feel right about it, but he did make sense. All right, you wear clothes in public but why all the time in your own home? Then, as time went on, he sort of let himself parade around a little without clothes on, like after a bath or something, and I did, too, not that I think people really saw what we were doing. It was like a little game we were playing to get ourselves relaxed with each other, although I pretended to myself it was to get me more comfortable with my body. I began wearing short shorts. He'd come out of the bathroom naked, and I was sort of surprised 'cause he wasn't all that disgusting. In fact, it was kind of interesting to see an older man. Whatever it was, it was like doors opening up that had always been locked. I was seeing more of him *and* me, and feeling all kinds of things I never knew before. I convinced myself I was growing. We were both very casual about everything, as you can imagine. He'd come in when he knew all I'd have on is a pair of pants and ask, did I know where the toothpaste was, which he probably hid somewhere. And I'd say, oh, is it gone? and go looking for it, which meant he could look at me half naked and I could pretend not to be looking at him. Everything very casual. Some casual!

"I don't think I want to go through all the details. It went from there to massage to, well, all the way on one or two occasions. By that point I guess I didn't know what to feel anymore. You know the famous expression about how suddenly I went numb? Well, I *never* went numb. I knew what was going on *all* the time. Was it right or wrong? I was beyond thinking like that, I can assure you, but I didn't know anymore how to feel about it. I knew I had to stay sort of sexy for him, and keep the whole thing not only a secret, of course, but casual. Casual at all costs. We could pass each other in the kitchen, like, less than a minute after hugging without clothes on and you'd think we were strangers. My mother never knew. No one had the slightest hint of our secret. He once stayed home from work ill—hee-hee—so he could have an afternoon with me. *That* did scare me, so I stayed at school until dinner. You should have seen me trying to think up excuses for why I was hanging around school when I never did my entire life. I remember I wanted to be around lots of people, like a real *gang* of people, which isn't like me at all. The other kids saw this, too. It was a primitive sensation, of wanting to be protected by lots of people, not that I ever felt my father would hurt me. He has a thing about my back, my back parts really. I always had to lie down on my stomach, but even then I didn't feel afraid he was going to attack me, or hurt me. Well, maybe in the beginning I might have, but not for long. I think that's normal in every girl.

"I used to close my eyes when he'd get close and tell myself, to sort of get prepared I guess, now Brenda, all these things are in words. One word is 'father' and the other word is 'daughter.' Switch them with any other two words in the English language, or make up your own words and nobody could say you were doing anything wrong. Call him 'house' and me 'cloud,' and then what's the big difference if 'home' is hugging 'cloud'? It sounds like an Indian prayer. Big Home holds Little Cloud. Say father sleeps with daughter and the windows begin to clatter. It's very strange. People write about why these things *don't* happen. Children want them to sometimes, but they grow up feeling guilty about it, guilty even thinking about it. But where does the guilt come from? Partly from the words. Then you always add on, but somewhere inside the child *knows* it's wrong. Or he *senses* it's wrong. What do they mean he *knows* it's wrong? All that happens is that he's *taught* it's wrong. The whole thing can be *untaught*, you could say, the same way it was *taught* in the first place. And the teacher, which is the important part here, is the same person: good old Daddy, or good old Mommy.

"Okay, so they write in the books that it serves some purpose to not let this business go on. Incest. It keeps the family safe and sound to keep Daddy in *his* bathroom and Brenda in *hers*, right? But that makes a lot of assumptions. Like, if Mommy and Daddy both like sex, particularly with each other, then when the little daughter and the little son grow up to be a little sexual themselves, Mommy and Daddy don't really notice them all that much and Daddy lets daughter go out with the boys *she* wants to go out with. But in my case, there was a good reason for this to get started, not that I'd argue we solved it the right way. My father kept telling me, for God's sakes let me at least look at you. You *are* my daughter, aren't you? Later he told me he never looks at my mother. She never lets him, and if she did now, after all these years, he probably wouldn't even want to. That's the part that really got to me those first times. Then, you know, when I'd maybe rub his back, he'd tell me how much he liked that, and I knew, oh brother, sex is just around the corner; I can smell it. Of course I should have gotten out of the whole thing, but then he'd say he never had anyone to rub his back. The idea sickened my mother, or maybe she refused, or maybe he didn't even ask her because he couldn't. So it became like some new family responsibility, something I *had* to do to keep my family happy. *I* was making *their* relationship better. I didn't want him going to prostitutes, which is what he sort of threatened he'd do if things kept on like they were. *That* idea was really disgusting, going to some stranger and paying her to do it. He told me the reason he hated the poorer-looking kids coming around is because they made him think, I'll bet those boys are the sons of prostitutes. Cheap, ugly-looking people with fathers they don't know, who could be him, or his neighbor. I certainly didn't want him having an affair; I've seen too much of that. It always starts out quiet enough, wife doesn't know or husband doesn't know, and certainly the children don't know. But then everybody *does* know; the kids are walking around with their great secret that Daddy has a lover and suddenly the whole school knows. Or the parents get a divorce. Divorce was a possibility for them, but what would it have solved? It would only have made more problems. They're unhappy in one area, that's all. All the rest of the time—you've seen them—they're really not that bad together. Fact, they're probably better than most couples. But when they're alone, they have problems. So maybe I helped to keep them together. Or maybe that's all my imagination, the mind working to keep away the guilt, and some of the tears.

"I've never cried about this. Maybe someday I will, but up to now, nothing. I've never revealed anything, and I certainly haven't broken down. That's probably why I had to tell. I can convince myself, all right, so it happened, thunder hasn't hit the home, the earth hasn't split and all of us fallen in. The days go on like they did before. B.C. and A.D., I tell myself: Before Crisis, After Daddy. It's a dramatic thing, but it doesn't seem *all* that much. I mean, I'm sophisticated enough to know incest isn't in the cards for every family. But it also wasn't a car crash that left me a vegetable without a mind. I know I'm supposed to feel I should be punished, or that magically I will be, which is what the myth of incest is supposed to be. I guess I feel a little bit better talking about it, but it doesn't feel like I thought it would. It's like something dramatic, but I keep thinking the way I am makes it more dramatic than it really is. *I'm* the one building it into something. I thought it would make me feel better getting it out, but all I feel now is that I've made it into something bigger than it's worth; I feel embarrassed and disloyal to my father, since you're friends with him, too. *And* my mother. She's still my mother and married to my father, so what exactly did I accomplish by this confession? Not much at all, I guess. I'd have been better off not doing any of this, but now that it's done, and I hope buried, I think I made a mistake saying anything. Now I really *do* feel like the bad little girl. It wasn't very nice of me. If the whole thing isn't buried by now it should be, and people aren't supposed to speak about the dead, particularly if they don't have nice things to say. Believe me, you learn about speaking unkindly about the dead when you learn the terrible evils and sins of incest. More lessons from Mommy and Daddy."

Part III

FINANCIAL MATTERS

"The Myth of Affluence"

FIVE

Debt and Bankruptcy

To introduce the underlying theme of this chapter, the Myth of Affluence, I have chosen to recount a moment of personal history.

My family and I while traveling in Ireland had rented sight unseen, a house near the western coastline. When, after a long drive on a cold and rainy evening, we reached the house, we found it to be almost untenantable. It was not a matter of personal taste only or some deep-seated allegiance to American affluence that affected our judgment; we simply were unwilling to accommodate ourselves to the house, which, as I say, was just this side of livable. In the end, what probably kept us there, besides the fact that alternative living arrangements were scarce and we had committed ourselves to rent the house, was our oldest daughter's terse remark: "We'll live." How right and reassuring were her two simple words. We *would* live, as most all people survive in conditions far worse than what we had met. But all of this is by way of background. Of course, I knew we would survive, and of course I recognized how my imagination had betrayed me; it had created a gorgeous bungalow high on a cliff overlooking Dingle Bay. What gnawed at me, however, was something more perplexing.

Before renting the house, we invited a friend to visit us. He said he might accept our invitation as he, too, was touring the south and west coasts. If he ended up anywhere near us, he said, he would sleep over. The invitation was not at all perfunctory; we hoped he would join us. Yet when I saw the house the first thing to cross my mind was how much I *feared* he would arrive and discover this house, and us in it. Even as I was inspecting the lugubrious rooms and bemoaning our fate, I was conjuring up excuses for my friend, who surely would be mortified by the spectacle. As temporary as the condition was, it somehow hurt me, or let me say, affected the way I wish to be seen, as difficult as this is to admit. Of course our friend wouldn't judge us, yet in some way, I imagined, he would be obliged to. And I would be lessened.

The point of the vignette is evident. One of the most common human concerns is to be perceived by others as living comfortably if not affluently. The myth of affluence often substitutes for the real item, at least for an afternoon or evening. Much of the feeling of affluence is idiosyncratic: Some may feel uplifted in new clothes, or sitting behind the wheel of a gorgeous automobile, even if one recognizes it is all a sham, and that financiers and bankers are about to repossess one's entire world. Still, one feels uplifted. The feeling also has its social implications. One has special feelings about oneself when standing in handsome surroundings. Indeed, the very word "standing" rings with stature, height, position. No matter how one defines standing, affluence all too often underwrites it. Quite remarkably, we forget that people may feel ashamed of their "low standing" in the world, their shabby clothes, their barely tenantable homes. We forget, too, that shame is evoked in the presence of one's own family; it is not, in other words, only the "outside" world that winces or looks away when one makes public one's circumstances or social position. One's family members may evoke the shame. The words of our daughter, "We'll live," also could be interpreted as meaning, "Daddy, we all know this is unusual; the other fifty-one weeks of the year you keep us at a lovely level of affluence that never embarrasses us!"

The shame of poverty, or more precisely, the fall from affluence, which is the theme of this chapter, has been experienced by many families. Americans, preoccupied with economic achievement and advancement, tend to recoil from accounts of bankruptcy, financial collapse, or cases of people gradually but perceptibly declining in their material standards. My own research with families has taken me into homes of genuinely rich people. I have also visited in homes where people were living "above their means." (The Kellehers represent such a family.) I say this not as a judgment, but because all too many times they made the point abundantly clear to me. Still, with families like the Kellehers, the outsider hears about and, perhaps, senses some strain, but never does one have the feeling that the family is on the rim of collapse. If they have to pull in their belts, as one of America's less relishing expressions goes, then neighbors will not discern major signs of economic decline.

There is, however, another group of families, represented by the people presented in this chapter. These are people who are neither excessively rich nor faced with the manageable though slightly distasteful task of pulling in their belts. Instead, they find themselves in a slide from affluence to barely livable standards of living. It may be more accurate to say that many of these families have reached the bottom of their slide. Whether or not the slide came quickly or dragged on for a painfully long duration, they continue to live as though the slide were merely a bad dream. One reads of these families in novels or witnesses their stories in television shows. In thinking about these families, I invariably ask myself the same question: All right, lie to the outside world if they must, but can they not see the stupidity and futility of lying to one's own spouse and children? Aren't they being a bit carried away believing they can keep the truth from the people with whom they live?

My Irish experience taught me something about this matter of falling from affluence (even on holiday). I wanted to keep our embarrassing predicament from my friend, but I also wanted to hide it from the very people sharing it with me. As preposterous as this sounds, I began to recognize some of the social psychological forces that cause a man to feel so threatened and unsettled by a dip in self-esteem that he actually wished to keep the matter secret. Affluence may be seen by some people as being pernicious, and material wealth the evil that ultimately will bring down our culture. Others continue to perceive of affluence as the only sensible goal worth dying for. "Money isn't everything," a popular sign reads, "but it's far ahead of whatever's in second place!"

In between these extremes lies a host of attitudes, life-styles, ways of being in the world wherein affluence assures special significance. It is not that one lives and dies for the dollar, or even that some ideological posture dominates a family. More precisely, if one can even describe it, affluence defines a way of living where one assumes he or she will be financially better off each year, irrespective of fluctuations in inflation, and that when one reaches a certain age, one will be "well off." Now, while "well off" need not mean "set for life," it does mean that people are viewed by others *and* themselves to be, well, comfortable, which, as I have noted, means a trifle more than being comfortable.

STEPHEN CORNISH

The Cornish family, for example, lived this sort of affluent life. Walter Cornish was an accountant for a large corporation who, during his early years, took on additional clients so that by the time he reached forty, he was living well, by anyone's standards. He and his wife, Sylvia, bought a large house in a well-to-do suburban community and then, with close friends, invested in a mountain chalet which they used for vacations. Walter drove a car, Sylvia drove a car, their son Stephen was promised a car when he graduated high school, which was only two years away when I first met the family.

In attempting to describe the Cornishes, it is important to note that no one in the family was anywhere near being obsessed with wealth or material objects. Granted, the products and symbols of affluence were omnipresent, but material acquisition hardly dominated the family's routines. All three Cornishes derived pleasure from a variety of activities and were in no way garish in their tastes and spending styles. Granted, too, they had become more than accustomed to a certain level of gracious living, but they should not be portrayed as people voracious in their appetite for affluence or social standing. There were no country club memberships, elite fraternities, special society functions, or political positions. They led a quiet life, rarely attended large parties, assumed almost no role in community affairs, and publicly cared little about the social standing of their friends. Their house was large, to be sure, and decorated with handsome fabrics and warm colors; everything seemed tasteful. The word for the Cornishes was "relaxed." Nothing was undertaken in a mood of crisis. They led a good life taking the days as they came, yet all were quick to recognize that it is not difficult to take the days one by one when people live in affluent surroundings.

Then suddenly, Walter Cornish's business began to go downhill. I heard talk of some unethical transactions, and all too quickly his position was more than jeopardized; it was critically damaged and he knew it. So did his wife and son. But the story did not end there. The slide came swiftly, according to Sylvia, and grew in intensity like the proverbial house of cards. One collapse led to another; the termination of one contract led ineluctably to the nullification of another. The predicament was serious, and tragically, the more Walter Cornish tried to turn things around, the more horrendous the situation became. Desperate, his lifelong capacity for calm and reserved decision making vanished. His easygoing style and charm gave way to brittle arrogance and what Sylvia described as a pitiful mood of supplication. He was reduced to begging before everyone for even a morsel of business.

What saved the Cornishes, at least for a while, was the wise and conservative manner in which Walter had managed the family's estate. They owed little money, and their investments, although nowhere near as large as Stephen imagined them, provided a modest income. In fact, a major problem facing the Cornishes was how to survive in their home with the two cars and all the rest. A severe drop in living standards in the form of a move to a small city apartment, along with selling at least one car and a good many of their possessions, might have solved many problems, but Walter Cornish would part with nothing. That was the whole point, he told Sylvia: "To sell out, change one's life even one iota, was the ultimate sign of ruin. And it's not merely a psychological thing," he argued. "Once you fall from the top, you never pick up the pieces in the business world. Poor people don't use accountants, only rich ones and corporations do. And where do they look for their men, in the slums? In tiny city apartments? Do they go to people who can't even afford a reasonable business address? Hell no! They go to the accountant whose life-style, business, and home addresses confirm the fact that this is a successful man. When you hire a cleaning lady you call up for references. My addresses *are* my references. You live in a home like this, you *must* be successful. That's why Stephen is to breathe none of this to anyone. If I commit suicide, he can tell everything he wants. If I slide out of the business world, it won't matter what he does. But right now he keeps quiet!"

So the secrets were born; and the Cornishes refused to concede they were lying. They were merely acting in diplomatic fashion for business reasons. Sylvia's car was sold, they announced, to make room for an expensive car already ordered from Europe, although the delivery date kept being pushed back. They sold their share of the vacation chalet to amass capital for a larger vacation house on an island. "No one has to know the real truth," Walter admonished his wife. "And something else. If anybody showed signs of cracking under the strain of living in a manner to which none of them could grow accustomed, they'd have to keep their cracking to themselves, too. No psychiatrists, no close friends, no early morning telephone calls. There were to be no leaks, not until they reached the point of recouping their losses so they could laugh at the past, or until something dreadful happened." All of this went for Stephen as well.

Obeying his father's wishes was one matter; making sense of them was something else. In every conversation with Stephen Cornish, I heard his confusion and bewilderment. There was no question of his remaining loyal to his father, but what his father was doing made no sense to him.

"My father wanted me to keep a secret, the big secret I've always called it. I'll keep it, although I have these dreams where some men have me locked in a cave. They're beginning to torture me to get the information out of me. But I won't talk. They start pouring hot oil on me. Then they take these pliers and pinch my fingers until the tips of my fingers break off. Then they shove hot sticks up inside me. Ugly dreams, but no one gets me to say a word. I wake up so relieved they're only dreams I almost begin to cry. But in the dreams I never confess a word. I don't even know what they want out of me. They're always shouting at me: 'Tell us, tell us.' I don't tell them anything. But all I want to do is ask them, 'What do you want to know?'

"Dad came to me over a year ago. He sat me down like he was either going to tell me the facts of life or announce the world was coming to an end tomorrow morning, which isn't so far from what he really had to say. Except that's where I disagree with him. For *him* it's the world coming to an end, but he could make a lot of changes; he's just too damn proud. He can take all this business nonsense of how important it is to have the right kind of home and the right address and put it on a flaming stick and jam it up *his* inside. We don't have to suffer from that. I'm used to living like we do but I can change. People aren't born feeling rich; they're taught all this. I can give it up; I don't want to lead my life like some big charade. I don't know if you grew up like this, but from where I sit the best part of life was feeling I was for real, if you can understand what I'm saying. I could be what I wanted to be, not because we were rich, although that's part of it, but because we were real. I thought my parents were terrific because they were real; they never pretended to be something they weren't; they did what they wanted to do. I know what's going on in the world. But all of a sudden my father tells me the facts of life. He tells me how all of it *has* been an act, everything planned out, everything calculated. In my dreams of being tortured

I'm always some low-rank soldier who seems to know things only generals are supposed to know. I'm sure that means I know my father's business affairs, but I don't want to. Well, in a way I'd rather know what he's told me than be kept in the dark. I get that military business, I'm sure, from the way he's leading his life. It's all been some big strategy to make us all, and especially him, very, very successful. No, I should say make him *appear* successful. He doesn't care about me. I thought he did. I thought he was for real, too, but it's a giant charade.

"We're a family that's always put up the perfect act, worn the right clothes, and made ourselves look perfect in case the phone rings and America invites us to a come-as-you-are party. The act was great; they both did it so casually I didn't even know there *was* an act going on. That's my mother's doing. My father's just *one* of the generals. He plans the battles and moves the troops into position. Then the other general comes along and makes it seem like everything's run-of-the-mill, real casual. Casual clothes, casual plans, casual furniture. No one could possibly think, seeing the way *she* operates, that the other general is planning his nuclear bomb explosions. And me, I'm the foot soldier, going along like these poor guys in Vietnam. Can you imagine dying for reasons you don't even understand? I'm the sucker. I got caught in all that casualness. I didn't know for one minute I was dressing myself like they wanted me to in case the phone rang with the big invitation.

"I told my father, right to his face: 'I wish you were telling me you were getting a divorce. I wish that's what this discussion was all about. I'd rather keep *that* secret than this one.' He nodded his head like he understood what I was telling him, but he didn't understand, and I didn't have the guts to explain it to him. I wished it was only a divorce because all it would have meant was that he didn't love my mother anymore and they made a settlement. *This* way, the secret tells me he's a fraud. Not loving someone anymore is one thing; being a phony in *every* part of your life is something else. I wish he was a crook. All right, it's humiliating. You probably have to leave town or visit your father in prison, but it's out in the open. And it means he only did *one* thing wrong. This business, my great secret, means he's done *everything* wrong!

"No, that's not it. It's worse. He didn't do everything wrong. In fact, I don't even know *what* went wrong. Maybe none of this is his fault. I don't know for sure about the ethics part. Honest to God. I don't know about it. Christ, when you keep a secret like this, or break it, you think everything you're saying could be a lie. *I* don't even know anymore if *I'm* telling the truth. Jesus, maybe *I'm* the guy trying to torture the soldier to make him give up the information. My father's life before this wasn't phony; he's made it phony now, so now I have to see *my* whole life as being phony the same way. Like they say, you can tell a man by the way he reacts to a crisis. I've never been through *anything* that looks like a crisis. But here's *his* crisis and boy, has he ever folded. His business hasn't collapsed, *he* has. He made a choice, too. He doesn't see any of this, or maybe he has and doesn't talk to me about it. But he's *chosen* to fall apart, and that's colored his entire life over. He's done the worst thing he could do for his business, too. He should never have asked me to keep this bottled up like some wartime secret. First off, people are going to talk anyway. Second, it puts him in an impossible position with everybody, especially us. He may not know it, but he's showed the world he's a fraud, that everything he is is a lie. He should have told me or not told me the situation, that was decision number one. But if he decided to tell me, he shouldn't have said keep it a secret. He should have explained why public knowledge of this could hurt him. I would have decided to tell no one. Nobody likes going around bad-mouthing their parents when their parents are in trouble. Sure, kids my age find fault with their parents, but no one's going to go out and purposely make it bad for their father. What the hell, it's *his* money that buys me what I want, so why would I want to hurt him? Sometimes when you ask someone to keep a secret, you're only asking them not to tell anyone what kind of person you really are. That's what I mean by him putting on the big charade.

"Then there's another part: being rich. I can't say too much about all this because I don't know another way to be, although I gather if things don't pick up I'll be learning about the other side of the tracks faster than I thought. But you can't say it doesn't matter if you're rich or poor; it matters a lot. I suppose it matters, too, if you're in the middle, because then you don't know if you're about to push forward or fall backward. My father never knew either, but he wanted people to think he was always moving forward. It's too bad, but maybe it's easy for me to say this. When you're young you tell yourself you want to lead an honest life, but how can you be sure you'll be able to? When you get to be his age, you see things differently. I'm pretty protected from just about everything; he's set that up for me. I hate to give that up, I almost said give it back, like we were rich on loan; like any minute they could come and take it away. Maybe the big secret in my father's life was not knowing when they were coming to take his *whole* life away. They sure picked a good time to do it. The way my grades have fallen down, I'll be lucky to get into a technical school somewhere. I have to admit, one of the reasons I decided I'd tell you about this was because I hoped if I gave *you* the information and you promised to give it to no one else, I could be free again and go back to studying the way I should. So far, none of my teachers has said anything, although they must be noticing I'm not doing as well as I was. Maybe the school's so large they don't even know if I'm there or not.

"I want my father to be rich, and successful. I could live with it all right if he were different, but I'd rather be poor all my life than rich part of it and poor the rest of it, not that I couldn't try to do better than he did, although even that's a scary idea right now. It's the falling back that's really hard. It's like losing fifty yards on your first two plays and kicking on third down. You're going the wrong way. You dream all your life about moving up, flying, taking off. Now *this* comes along. It's like this big foot has come out of the sky and kicked us way, way back. Maybe another reason it bothers me is because I'm being pushed back and I don't even get a chance to get into the game. I kind of want to explain to people, hey, *he* may be falling down but I'm not falling down with him. It's nothing *I* did. Blame it on the generals. I don't need to protect them; they're not the children in this family. *I'm* the children. I'm the one who's supposed to get the protection.

"It's really absurd. Here I am with every break I've had made possible by a guy who's now in so much trouble he won't even let people know about it. He's being punished plenty; a part of me wants him to be punished a little bit more because in a way he's being kind of a child about it. But I'm being a child, too. Look, money means a lot to me. Just because you don't think about it all the time doesn't mean it isn't important. It's goddamn important. You have to work hard when you don't have it just to get to places where I can get without even thinking about it. You want the truth? I *hate* the idea we could become really down and out somewhere. I *hate* the idea of living in a small apartment. It wouldn't even be a bad one, I know that. We'll never be poor. But I don't like the idea of falling back any more than he does. I hate it. There are people wondering why we sold a car. Some of my friends, I'll bet, would love to ask me. I couldn't face them and say, we sold it 'cause my Dad is going under, and we're going to sell the TV and the dining room furniture, too, because there aren't dining rooms where we're moving.

"I'm really the American suburban snob, aren't I? What can you think when I tell you I honest to God hate the idea of giving up our dining room, not that we use it more than twice a week? But it's wonderful knowing you *can* use it, that you can *act* like you were rich when you want to. How can you act when you don't have money? I tell myself, you have to be a real and genuine person, but all that's a load of crap. My father's money makes it possible for him *and* me to act any way we want to. What the hell, *I'm* the king of casualness. I probably taught it to *them*. Wear the same clothes every day, like the poor little boy couldn't afford to buy a new pair of pants, and I could buy the store if I wanted to. Maybe the secret information those guys are trying to get out of me is the fact that I'd kill someone for taking *it* away. We may be slipping financially; we *may* be? We *are* slipping, on our asses, all three of our asses. But I'm falling, too. My insides and outsides, it's all falling down. And all the king's horses and all the king's men . . . right?

"There's no way you can be happy, I suppose, when you know things could be different, financially, I mean. Maybe that's what the big secret is. If you can really rise up, you become anxious, you think, this could be the moment. And when you don't have strong financial security, like I guess we don't, then you go around every day wondering what's the mail going to bring, what's the telephone going to bring? It's like waiting for your grades or examination scores every day, every minute. So you keep all these secrets, pretending it doesn't matter when it does. Like, if you fall forward or backward, it's all the same to you. Like *hell* it is. Kids growing up in suburbs may never think about it, but you just tell them it's all going to be flushed down the toilet. Truck's coming tomorrow to take every last bit of it away, and you'll see them fall down on their knees and beg you to leave everything just where it is. I think, what if our cleaning lady knew about this? She'd be upset 'cause it'd mean she lost her job. My mother would go begging before she'd give up Mrs. Conners. But if Mrs. Conners found out and got a new job, she'd laugh at us. Oh my God would she have a great laugh at our expense. We'd be providing her that laugh and I *would* feel like shit.

"Being rich then suddenly losing it is like eating beautiful food and letting yourself think about the fact that a few seconds after you even put that beautiful stuff in your mouth—and you can see people who refuse to eat something even if it tastes all right because it doesn't *look* all right—it's already being turned into shit. Excuse my language but that's what it is. It seems to me that's what's happening to us. We don't want to make it public, but all of us are turning into shit. We'll start smelling, too, if we're not careful. Pretty soon they'll be flushing us down the sewers, or maybe I'll come up, in another life, as a flower growing over a neighbor's scptic tank. That'd be a laugh, wouldn't it? Or maybe we'll just ooze into some grave somewhere, or turn into the dirt they shove into graves.

"I know it's maudlin, but without money you're next to nothing. Money keeps you living on *top* of the septic tank. I don't want to be in the gutter, not my gutter, your gutter, anybody's gutter. Maybe I could do something to pull all of us back up, but I don't want to get in there for a minute because I've seen people like that and they never get the stink off them. Or like me, they keep it a secret. Even if you can't smell them, they can smell themselves, and that's worse. I can smell myself now and I'm beginning to hate it. Okay, it may be I'm smelling myself for the first time, but I didn't mind it when I didn't smell at all. I liked it one helluva lot better, I can tell you, when the generals were winning the battles. The first thing children in this country learn is it isn't how you play the game, it's whether you win or lose. People like us don't want to admit it, but there's no place in a suburb for pcoplc who lose. I guess what I just said says it all, whether you want to admit it or not. I don't want to, and neither does my mother or father. So the only possibility for us is to keep our mouths shut and hope the smell blows away in the wind. Maybe we'll get lucky and some innocent home down the road will get the smell and we'll be saved for a while. Like, if the people across the street got involved in some serious divorce, maybe no one would notice us flowing down the sewers.

"Money, money, money . . ."

It is difficult, and dangerous, to reduce Stephen Cornish's story to a few words, a few concepts. Still, in reflecting on his account, several words do come to mind. Shame, pride, humiliation, and that inevitable distinction between appearance and reality capture some of his message. One is struck by his references to a "fall" from affluence and how this would yield a corresponding dip in self-esteem, indeed a fall from grace. To suddenly become poor, Stephen indicated, was partly to be publicly disgraced, as if one, in fact, had slipped and fallen on one's behind. Partly, too, it meant being punished, as though by God. I think, in this context, of his image of the large foot coming out of the sky to boot him in the pants. I think, too, how a child might feel when he is spanked. A punishing parent must seem larger than life; and the pain and humiliation of the punishment must be excruciating especially if a child feels, somehow, wrongly accused. Surely Stephen, in bemoaning his fall from grace, wished to blame "the generals." So, along with shame and pride and the fall from affluence we add the concept of innocence.

In raising these terms, we should note the complex relationship between social status or wealth, on the one hand, and an individual's sense of esteem, literally *worth*, on the other. Stephen Cornish had learned in the proverbial hard way that one's sense of worth stems in part from an economic and social structure over which one has little or no control. Admittedly, his state in the world, and with it much of the substance of his self-assessment, was based on his parents' accomplishments. In his words, he was merely the foot soldier experiencing the pain or pleasure of his parents' defeats and triumphs. In this one sense, therefore, he was innocent. Barely aware of his parents' economic situation, he rode their successes, as do all young people living in affluence, masking the fact that his was purely an inherited wealth carrying with it a style of casualness. His parents, seemingly, could have cared less what would happen to them; they cared very little, moreover, about how they had reached their present position.

Yet even in the innocence and casualness, Stephen recognized his own deceit. If his parents, and particularly his father, had created a charade for the family, then Stephen, too, felt his own life to be a sham. He used these terms—sham, charade, phoniness—so regularly with me, it was difficult to tell just how ingenuously he believed in them. Whereas his perceptions of the affluent life-style were trenchant, he repeatedly remarked on the precarious nature of affluence and hence a child's belief in the possibility of all of it vanishing, or being taken away. Some of this sentiment may have grown out of a fear his father actually never expressed, of people's envious delight in the fall from affluence of an acquaintance. Stephen's own sense of humiliation was affected by this sentiment. No matter how casual his attitude toward his handsome life-style, he knew he adored everything money provided him. As much as the attitude may have sickened him, he felt *entitled* to affluence, even though this, too, caused him to feel counterfeit.

In certain ways Stephen Cornish as well as his father represented for me the classic literary hero. Proud, accomplished, successful, men of this rank walk the earth with modesty and casual manner until the fates—God, the devil, circumstance—strip away their frail cloak of fame and achievement and leave them naked and humiliated. The world, apparently, has turned upon them, in this case in the form of economic demise, and punished them for their albeit concealed pride and not so concealed fortunes. Stephen, of course, never spoke in such lofty terms, but there was no doubting his identification with fictional heroes. Often he was reminded of a likeness between himself and literary figures, a likeness that tended to exacerbate his sense of personal inauthenticity, as well as his sense of being punished for someone else's fate. As I say, his use of words like sham, charade, fraudulent (which might also have referred to some of his father's business transactions) was persistent. But there was another set of words and images he employed, a set that caused me to reflect on some rather traditional psychoanalytic coinage.

In looking back at my notes taken after visits with Stephen, I could not help but remark on the frequency with which he resorted to so-called anal imagery. People were being kicked in the ass, having hot spears shoved up inside them, and being stuffed or stopped up with things, notably lies. If these references were far-fetched, then his concluding words about the smell of feces, the stink of richness and poverty, along with allusions to crap, shit, septic tanks, and sewers, could not have been more explicit. From his accounts, I pieced together the idea that Stephen felt his secret to be the central core of his life. He himself likened the chat with his parents when he was advised he must not reveal the family's financial troubles to a discussion of the facts of life. From the idea of the secret as the fulcrum of his personality, I drew a picture of Stephen being either pregnant with or constipated by his secret. While lying is associated with the feces he wished he could flush down the toilet, there was also a theme in his account of giving birth to the secret as if the secret-child might return the pride and self-respect connected with affluence now lost to the Cornishes. Pregnancy and constipation, which are generally allied in children's minds (children often imagine babies growing in the stomach and being delivered through the anus), reminded me, moreover, of another aspect of Stephen's account. Continually he reasserted the distinction between being willing to keep a secret (which I likened to constipation) and being forced to keep one, which more closely resembles pregnancy or more precisely conception, in that something is put inside the body, possibly even against one's will.

Similar or not, the processes of constipation and pregnancy reveal how deeply felt and internalized was this one dreaded secret. Weighing him down and preventing him, in personal as well as economic terms, from progressing, Stephen had conceived two possible outcomes: Either a bomb would explode, suggesting his body could contain its dirty material no longer, or he would die from the poison emanating from his waste materials. When "they" come and take back your money, essentially they are taking away your very life.

Stephen said as much. In the same vein, he had likened wealth to feces. Money must be "there"; it must be part of one's everyday living and being, but it also must remain invisible. Ugly, dirty, cheapening, even counterfeit, money nonetheless remains the substance by which people grow and develop. Little wonder, then, that he should associate it with manure and imagine himself returning in a future life as a flower. Then again, it is difficult to say if Stephen found money or the idea of money ugly, or whether it wasn't the bribelike quality of his father's demand that he remain silent that he found ugly and demeaning. Or was it that money (shit) lay behind his own sense of autonomy, pride, and manifest self-sufficiency? How much his parents' money created a counterfeit foundation on which his own life perched cannot be accurately determined. We have noted how he felt obliged to participate in what he relentlessly labeled a charade. What we do not know is the degree to which Stephen's overriding sense of personal doubt also related to money, the family's fall from affluence, and that frustrating recognition that fate seemed totally out of his hands. Life had reached the point where his eating and defecating habits were no longer under his control. To remove this sense of control, and with it, seemingly, his entire future, constituted a most destructive and torturous punishment. It left him with the wholly ignominious fantasy of killing his own father for money.

I feel self-conscious advancing these notions on the heels of such a poignant account. Still, it seems essential in this exploration that from time to time we look beyond the child's account to the more subtle psychological meanings generally associated with keeping secrets. Stephen Cornish's words unquestionably point to the life and death, shameful and prideful aspects inherent in secret keeping and financial affairs. But again, if the reference to life and death matters seems excessive, or metaphorical, then the following account renders these matters all too literal.

THERESA BARBERI

Theresa Barberi, sixteen, lives almost two hundred miles from the Cornishes. Her family has no connection with the Cornishes; Theresa herself has never heard of the suburban community which means so much to Stephen Cornish. The two young people, moreover, do not physically resemble each other. Theresa's pitch-black hair and dark brown eyes present quite a contrast with Stephen's pale blue eyes and long blond hair. The two families, presumably, will never meet or learn of each other's circumstances. Yet the two children would have much to talk about, for Theresa Barberi, one of six children, was also going through the fall from affluence, the fall that had made Stephen Cornish so unhappy.

Like Walter Cornish, Louis Barberi had worked his way into a position of not insignificant rank and affluence. In some respects, his climb in the exporting business took a chapter from the classical rags-to-riches story that his father, Louis, Sr., had memorized when he immigrated to America at the turn of the century. Like many immigrants, Louis Barberi, Sr., knew the measure of his success would be demonstrated by the accomplishments of his children and grandchildren, and more than anything else, by their social position as well as earning and spending power. He was not surprised, therefore, when his first son, Louis, Jr., turned out to be a successful businessman. Even as a child, young Louis had exhibited shrewdness, charm, and a strong will, the very ingredients, Louis, Sr., always told his wife, that guarantee success, especially in a country like America. Young Louis, however, was also a mischievous boy. He constantly flirted with trouble, and as an adolescent, associated with people who his parents feared were a dangerous influence on him. Still, the boy did well in school, and never desired to be a leader of the groups with which he associated. Anyone could see that he was the most intelligent and ambitious one of them; there was no way they would lead him astray.

By the age of twenty-eight, after some rather precarious years, Louis Barberi, Jr., had shed the negative influences that troubled his parents and established himself in a handsome business position. Louis, Sr., would live long enough to see his son sitting behind an enormous walnut desk in a richly decorated office. The stories about American achievement were true, he would tell himself. The image of his son basking in the warmth of success was what he, Louis, Sr., had lived his life for. Only one thing disturbed the old man: Hadn't the young man's rise come awfully fast? Sudden success was peculiar, even for American-born Americans.

I learned a bit of the Barberi history from Mamma Barberi, as everyone called the elder Louis' widow. Mamma told me colossal tales of the old country, and the new one, but she grew discreet when speaking about her family. Five children were alive, two had died, one as a child, one as a teenager in an automobile accident. Born and raised in an orthodox Catholic family, Mamma went to mass twice a day, praised her children who did likewise, and said nothing about Louis and his brother Carlo, who rarely if ever entered a church. What they did was their business, but Mamma Barberi would not have uttered such a phrase. When I asked her about her sons' religious practices, she commented, "They are not boys anymore. When they lived in our house they did as they were told. Now their children do as *they* are told in *their* homes. They're good boys, the both of them." Louis, Jr., was a decent man. He was also a good boy in the sense that he retained much of his youthful charm and mischievousness. In all my years of visiting families, I never met a man who treated his wife and children with more kindness. Naturally, he could be stern with the children when a situation called for him to be, but this took nothing away from his obvious love for them.

Unlike an intriguing short story, the conclusion of this brief account of the Barberi family is already known to the reader, for we are addressing accounts of children whose parents are either bankrupt or in heavy debt. Like Stephen Cornish, then, Theresa Barberi, whose eyes often seemed so dark and solemn their look frightened me, had a powerful secret to keep. Unlike the secrets kept by the other children in this book, however, Theresa's secret had become a matter of life or death. What people like Stephen Cornish and Brenda Kelleher feared they were rendering melodramatic was only too real for the Barberis.

As I heard it, Louis Barberi owed a great deal of money and was having difficulty paying it back to a group of men who felt their generosity had been overextended. By the time I learned of his problem, Louis Barberi had sold whatever he could to pay his debt, but he had not fully extricated himself. In his own words, his time was running out. Initially, I found the phrase excessive, a throwback to the predictable television scenario. Mamma Barberi advised me in her characteristically quiet but strong manner that people like Louis do not use such words for mere effect. Louis' life had been threatened, she said, and for some reason Theresa was the only child who had learned of the threat. It was for the child's sake, Mamma whispered, that I must talk to her.

To observe Louis Barberi was to discover not a trace of anxiety. Theresa, however, was unable to mask her terror. She consented to talk with me because the secret was beginning to make her physically ill. She was eating little more than bread and tea and had lost fifteen pounds from an already thin frame. Her cheeks were sucked in, and her skin color, always pale white, was now ashen. Her parents were concerned, but they had more pressing matters on their minds.

I recount now some of what Theresa told me. As I made clear in the introduction, all the people appearing in this book granted me consent to publish their words after they had read my written accounts. The reader also will recall that the subjects of these life studies reserve the right to strike possibly damaging passages, as well as correct errors of content and tone. In this case, the Barberis, although not Theresa, requested that certain details of the account be omitted. Here, then, is a portion of Theresa's account:

"There's nothing complicated about it. I went into Daddy's study one day looking for tape. I had an assignment for biology, and I had to put together this notebook. I knew there was tape somewhere in his room because someone's always using it. So I started looking in drawers and the first drawer I opened I saw this letter. It was wrinkled up, like he was going to throw it away but then he saved it. Even then I probably wouldn't have looked at it but it was written, like, by a child. I thought it was one of my younger brothers, so I read it. In the letter they called him Nino, which is a name I know he hates, but only people who know him for a long time would call him that; none of the children would call him Nino. The letter was very simple. They said he owed so much and had this amount of time to pay or they would kill him. I always imagined those letters had certain expressions or clue words, but this just said or we'll kill you and your wife can pay us. It ended up saying you're lucky we waited this long. Then it had a P.S., something about, do you remember Lorenzo? I didn't understand that part since no one in our family's called Lorenzo.

"I couldn't believe it. It was like a movie. I began to cry. I put it back and ran to the door, like in a story. When I got to the door I said to myself, where are you going? It was like I knew I couldn't tell anybody I'd seen it, which meant I also couldn't go anywhere. I don't think my father would have been upset if he knew I was looking in his desk. He has a safe, so I thought, maybe it's not for real, but that was the only time I thought that. You know somehow these things aren't jokes. And you know the first thing I thought? I remembered a Thanksgiving dinner in Pappa Louis' house, a long, long time ago, when my father was starting to be sort of rich. Well, not rich, but you know. There was this lawyer there with his wife, and they brought their dog. After dinner Pappa Louis and the lawyer were talking and I was playing with the dog. Nobody else was in the room. I don't remember what they were talking about but I heard all my life how Pappa thought my father made too much money too fast. Like maybe people had set him up in business and my father had never told people all the deals he had to make. Pappa was always worried about my father. He was pleased he was doing well, but he worried, like he smelled something and he sort of knew what it was but didn't want to say anything.

"Nobody in my family wants to make trouble for anybody. I've never heard Mamma say anything bad about *anybody*. She keeps everything to herself; you know she's thinking a lot of things. I take after her. I told myself, I was standing in the door to my father's room, I *better* take after her. I wondered what Mamma knew and whether I could talk to her. I didn't say *anything* to my mother. I didn't know if she knew about the letter. Probably she did. Maybe Mamma knew, too. Maybe *everybody* knew but me. But the younger kids wouldn't have known. They weren't different, and they would have changed a lot if they knew what my father was keeping from them. I never thought it was a joke. Nobody we know jokes this way. Nobody would have used that name, Nino. And my father would have thrown it away like he must have started to when he crinkled it up. Dumb me, I was scared. It's like you want the clock to go backward so you could do it all over again and you wouldn't have looked in the drawer. But if the clock went back, it wouldn't mean the letter wasn't there. I didn't want to think about what might have happened, or what my father did to get someone so angry they wanted to kill him. Dumb me. I checked to see if anyone was around and went back and stole the letter. I took it outside and ran to the end of the street where there's that little bridge, you know, and burned it. I lit it and watched it burn. I even buried the ashes. Then I thought, maybe the police would want the letter for evidence, or lawyers would want to see it. That's what you think first, but I knew that was just me wishing. I think my father is a very good man. I'm sure he works hard. We don't see him a lot and we almost never take vacations with him because he's so busy. But somehow I knew if the letter wasn't a joke, which I was sure it wasn't, the police would not be part of it, you know what I mean? Children sort of know what's going on. They don't use lawyers in things like this. They either pay the money—although I don't know anything about how they get it—or someone probably does come and kill him.

"I can't eat knowing my father could be killed any moment. Nobody could. He won't run away. I don't know if they really mean it. I don't know why he owes the money. I don't know anything. To look at the two of them you'd think, well, not that everything is perfect, but whatever's wrong isn't all that serious. But you can tell they decided it was important the children didn't find out. They're keeping the secret from me, and I'm keeping the secret from them. And the secret is, when is he going to die? Can you believe! That's the secret. I'll bet every child in the world wants to know the answer to that question. I remember asking my mother when I was going to die. Not for a long time, she said. That's what all parents probably answer. When are you and Daddy going to die? Hopefully not for a long time, too. Don't worry. They always put that one on, too: Don't worry. Now I can't do anything *but* worry. I'm going to be without my father. Some night, some day, some morning, maybe it's happening now, someone's going to come and kill him and I'm going to go about my little life and not say anything to anybody. What can I say? I can't do anything but keep my mouth shut.

"I want to feel sorry for myself. I want to forget about what's going to happen to him and only think about what's going to happen to *me*. If he dies I won't be able to say anything to other kids, will I, because they'll think it was an accident or something. I can't go and tell them it wasn't an accident. Daddy owed a lot of money and couldn't pay so they killed him. I could probably talk to my mother. Mamma won't say anything. She'll pray and make me pray and I don't want to pray. I'm like my father. I have my religion but I don't have to show it around all the time. I wish I could burn my brain up, too. I go to church actually. I pray they won't kill him. I can barely listen to myself saying the words. I tell God, please do me a favor and don't let them kill Daddy. I imagine God's thinking, I don't like people to die, but if he owes the money something has to happen to him.

"I thought, I could go to confession, but why do I have to? *I* didn't do anything. Father, I've sinned. I burned a letter that wasn't mine. What is *that* supposed to mean! I guess in my own pitiful way I'm like a nun. I don't eat, I don't sleep, I don't talk much with people. Maybe I've become more religious than I thought. I wonder if my father goes to church, and confesses, as if that would do any good. He needs money. I wish I had it for him. I wish Pappa left him a lot of money. I wish and I wish and I wish. I'm not very mature about this, am I? I tell myself, I won't die if he dies. It would be a stupid waste if he does, but I'll still be around. And my brothers and sisters will be around. I'm not going anywhere. It's a world full of secrets. I think someone we know, someone close to my father, wrote that letter. I may have talked to the person who's going to kill him. I might even break down at the funeral, or right after, and the person holding me, I mean, might be the one. Or some man comes up to me and says, Theresa, you've never met me, but I grew up with your father. I'm so sorry. Maybe *he's* the one. Maybe all the people who grew up with my father, everyone who knows they used to call him Nino, maybe they'll *all* know. Maybe the police will know, too, only they won't do anything, and all the lawyers, too. Maybe that's what happens in families like ours where something goes wrong. They *all* know, only they don't tell anybody, just to protect them from it. Maybe Mamma *does* know. I'm sure she does, too, now that I think about it. Nobody tells. It's like a test, or initiation into some special club; the Barberi club.

"We all have our little secrets. Maybe we don't tell anything to anybody. Maybe we're always covering up for one another. How can I know anymore? How can I trust anyone? 'I'm so sorry your father died,' and he's the one who might have killed him. I can't trust anyone anymore. I can't even trust the food I eat, or used to eat. Maybe they're planning on poisoning him. Maybe the whole family but me will die of being poisoned. Then they could blame it on me, since I was the only one who lived. It must have been Theresa who wrote the letter, that's why she burned it. Maybe there wasn't a letter at all. Maybe that's just her excuse. Maybe then they really *would* bring in the police. Oh, I talk and talk and my father's going to be murdered."

Theresa was sobbing.

"It's the first time I said the word, my secret word."

Five months after this conversation took place, Louis Barberi, Jr., disappeared. His whereabouts, presumably, are unknown to his family. Mrs. Barberi and her mother-in-law continue to assure Theresa and her brothers and sisters that their father is alive and that they will see him again. Most of the children believe this. Theresa, however, is convinced her father is dead. She continually asks for proof that he is alive, but she receives none. It is now more than three years that Louis is gone.

SIX

Unemployment

It goes without saying that unemployment has the most profound implications for an individual and his or her family. Unemployment makes one redefine one's sense of masculinity and femininity. It turns people against their spouse, parents, and children, as well as themselves. It deeply affects one's health and well being, and in perplexing ways, demands that people devise new philosophies of living and dying, philosophies that either justify their struggle to survive or end their lives.

While the quantitative data on unemployment are familiar to many, it seems worthwhile to review some of them here.

As of January 1979, the Monthly Labor Report indicated that 6.7 percent of America's labor force, or approximately 8 million people, were out of work.[1] Generally, unemployment is highest among people sixteen to nineteen (19 percent) and specifically among blacks of this age group (37.1 percent). Black men of twenty years and older show a 10 percent unemployment rate. In addition, 10 percent of women who head families are out of work, as are 8.1 percent of full-

[1] On a monthly average, 3 million people lose their last job. Some 900,000 leave their last job, while 900,000 seek their first job. Also on a monthly average, 2 million people reenter the work force. But let us be reminded that each month the work force increases, so even if unemployment percentages remain the same or dip slightly, actual rates of unemployment may be increasing.

time workers and 7.9 percent of married women whose spouse lives in the house. In terms of occupation, blue-collar workers (9.4 percent), operatives (10.8 percent), nonfarm laborers (15.6 percent), construction workers (15.6 percent), and agricultural wage and salary workers (11.7 percent) reveal the highest unemployment rates. Not so incidentally, veterans of the Vietnam War also show high unemployment rates. Over 500,000 veterans remain out of work, with the highest rates occurring among veterans twenty to twenty-four (11.3 percent) and thirty to thirty-four (5.1 percent). Unemployment, moreover, runs higher among black veterans (30.5 percent in September of 1977) than white veterans.

In general, the average duration of all unemployed people is 15.8 weeks.[2] Normally, 15 or more weeks is called long-term unemployment, while 27 or more weeks is called very long-term unemployment.

In contrast to the typical picture of poor and working-class people out of work is the surprising number of unemployed people in middle- and upper-middle-class communities. Granted, as Kenneth Keniston has observed, all families in the United States and especially the poor ones experience extreme pressures of one sort or another.[3] But the fate of poor families must not obscure the destructive quality of unemployment among more affluent families. The data on unemployment rates among affluent families are far from precise. Paula Leventman reported that in 1971, 20 percent of America's technical professionals—scientists, engineers, data analysts, etc.—were out of work.[4] According to Leventman, many of these professionals never got "hooked back" into jobs after their initial layoffs. Indeed, of the approximately one hundred unemployed men she interviewed in 1971, 80 percent still had not settled securely into new jobs when she interviewed them again in 1975. Many had found work on contract jobs ranging in time from several months to a year, but contracts afford neither job security nor fringe benefits.

While critics of Western society have faulted America's possibly

[2] On a monthly average, one finds an almost equal number of people (some 2,500,000) unemployed for less than five weeks, for five to fourteen weeks, and for more than fifteen weeks.
[3] See Kenneth Keniston, *All Our Children* (New York: Harcourt Brace Jovanovich, 1977). See also Joseph Becker, ed., *In Aid of the Unemployed* (Baltimore: Johns Hopkins Press, 1965).
[4] See her *Professionals Out to Work* (New York: The Free Press, in press). See also her "Nonrational Foundations of Professional Rationality: Employment Instability Among Scientists and Technologists," *Sociological Symposium*, No. 16 (Summer 1976), 83–112.

obsessive and extreme work habits,[5] the fact is that being out of work has far more serious effects on people than the phenomenon known as workaholism. It well may seem, as Alan McClean once suggested,[6] that the great madness of life has to do with adjusting to certain work organizations. Yet the choice for most people between this brand of madness and the hurt of unemployment is all too easily made. To be sure, the process of living is a process often underwritten by biological, psychological, and sociological stress.[7] The human organism is constantly having to cope with stressful situations and environments. This fact holds true at the level of the cell just as it does at the level of the whole person being in the world.[8] Among the many sociologically rooted areas of stress are those connected with the quest for status and position.[9] Again, however, the basis of this quest is work, regular employment, if not steady improvement in job conditions and wage.

The effects of unsatisfactory work conditions and unemployment are best observed in studies of longevity. Palmore, for example, found that the best predictor of longevity was work satisfaction.[10] The

[5] See, for example, Branko Bokun, *Man: The Fallen Ape* (Garden City, N.Y.: Doubleday, 1977); Philip E. Slater, *The Pursuit of Loneliness* (Boston: Beacon Press, 1970); *Work in America*, a Report of Special Task Force to the Secretary of Health, Education, and Welfare (Cambridge, Mass.: M.I.T. Press, 1971); G. Friedmann, *The Anatomy of Work* (New York: The Free Press, 1961); A. Tilgher, *Work: What It Has Meant to Man Through the Ages* (New York: Harcourt, Brace, 1930).

[6] Alan McClean, *Mental Health and Work Organizations* (Indianapolis: Rand McNally, 1970).

[7] See R. S. Lazarus, *Psychological Stress and the Coping Process* (New York: McGraw-Hill, 1966); Ely Chinoy, *Automobile Workers and the American Dream* (Garden City, N.Y.: Doubleday, 1955); A. M. Okun, ed., *The Battle Against Unemployment* (New York: Norton, 1972); H. Basowitz et al., *Anxiety and Stress* (New York: McGraw-Hill, 1955); E. Gunderson and N. Rahe, *Life Stress and Illness* (Springfield, Ill.: Charles C. Thomas, 1974); F. Janis, *Psychological Stress* (New York: Wiley, 1958); L. Levi, *Society, Stress and Disorders* (New York: Oxford University Press, 1971); J. W. Mason, "A Historical View of the Stress Field," *Journal of Human Stress*, 1975, 1, 22–36.

[8] See, for example, T. S. Langner and S. T. Michael, *Life Stress and Mental Health* (New York: The Free Press, 1963). See also Arthur Kornhauser, *Mental Health and the Industrial Worker* (New York: Wiley, 1965); G. Brown et al., "Life Events and Psychiatric Disorders: Some Methodological Issues, *Psych. Med.* 3, 1973, 74–87; M. R. Eastwood, "Psychosomatic Disorders in the Community," *Journal of Psychosomatic Research* 16, 1972, 381–86.

[9] See R. J. Kleiner and S. Parker, "Goal Striving, Social States, and Mental Disorder," *American Sociological Review* 28, 1961. See also S. Levine and N. Scotch, *Social Stress* (Chicago: Aldine, 1971); B. D. Dohrenwend and B. S. Dohrenwend, *Social Status and Psychological Disorder* (New York: Wiley, 1969).

[10] E. Palmore, "Physical, Mental and Social Factors in Predicting Longevity," *Gerontology* 9, 1969. See also E. Palmore, "Predicting Longevity: A Follow-up Controlling for Age," *Gerontology*, Winter 1969.

next best predictor, incidentally, was overall happiness. Several researchers,[11] furthermore, have demonstrated significant frequency of heart disease and high blood pressure among people reporting job dissatisfaction, occupational stress, lack of job stability, and of course unemployment. The number of human problems associated with unemployment is seemingly endless. Research has shown it to be correlated with interpersonal problems in the family,[12] alcoholism,[13] and drug taking. In sharp contrast, stable and rewarding work conditions often prove to be a rehabilitative if not outrightly therapeutic measure.

Even this brief literature review reveals how great is the cost and how widespread the problem of unemployment in the United States. Yet our concern here is with something of a more personal nature. I have presented these data to show first, how widespread unemployment in America has become, and second, to demonstrate the physical and psychological effects of unemployment on men and women. There is therefore, a human matter at stake here. It is captured, I think, not only in a person's reaction to being out of work but in a child's reaction to his or her parent, or parents, being out of work.

The account of Davey Sindon that follows offers a slight deviation from most of the other children's accounts found in this book:

[11] See J. French and R. Caplan, "Psychosocial Factors in Coronary Heart Disease," *Industrial Medicine* 39, No. 9 (September 1979); J. French, "The Social Environment and Mental Health," *Journal of Social Issues* 19, No. 4 (1963); *Work in America*, op. cit.; S. Cobb, *Some Medical Aspects of Unemployment* (Ann Arbor, Mich.: 1971), Institute for Social Research; S. Seashore, *Group Cohesiveness in the Industrial Work Group* (Ann Arbor, Mich.: 1954), Institute for Social Research; A. Pepitone, "Self, Social Environment and Stress," in M. H. Appley and D. Trumbell, eds., *Psychological Stress* (New York: Appleton-Century-Crofts, 1967); S. M. Sales, "Organizational Roles as a Risk Factor in Coronary Heart Disease," *Administrative Science Quarterly* 14, No. 3 (1969); S. Levine and N. Scotch, *Social Stress* (Chicago: Aldine, 1971); M. Harvey Brenner, "Personality Stability and Economic Security," *Social Policy* 8, No. 1 (May/June 1977), 2–4; J. Brod, "The Influence of Higher Nervous Processes Induced by Psychosocial Environment on the Development of Essential Hypertension, in L. Levi, ed., *Society, Stress and Disease* (New York: Oxford University Press, 1971), 312–23; J. P. Henry and J. C. Cassel, "Psychosocial Factors in Essential Hypertension: Recent Epidemiologic and Animal Experimental Evidence," *American Journal of Epidemiology* 90, 1969, 171.

[12] See J. Veroff and S. Feld, *Marriage and Work in America* (New York: Van Nostrand, 1970). See also V. Tauss, "Working Wife-House-husband: Implications for Counseling," *Journal of Family Counselling* 4, Fall 1976, 52–55; D. E. Gil, *Violence Against Children* (Cambridge, Mass.: Harvard University Press, 1973).

[13] See, for example, P. M. Roman and H. M. Trice, "The Development of Deviant Drinking Behavior," *Archives of Environmental Health* 20, March 1970; McClean, op. cit.

namely, the secretive aspect is a trifle more subtle than we have been accustomed to. Oliver Sindon's unemployment was certainly well known to his family and friends. No one, moreover, ever admonished Davey for talking about his father being out of work. Yet something about the family's situation and their transactions made it impossible for this one young man to speak freely of the problems he and his parents and sister, too, were encountering. I should add that my relationship with Davey Sindon was never one to suggest that he was keeping secrets from me or anyone else for that matter. And this is what made the atmosphere in the Sindon house that much more complicated and disarming. Something was eating away at this young man, and what it was stood right before our eyes in the form of Oliver Sindon's history of unemployment. Still, even knowing this did not change anybody's behavior, or lessen any tension. Pressure, I am tempted to say, grew from a source we recognized only too well. Or perhaps a better metaphor would be that Oliver Sindon's unemployment had become a billowing smokestack, and all the Sindons were caught in the fumes and filth of his bitterness, anger, and utter helplessness. I debated a long while before selecting the following account for this study. Now, in reflecting on all that we have heretofore considered about children's secrets, I would submit that this one case, illustrating the effect of one man's unemployment on his entire family, may well be the quintessential account of children's secrets, private matters, and public shame.

DAVEY SINDON

When Davey Sindon was small, his mother used to put him on her lap and sing, "Davey Sindon's gone to sea, leaving his father and his sister and me." No matter how often she did it, the little boy laughed and bounced up and down, giving all the signals he could conjure up to get her to repeat it. By the time he was five, he couldn't remember his mother Victoria ever singing to him. As for the verse, Davey Sindon's gone to sea, he wasn't even certain what it meant. "Is Daddy a sailor?" he would ask his mother earnestly, not sure exactly what a sailor did.

Like his older sister, Effie, Davey gave his mother great pleasure. Indeed the two children were Victoria Sindon's only source of pleasure. She could be tough with them, though never mean, but she never did anything that would make her children question her love for them. The rule for Victoria was constraint. She never left the children unattended, never surprised them with changes of mood or deviations in the pattern of their lives. People wondered how she did it, in light of the ferocious world in which she lived, married to Ollie Sindon, but Victoria always said, "It's easy to be a gentle boat when the sea is roaring. If the sea roars, boat don't have to do nothing but hold on to its course." Her friends would smile. Victoria had a way with words. She also had a way with people, that rare ability of making the hard times seem easy, the rare ability of making human survival during its most precarious moments seem effortless. She also had that special capacity of keeping people from asking her pressing questions when they knew she was ducking away from personal turmoil. All one had to do was walk past the Sindon house when Ollie was going through what Victoria called his "complaining lessons," and one knew her life was difficult to the point of becoming a disaster.

The problem wasn't Ollie Sindon's mercurial temperament, his fiery responses to everything from politics to changes in the weather. Rather, the problem was his being out of work. The problem was his moroseness and anger and sickness caused by his being turned down by employers, from being lied to, from having his few little hopes shattered. "They're bombing me out," he'd roar, if he wasn't weak from drinking. "Bombing me out with their promises and their bullshitting. I had it with those folks, *all* them folks long, long time ago. They hate us niggers till it just about kills them to have to look at us. Give us a job, shit, they'd just as soon give what little they got to an animal 'fore they'd give us a look. Go in there with them white faces looking at me. Oh-oh, here comes another nigger wanting to be lazy on another job. Close the door on him 'fore he gets in too far so's we can't throw him out. You got a family, man? Damn niggers don't give no shit for their families. His old lady's probably doing it with some son of a bitch right now, so what's this guy care. He don't care. *Do* you care? You goddamn right I care, Mister White face or black face. You goddamn right I care. 'Cause I ain't working. You hear me? I ain't working, and if I ain't working, ain't living, 'cause I don't live if I don't work. You hear me, man? I'm not living no more till you give me a job. You got to give it to me."

Victoria would stare at him as hard as she could and without raising her voice she would warn him: "You don't talk that way with me or I take those children and I leave. I am just as nervous and upset about your not working as you are, but I will not have everybody's life being spoiled by your problems. We live on what we have, what we'll get. But don't you go on playing those plays of yours. I will not be your audience anymore." Then she would leave him before he had a chance to speak, and by his own admission, he would be happy that she had silenced him, for his complaining hurt him almost as much as his not working. And there *was* hope. Jobs had turned up in the past, they would turn up in the future. "Just let the future come quick," he would whisper, following Victoria into the back room, the single bedroom in the apartment, where the children slept. What a feeling to look down at the two of them, so little, asleep, breathing so slowly and regularly, the two of them so wondrously unaware of his problems and the miserable times they might be facing.

Ollie Sindon knew perfectly well that he wanted to share his agony at being unemployed with his children, despite the fact that they were too young to understand what it meant. He wanted them to say, Dad, you got the rawest deal any man on this earth ever got. But you'll see, if things don't turn out better, we're going to *make* it better for you. We're going to stay by you no matter what, even if it means we'll *never* get married or move away. You did the best you could for us and we're going to do the same for you. But no matter what happens, we'll never see you as a failure. It's the country, the world, the society that's at fault; not you! You did the best you could. Ollie Sindon wanted so much to be happy. He saw his life as being complicated, but he never gave up the idea that he could be satisfied. He was willing, he told himself, to settle for very little, but one requirement was steady work until he was sixty-five and ready to retire. He dreamed of the days he would be too old to work and he would say to his son, Well sir, Davey, the load's all yours. From now on, *you* look after this family. And Davey would say, You worked steady all your life, Dad, now it's my turn. The daydreams were plentiful, all of them realistic, all of them with happy endings, but each one based on the idea of a man working his forty good hours a week and bringing home a paycheck for his wife, his children, and himself.

Victoria Sindon was the only one who knew about Ollie's fantasies. She used to tease him about them, at least when she was certain his mood was strong enough to take her chiding. She would say: "You know, my husband, for someone who spends as much time dreaming all the time, your dreams aren't too rich, are they?"

"What do you mean rich?" he'd ask her, obviously insulted.

"Well, if *I* was dreaming, I'd put us in a big house somewhere, but all you see is working steady forty hours a week."

"That's all I see," he'd answer quietly.

"Maybe that's all any of us have the right to see. Well, maybe someday you should think big, dream about working steady forty-*five* hours a week. Then we'd have that little bit of extra."

"Listen, chum," he'd say, both of them starting to laugh, "if I start dreaming really big, I'm going to dream about working steady *twenty* hours a week and still end up better than what I got right now."

"Bet you would, too."

"You *know* I would. Then I'd add a little more. I'd add that I could see my boy working even less and getting even more. No. Let him work just as long as I did, only let him come out of it a whole *helluva* lot better than I did. I wouldn't want no one to repeat what I went through."

Ollie Sindon's wishes never came true. His career was at best spotty; his periods of unemployment were frequent. He was never a skilled laborer but no one could work harder. He rarely looked at his watch. When the job was done he quit, even if it meant coming home a few hours late. Victoria never liked to add to his burdens, or shake his luck, but when he was working and the job looked like it might last, she wouldn't hesitate to ask about his long hours. "No one's asking you to work more than eight hours a day," she'd say when he came home, exhausted and dripping with sweat. "You aren't that young that you can go on like a boy."

Ollie loved to hear her talk this way. He loved the feeling of being exhausted from a hard day of work and knowing that no one in the world could tell him he hadn't put in one amazing day. "I got pride," he'd tell his wife. "I may not love what I'm doing, but I'm working, and working is the great act, the act we're put on the earth to do."

"Glad you told me," she'd wink at him, " 'cause a person like myself's always happy to know why we *were* put on the earth. Now that I know it's because we get a chance to dig ditches for some rich white man, I suppose all of us can sleep a whole lot better tonight."

"Don't you fool yourself, Victoria. Everyone gets the most gratification out of his work he can. Doctor gets his kind of gratification, butcher gets his kind, even an old woman like you gets her kind. You work 'cause that's what we're meant to do. Some folks use their heads, some folks use their hands, but it don't make no difference 'cause the society needs all of us to be doing our work, even if the work's so terrible we can barely get ourselves out of bed in the morning to do it. There is no world without people working.

I'm digging holes for telephone poles. Wouldn't exactly call it the greatest job in the world, but it's important. If I don't do it I don't stay alive."

Victoria Sindon was happy when her husband worked. Her children, too, she imagined, seemed healthier when he was working. They ate better, and it was good knowing there was a little money left over to buy those special treats the family liked. There wasn't a man in the world who liked steak like Ollie Sindon, steak followed by strawberry ice cream. It was there when he worked, it was never talked about when he didn't.

By the time he was eleven years old, Davey Sindon knew all about his father's difficulties in finding jobs. He knew it was bad luck to say anything about a job his father held or might get, or announce where his father had gone on a particular day. His father arrived home around six o'clock. Maybe he had worked, maybe he hadn't, but one waited to see what Ollie would say. His children didn't ask questions, nor did his wife. Most days no one had to ask; it was clear he had not worked. His eyes and posture told everything. Maybe he would ask Davey if he wanted to throw a ball around. Davey would grab their mitts and a ball and be downstairs on the street in seconds. His father would follow minutes later, walking slowly, wearing his suit jacket, and they would throw the ball back and forth, his father's mind clearly on something a million miles away. It was better, naturally, when Ollie was in a good mood, when he was working. Then there was real excitement in the game. They pretended to be professional ballplayers and Ollie would do a play-by-play description of their game.

"There's a ground ball in into the hole," he'd shout out, rolling the beaten-up old ball down the sidewalk. "Sindon over to his right, makes a great pick up and throws him out. What a play, what a play!" Then Ollie would tell his son, "Put your foot behind your hand on grounders. It's added protection." Davey would lean down and try it. "The other hand, the one with the mitt."

"Do it again," his son would order.

"Ground ball to Sindon. He hasn't much time, Morgan can fly, but he throws him out. Get down lower, David. Lower to the ground." Davey tried to follow his father's instructions. "Lower still, that's it. What, you afraid the ball's going to hit you in the face?" Davey had to admit he worried about the ball skipping off the concrete and hitting him squarely in the mouth. "Hey, listen," his father would shout at him, his hands on his hips, "you want to be a major leaguer, you got to take the chances. It's just a job, with its own kind of chances. Man digs holes there's the danger he could fall in one of them. Man digs for coal, there's a chance he can get caught in the collapse. Man flies a plane there's a chance he falls right out of the sky. You go for a grounder, someone leaves a little bitty stone out there, that ball's going to pop up right over your head. Got to have fast hands, fast hands."

"You play ball, Ollie, when you were a kid?" Davey would ask, for when they played together he pretended they were teammates rather than father and son.

"Did I play ball when I was a kid?" Ollie would shout back in disbelief. Victoria would be watching them from the window, barely able to hear them, and making certain Effie didn't fall off the ledge. Effie always cried because Davey would never let her play when he was playing with his father. "Did I ever play ball when I was a kid?" Ollie's deep voice would rush in through the window like thick smoke. "Who do you think taught Billy George Blatter everything he knows about baseball?"

"Billy George *who*?" would come Davey's little voice. No matter how many times Ollie pulled the routine, Davey went for it.

"You don't know Billy George Blatter?" Ollie would say with exaggerated incredulity.

"No. Who's Billy George whatever his name is?"

"Victoria," Ollie would shout up to his wife. "This boy of yours doesn't know who Billy George Blatter is."

"Suppose you just tell my son then who he is."

"Tell him yourself," he'd shout, laughing to the point where his mitt would fall off and he would drop the ball, which only irritated Davey that much more.

"How the hell should I know? Anyway, hurry up because the steak's almost ready."

"Steak!" Davey would scream, forgetting all about Mr. Blatter, and off he'd dash leaving Ollie to carry the mitts and ball upstairs. At dinner he would tell Davey that Billy George Blatter was a little boy who went to the same church as he when he was a little boy. Truthfully, he couldn't figure out why that name had come into his mind, but one thing he did remember about little Billy Blatter was that he was the worst athlete in the neighborhood, maybe the worst in the state. Ollie even remembered hearing the boy's father say that Billy George was so bad at sports, he must have had white blood in him. He was going to speak to his wife about that. The thought made Ollie Sindon laugh out loud. "I think even Effie could have taught that boy a thing or two about playing baseball."

Davey would have lost interest in the story by this point. His father's enjoyment at such a foolish story irritated him. "We ought to have steak every night," he would say.

The remark would quiet Ollie. For a few minutes the family would eat in silence.

In the beginning, no one knew exactly what had happened to Ollie Sindon. Merely remembering the event was difficult enough. It was a Wednesday morning, *that* Victoria knew for certain. A Wednesday morning when he was out of work. He awoke and found he couldn't get out of bed. Victoria told him to quit joking, but he insisted he couldn't move his left leg. Soon he realized he had lost all sensation in the leg. Victoria was terrified. Fortunately the children were at school. A police ambulance arrived and two attendants carried Ollie down the stairs. In time he recovered most of the feeling in the leg, although no amount of therapy healed his limp. The leg never was as strong as before, and while he tried to hide his slight handicap from potential employers, the few job possibilities he had accumulated grew even more thin.

The minor stroke Ollie Sindon had suffered occurred when his son, Davey, was thirteen and a half. Victoria had taken on odd jobs, sewing, housecleaning, laundering, when she could find them. She disliked being away from her husband, who had grown depressed after his illness. The little bit of energy he had always been able to draw upon during the long weeks and months of unemployment had vanished. He would threaten suicide, go several days without speaking to anyone, demand to be fed when he knew there was no food in the house. When Victoria offered to go shopping for bread and the kind of cheese he liked so well, he would yell at her for leaving him alone in the house. What if he needed her suddenly? What if he fell, or suffered another stroke?

"Get someone else to go shopping for you and arrange your life better to shop when Effie's here. And how come Davey isn't home at night? Why don't you talk to him about why he's never home when he's supposed to be? Just 'cause I'm not working don't mean he's supposed to be playing around all the time. What do you tell him? His father's a cripple? That his father's a bum? That why he's not here? What is it with all these kids anyway, that they get so damn disrespectful? Girls, too. Who they think they are anyway, acting like they're superior to everyone, wanting only this kind of food or wearing only that kind of clothes? I'd like to tell them about what *real* hard living's all about. I'd like to see them do a whole lot better what with the conditions I had facing me. Big time, that's all they want, the big time. Hell, I'll bet they sit around talking about me. 'My father don't work no more 'cause he's got a bum leg that keeps him home. Course even if he didn't have it he wouldn't work anyway 'cause he always had trouble. Probably didn't want to work neither. That's the real story behind it. Never saw an old man so lazy. Hell, he didn't even have time to play with me when he wasn't working. Told my mother, you're not supposed to work, then he didn't work himself. So what'd he expect, *us* to work, me and my sister? Laziest nigger in the city, my father. Wasn't even a good ballplayer.'

"*Victoria!* Where the hell are you?"

"I'm here," Victoria would scream right back at him. "I am goddamn sick myself with all your complaining. You've complained about one thing or another from the day practically we got married. Now, what the hell is it now? You want to eat, I told you I'd go to the store. You want to talk, we'll sit here and talk. But if it's the feel-sorry-for-the-poor-old-man bit, I have had it up to here. You want to complain about how you're the only person in the world who's got problems, you go right ahead, but I ain't listening to it and I'll be damned if I'm ready to tell my son he has to sit here at night with his father and listen to all the garbage that flies out of your mouth. It's just garbage and I don't want to hear it no more!"

Ollie Sindon listened to his wife when she spoke to him. He felt increasingly sorry for himself and wouldn't let her gain an inch of advantage over him. He fought her, defended his position, but he listened to her, because, like her, he blamed himself for his troubles. Still, he fought her.

"You don't want to hear me talking, that's fine. Why don't you just pack your little bag and take all your junk and get out of here. Take the children, empty out the kitchen, take all your friends for all I care. I'd be better off without them floating in here all the time asking me about this job or that job, or saying it don't look to me like you got any problem with your leg. Take 'em all. Or maybe you'd like *me* to leave. That's it. I'll leave. I'll run out of here. Why don't you go down to the five-and-dime and buy me a track suit and I'll run out of here. Give all of you the big laugh you want out of me. What the hell, you laugh at me behind my back, might as well do it in front of me. I sure would love to know one of these days just what it is you tell that boy about me."

"What the hell are you talking about?" Victoria would come into the living room and stare at him, but Ollie would pretend he didn't know she was there.

"Well, son," Ollie would begin, "it's like this. Your father's a big bust. Just another one of those dumb niggers that didn't spend enough time in school, so here he is a big failure, not that anyone ever thought he'd come to much more than what he is. He tried. Even thought he'd be able to make it, but it didn't work out. He's just a two-bit bum! Tell you, son, there's only one thing a man's supposed to do, and that's work. If he don't work, well, he just ain't a man. So you see, son, your old man ain't a man at all. He's just a dumb old *nigger!*"

"Shut up," Victoria would cry out. "Just shut up or I *will* leave."

"Go on. Who the hell needs you around here anyway, all you do is mother people. Hell, you been mothering me like I was the boy's *brother* instead of his father."

"You act like you were his *baby* brother 'stead of his father. That's the first true thing you said all day. 'Bout time you started acting like his father."

"'Bout time you shut your face up."

"I don't see where just because you ain't working don't mean you can't take a little fatherly interest in him."

"A little fatherly interest in him," he would mock her.

"That's exactly what I mean. A little fatherly interest."

"A little fatherly interest," he'd mock her again. "You know something, Victoria, you're beginning to sound like some of those high-class white folks you been working for. Maybe that's what you want, too, since you *are* the man of the family. Ain't that it?"

"What you want to eat?"

"You didn't hear me?"

"What do you want to eat?"

"I'm asking you a question," he would scream at her.

"What do you want me to say?" She could not have sounded more bored.

"I want you to say that because I don't work and never worked regular like a man should, I'm only his father by title. That's all. I carry the title, just like I carry a card that says I got a right to work. Neither of them does no good. I'm a shit-ass father, man, and you know it. World's number one worst father, to both of 'em. But I ain't got no excuses. I ain't making excuses to nobody. I don't care what happens to either of them 'cause I come first, man. *I'm* the one. You get it? I don't have a job, there ain't no work in this country, bad leg or not, then I don't mess around with no children. That's *your* job. Ain't my job. Don't give a damn about them. Don't need to see them, don't need to talk to them, don't need them for the slightest goddamn thing. Boy wants to talk with some man, let him find somebody at his school. Better yet, let him go find one of those bullshit nigger ministers. You want real men with real jobs, hardworking men, men working their asses off for the community and just for the love of God, then that's who he can go talk to. That's your real man. Go in the church, man, with all those guys running around in there. 'Hey, man, what you do?' 'I work for God, man.' 'Oh yeah? What you do for God, man?' 'I light candles and keep people from sinning.' 'Yeah, that right, man?' 'Sure is, man. Get money for it, too, telling all the little children with fathers who don't work what to do.' 'Yeah, what you tell 'em to do?' 'I tell 'em how they got to have *compassion* for their poor old stumbling fathers. Got to have all kinds of *compassion*. Poor old dudes just sitting up there in their ridiculous little houses watching the walls and waiting to die. Got to *advise* all those little children so's they see the light of God.' 'Hey, man, that's one helluva job you got there working for the church. I talk to those children myself, man.' 'Yeah? Ones with the unemployed fathers?' 'Sure, man. I talk to 'em just like you do.' 'Yeah? That a fact? And what do *you* tell 'em?' 'Me? I tell 'em if you're old enough to see your old man ain't working, and you're old enough to understand that when he don't work it means he ain't bringing home a fuckin' dime, then you're old enough to get away from that man as soon as you can 'cause he *ain't* no man. He *ain't* your father. He's nothing, man, absolutely nothing. And the sooner you forget the sight of him, the better off you're going to be. Don't hang around him if he ain't working. He'll just bring you down with him.' "

Victoria would close the door to the apartment and start down the stairs quietly. She would be weeping. Then Ollie's big voice would bellow from the living room. "Victoria, Victoria," he would be yelling. "You get back in here at once. You come back in this house in one minute or I won't be here when you get back. You can just say good-bye right now. You come back here!"

Victoria would leave and buy strawberry ice cream for him, even though the doctor said Ollie would do better without high carbohydrate intake.

No matter how hard she tried, Victoria Sindon could never convince her husband that being out of work did not reflect on him as a man. He was a good man, a good father, she tried to assure him. But there was no convincing him. A job possibility would arise through some friend and his spirits lifted, but Victoria could see that he was scared now from the uncertainty and the months of inactivity. There were days when the little bit of hope she wanted to hold on to seemed real enough, but she knew nothing would last, for no jobs ever lasted, and Ollie wasn't getting any younger. Indeed, he seemed to be aging more quickly than anyone she knew, with the exception of her son.

At fourteen, Davey Sindon was an extremely strong young man, quiet, polite, but filled with anger. Several close friends spoke with him, but he let very few others know what he was thinking and feeling. Surely his father had lost touch with him, and while his mother believed she knew what he was doing, Davey insisted she hadn't the slightest notion of who he was. A deeply complex person with many talents and a rich intelligence, he dreamed of becoming all sorts of things, and was blessed with a miraculous memory. But in most conversations that focused on his life, the matter of his father's unemployment played a significant role. It was like a fire in him that never went out, a haunting demon. He himself could not define what it was, exactly, that infuriated him: the conditions of the country that made for widespread unemployment, or the mere fact that his father spent so much time out of work. He might start a tirade against America, its racism, the fact that the country allowed so many people to be poor, but soon he was haranguing against his father, calling him weak, a quitter, a man who rolled over and played dead with his own kind. He labeled his father the nice little nigger man in the company of white folks. Davey Sindon believed that since the odds were so stacked against him and his family, the only way to lead one's life was to not let anybody see you were afraid of anything and take the attitude that you have everything to win and nothing to lose, except the respect of a few people, like perhaps your own father.

Davey Sindon had grown up to be a tough boy. His manner troubled his mother, infuriated his father. "They're all fancy big shots," Ollie Sindon would growl at Victoria when Davey strutted out on a Friday night, dressed in clothes that Ollie disapproved of and believed to be stolen. "Phony big shots. Going out with phony big shots. Son of a bitch child looks down his nose at me and there he is strutting around as if he were the goddamn tax collector. If he disapproves of me so much, let him get his own goddamn home. He can do so much better without me, then let's see him try. They can both go, far as I'm concerned. Let him show this great big world he thinks he's discovering and all these people he finds to hang with to his sister. Then *she* can be a phony big shot, too. Where'd he get those clothes?"

Victoria wouldn't answer. She held the same fears as her husband about where her son went and what he did. Victoria's problem was to get Ollie to turn his attention from his own concerns to those of his son. No one needed to tell Ollie that he was a failure, that with each passing day the chances of him ever resurrecting his life grew slimmer. No one needed to tell him, as he himself said, that his salvation lay in making certain his children wouldn't share the fate he had known. But something always kept him from putting his own problems aside long enough to attend to his children, and especially his son. No matter how intensely he resolved to devote himself to Davey, his bitterness at being sickly and out of work never allowed him to carry out his wishes. He would try, but then Davey would say something and he would give up all ideas of befriending his son.

"You know where that boy's going to end up, Victoria?" Ollie would mutter when Davey would leave.

"I know exactly where he's going to end up" would come the voice from another room, for Victoria made it her business to overhear the conversations between her husband and son. "He's going to end up in jail. Won't be long now."

"Way you say it, makes it sound like that's what you want."

Victoria wouldn't bother to respond.

The thought that he might end up in jail had crossed Davey Sindon's mind as well: "Could happen, man," he would say, beginning to smile his smile of toughness and defiance. "Could happen all right. Steady work though, in jail, ain't it. I mean, you don't even have to go looking for it, or have some Mr. Nobody with a big stomach interview you or nothing. You walk in there and the cat says, your job's working in the carpentry shop. You got a job, man. They even pay you to work. That's true, ain't it? Pay you a little money, ain't much, but what the hell, working for peanuts is better than not working for no peanuts. You don't believe me, you just ask my old man. He'll tell you all about working. Man, has this country screwed *that* guy up. Sent him this way, sent him that way, scratching for jobs. Down on his knees, I'll bet, more times than he'd ever admit begging for people to give him a job. So what the hell if I am in jail. They give me the work, I'll blow out my time there.

"Course my old man, he'd be so angry 'bout me being in the slammer. Love to see that man's face when the cat comes and tell him, We got your little boy locked up for ripping off a bank. Son of a bitch kid, he'd be yelling at my mother. Told you he was no good. Told you he was the biggest bust this side of Africa. Yeah, but tell me, Copper, how much the boy rip that bank off for? Couple thousand maybe. Couple thousand, man? Shit. I may go into some prison somewhere, if they catch me. But if I go I ain't going for no two thousand dollars, baby. I go in for the kill. Six figures right up front man, or I don't even *talk* about the job. You see my old man starting to smile, laugh out loud. Hey, is that a fact? Old Davey boy ripped 'em off for six figures. Son of a bitch kid didn't do so bad at that, even if he is in prison. Hell, time will come when they got to let him out. Hey, tell me, Copper, they find out maybe he left a little money for his poor old mom and dad. Ain't worked in twenty years, man. Bet he left something outside for me. Hell, he did, old man. Told me to tell you you played the good little nigger part too long, man, way too long. You could have been in on anything you wanted to. Yellow shit bastard that you were. Sitting in that chair of his, bitching all the time 'bout this and that to my mother, my *mother*, man, like she was the governor or something.

"You get a load of that guy, man, begging in the streets so's he got the whole community laughing at him, and he's putting it to my mother? What the hell he think she's ever going to do for *him*. That son of a bitch walked, she walked *blocks*, man, more streets than you could count looking for the food he told her he wanted. You imagine that, man, sending that woman 'round the city shopping in just the stores *he* wants, buying him just the certain kind of ice cream he wants, 'cause you can't get the brand in stores 'round here? Son of a bitch worked, hell, no more than a few years all together since he was married, and he's pushing her 'round like some big king. Should have seen him too when he got sick, you know with that leg of his. Doctor told my mother he was fine. He went around acting like they took the leg off him or something. He's an actor, my old man. Makes everybody treat him special like he's somebody famous. Who the hell are you, man, Martin Luther King or someone that you're acting so high and mighty all the time? He's nothing, man. He can't stand to face it, but he's nothing. The more a man is nothing the harder it is for him to let on that he is. You want to bullshit the guys at the pool hall, let 'em think you ain't drawing welfare? That's okay, man. Nobody *wants* to be seen as a bum. Nobody says you got to advertise your losses, you know what I mean. But that man was acting like he was doing all right in his own home, in his own home, man. Front of me and my mother and my sister. Who's he think he's kidding?

"And that's another thing. All this time he ain't working, all he's thinking about is me, his famous son. Half the time I think he's trying to figure out ways I won't end up being like him. But the other half, man, I really think the son of a bitch was plotting how to have me end up in the same shit pile as him. Swear to God, man. I think

it'd kill him to see me successful when he failed so bad. There ain't
no one talked so bad as he did. But don't think once he's paid any
attention to my sister. I can't even remember him asking her what's
she doing, like at school. And that kid is smart, man, she can read,
man, like a son of a bitch. She reads out loud to my mother sometime at night, I tell her to shut up, you know, 'cause I'm trying to
sleep, but I'm only pretending 'cause I love to hear her read. Kid's
out of sight, man. Adult books. My mother gets her all these adult
books and she goes through them, zip zap zip, and she's finished. She
remembers 'em, too. I do, too, when I hear her reading them out
loud. She's terrific. But you think my old man has once said, hey, you
know what, Effie, you're the best reader in this city. I'm proud of
you, Effie. Good Effie. Fuck you, Effie. Don't say a word to her, man.
Man's got two things on his mind. He ain't got no job so he thinks
he's got the right to order us around. Nobody's told him you got to
earn your place in the house. You don't just get it for free.

"Other thing he thinks about is how soon it's going to be 'fore I
end up in the slammer. Shit, I got a mind to walk in on him one
day, you know, and say, Hey, Pop, I'm going to take a big load off
your mind. Listen here, I'm going to be in jail in less than a year, so
now all you got to worry about is feeling sorry for yourself. But don't
trouble yourself none, 'cause it wouldn't look right, somehow, your
getting off your sweet ass trying to find a job somewhere so's your old
lady might have a couple of nice days on the earth before she croaks.
And while I'm in jail, Pop, why the hell don't you introduce yourself
to the little skinny girl who lives in the same apartment as you. You
named her after your own mother so you must have been interested
in her once. Instead of sitting there trying to convince everybody you
can't walk and that's why you don't go looking for a job, have her
read out loud to you. You'll be surprised. Shit, man, I'm not so sure
my old man even knows how to read himself. I guess he must, I see
him with the newspaper every day. Don't do him a helluva lot of
good though, does it? Maybe he don't know they print jobs available
in it. Probably all he's doing is choking himself to death on the
comics.

"I don't know, sometimes I feel sorry for the guy. Tell myself, hey,
the world is tough, 'specially if you're black. Lots of folks out of
work. Lot of white folks out of work. Nobody cares all that much
about how many folks don't have jobs when it's just black folks out
of those jobs. Going around mumbling, can't get good help these
days. Ain't like the old days. Uppity niggers won't work for twenty
cents an hour no more. Terrible times. Then all of a sudden, like, all

these white dudes, they start losing their jobs, too, high-paying guys, vice-presidents, lots of 'em are out of work. Then all of a sudden that's all you hear about, unemployment, unemployment. Ten years ago nobody said a word. Now everybody's bitching and moaning. Who was looking out for my old man ten years ago? Nobody, man. They were just out there on the streets looking for the cheapest labor they could find. Hell, those bastards they knew they could buy men like my father cheap, and man did they ever give 'em the shittiest jobs in this city. Holy Jesus, man. They had my father standing waist-high in shit, honest to God. They had him up to his ass in shit, digging, and the son of a bitch came home proud of his work, telling my mother he did a good day's work. They paid him shit, man, for working in shit. And the man felt proud. He felt proud like he just done something fantastic. I can't believe it, man. I know it's what happened but I can't believe it. He used to come home—I remember 'cause most of the time when I came home he was already home, which meant he didn't work that day—he'd be smelly like you couldn't imagine. Me and my sister couldn't stand how much he smelled. We had to get out of the house, man. I mean we got out of there. My father, he and my mother pretended to be angry with us for walking out like that, but you could see they were only pretend-ing. Everybody was happy then, 'cause the man had work. When he was working, we were happy, 'specially my mother, no matter how much he smelled. I was happy, too. I was only little so I didn't know. I mean, I wasn't old enough to be ashamed of what he did for a living. What's your old man do? My old man's a lawyer. What's *your* old man do, David? My old man stands ass-high in shit and shovels it around, but he's happy 'cause he's got a steady job. Little kids ain't ashamed of their fathers. They don't know what being out of work is all about. They don't even know where the old man goes, or what he does or doesn't do.

"But all that's different now, man. He never works. We never have enough money, so I ain't got a single reason in the world why I should stay around that house. I might have thought he was pretty cute when I was small, but I don't see nothing cute about him now. It's my job to make sure my mother and Effie are going to be all right, 'cause he sure gave up on that job a long, long time ago. Man doesn't take responsibility for no one. He'll push my mother around, man, about the slightest thing that bothers him. Hey, Victoria, there's a fly buzzin' 'round my chair. Hey, Victoria, how come my shirts ain't clean? Hey, Victoria, how come your son's always getting into trouble? He's tough on her, man, like you couldn't believe. But she takes it. Maybe there's something wrong with her, too, I don't know, in her head I mean, to take all his pushing her around like that. Hell, if I was her I'd tell him, Hey, lookit here, man. You work for a living, get up off your ass one second of the day and I'll *think* about obeying some of your orders. But if you just sit there looking so goddamn mad at the world all the time, I wouldn't go across this room to open the goddamn window for you. She don't tell him nothing though, man. She just takes it. Almost like he's got some special right to be out of work. It's like he's always telling her, all these cats are out of work, so he ain't special. Ain't his fault. Lots of guys like him out of work. You can't argue with the man. Black folks are getting killed without jobs. They're getting murdered, man. They'll take a black man's job from him ten times faster than a white man's job. You got a bunch of cats working, say, on some big construction job downtown and the word comes down to cut off some men, who you think they're going to cut first? They're going to cut every black man off that job, unless the dude is so well trained, like he's in some specialized job they can't get along without him. But there ain't a lot of specialized cats 'cause they don't train 'em until they've trained all the white guys they can find. Then, if they got some good jobs left over and they can't find no white guy, they'll go train some black guy. Shit, jobs being what they are, you can be damn sure that cat's going to turn his back on his own brothers if he can save his job.

"So who's my father got helping *him* out in the world, man? He ain't got nobody, man. There ain't nobody out there, unless it's somebody watching him figuring out how he's going to take my old man's job, if he ever gets one. Guy don't stand a chance. He's got a one in million chance, man, just to earn a living. You imagine how that makes him feel? Man has to pull his body out of the bed every morning knowing he's got a one in maybe ten million chance to make his goddamn living. I ain't talking, man, of making a lot of money, not even the money he *needs*. I'm just talking about the man's chances of making *any* living. It's no wonder he got sick like he did. This thing breaks your spirit, your body, there's nothing left of the guy. When I was small, you know, and he was working not all the time but a helluva lot more than he does now, that man was fun to have around. Man used to play ball with me, cat was a stitch. He'd clown it up, make it fun for me, 'cause it sure couldn't have been too much fun for him. Hell, I couldn't catch the damn thing, and half the time I had him running in the street or down some cellar stairs. But he was a jive, man. He had everybody laughing. Folks used to stand around and watch him. He knew everybody, man.

After work, all the men would come down to watch my old man play ball, and all these little kids wanted to play with us. I didn't want 'em to, you know, but I didn't say nothing 'cause my father would probably say, you gotta share, you gotta share. But he knew I didn't want to play with 'em. He knew what I was thinking even without me saying a word. He'd tell 'em, Hey, this scene's just with me and my son. This here's our special after-work baseball game. Man, I felt fantastic. I'd think, son of a bitch, man has to be the greatest father alive.

"Hey, but you grow up, you learn what's really happening in the world. Hurts you to learn, but that's what it's all about. You see your father sitting home all the time, bitching 'bout that, moaning 'bout that, and no matter what he says about how black folks got it tough, and the world don't want no part of us, I see him not working. You know what I mean? Words are one thing, but what he does or doesn't do, that's a whole other thing. And the dude ain't working. Never. Just picking on my old lady, every day when I'm around, which means he's probably knocking hell out of her when me and Effie ain't there. But she don't say much. When he screams, she screams back, and the rest of the time she don't say nothing at all, man. I used to think to myself, why's she take it like that. I used to think, too, I'm going out to make money. I'll give 'em both all my money. You see me, ten years old looking for a job in this city? I think I'll be a president of some big company. Why not? Get me fifty, sixty thou a year and give it to my folks. Little kids and all their dreams, huh?

"I'll tell you, man, I really didn't know what to do with either one of my folks when it got so bad. I said to myself, I'm either going to run away or I swear to God I'm going to kill 'em both, 'cause they're both crazy. I'm watching my mother, this is like two years ago, and she's not well. Effie doesn't know what's happening but she don't look good to me at all. But I don't say nothing. What am I going to do about it anyway? I was waiting for my old man to do something, or say something, but he don't move up off his ass far as I could tell. This is when he maybe didn't work, like, one week out of fifteen, man. So's he bad off like always, but my mother's getting to be bad off, too.

"So one day I come home from school and I got to take a piss something terrible, man. So I run up the stairs thinking for sure I'm going to do it in my pants and I like fly into the toilet, and there's my mother sitting there crying, you know. She's surprised to see me, but the tears are all *over* her face. All of a sudden I didn't have to

piss no more. I mean, you see your mother and she's all by herself
and she's crying, that scares the piss out of you, right? So I ask her
over and over again, 'What's wrong, what's wrong?' and she keeps
saying, 'Nothing's wrong, nothing's wrong.' 'But you're crying,' I tell
her. 'That ain't nothing,' she says. 'I don't know why I was crying.
Something in my eye.' Yeah, sure; you got something in your eye you
ain't sitting in the bathroom looking like she looked. My father, he
was sitting in the living room like he always did, he didn't even know
she was in there, 'cause I went in there and asked him and he was
surprised. He even called her, you know, 'You crying, Victoria?' and
she comes out and says 'No.' She don't have to tell me not to tell
him no more. I can see plain as hell she don't want him to know
nothing about nothing. So I don't say nothing.

"Then nothing happens for a while. My mother's going 'round
acting like everything's fine and like what I saw in the bathroom
never happened. Then about a month later I heard my aunt talking
to my mother's best friend. They're outside on the sidewalk but I
could hear 'em 'cause I hid behind the door. I could see 'em, too. My
aunt is talking and she's telling Morane, that's my mother's friend,
how my mother's sick and what the doctors have to do, which is to
go, like, once a week to their place where she gets an X ray. I can't
figure out what they're talking about 'cause this was a couple of years
ago and I thought X ray was like when you broke something. But
this was something different. Like, they were trying to make her well
with it 'stead of taking pictures of her with it. Anyway, I figured
some of it out and Morane told me the rest later. You know my
mother had cancer, maybe she still has it, and she was afraid to say
nothing about it to my father 'cause she said she didn't want to
bother him about it 'cause he was too upset about his own life to
hear any *more* bad news. You believe that woman acting like that?
Shit, man, I get cancer and wonder if I'm going to die any minute,
I'd go crying to anybody I could find, and the first person I'd cry to
is my husband. He tell me not to moan 'cause he's got worse problems, I tell him to get the fuck out of this house and don't ever come
back. Ever!

"That woman hid that she was sick from him. He didn't know till
after she was done going for those treatments. Then she had to keep
going back to see if she was well. They can burn you up but good
and it still grows back. I learned all this from one of my teachers.
She said, 'You worried by all this, David?' I said 'No, what's to be
worried about?' She's only got it in one part of her body. I didn't
even know where she had it. Teacher asked me, but I didn't even

know, man. When I found out where it happened I almost threw up. I mean, I never thought too much about how women are put together, and then this teacher tells me how they do it and I imagined my mother lying there on this table and them putting this machine over her, man, and it doing whatever it does, and all I could think about was her sitting in that bathroom and not telling my father what was happening 'cause she was worried about *him* all the time. About *him*, 'cause he was always so down about not working. Still is down. He's always down. But with her, it was always my father who was the bad-off one. Shit, I'd have killed the man for acting like that with her being sick. Never got her flowers or nothing, or bought her a present or helped her in the house. The both of them were just walking around pretending nothing was wrong with her. I couldn't believe it, man, and the worst thing was like Effie didn't know nothing about none of it. Didn't even know my mother was sick and I didn't know if she was better from all the treatment. I had to ask Morane, who had to ask my aunt. Even my mother didn't know for sure Morane knew about everything that was going on, and she for sure didn't know what *I* knew. I had to tell my teacher, be sure you don't tell either my mother or father what you been telling me. You want to hear something? When I told my teacher, you know, not to say nothing to my folks, she goes, 'I didn't even know your father was alive. You never say nothing about him.' It was true, too, 'cause most of the time at school I was always so ashamed about him never working I pretended like he was dead 'cause I never wanted no one asking me about him.

"But the thing was, my dad was upset by everything going on. He got scared about my mother same as I did. Then he got feeling really sorry and bad 'cause he'd been such a bad husband to her. That's all he could say for months. 'I been bad, Victoria. I been bad.' He was like a little kid. I didn't know whether to feel sorry for the guy 'cause he had no job and his wife might be dying, or angry with him 'cause he was acting like a baby. He never made it easy for any of us to know how to feel about him. You could love him or hate him practically in the same minute. Hell, I got so frustrated from seeing him acting like he did, I decided I'm getting out of that house as much as I can, all the time if I have to. I know my father real well, and I know what he was thinking. He was thinking, Dear Lord, let me find a job with my wife sick. Anything. I'll do *anything* but I need a job *now*. But he couldn't get nothing, man, not a dime's worth of work anywhere. So between him not working and my mother lying on that table once a week with that X-ray machine burning her insides out, where a woman has her baby, you know, shit, you can imagine how we were doing.

"Effie, though, she was doing fine, which sort of made me happy. She'd come home and read and read and help my mother, or whatever she'd do. You couldn't tell by looking at her she knew anything different from before. Fact is, I was certain she didn't know nothing. So one day I took her with me outside, you know, and I said to her, 'Effie, you got any idea what's going on in our house?' 'You mean Dad not working?' she goes. 'I say, that ain't new.' 'You mean about Mom and the X-ray treatments?' 'Yeah. You know where she's getting them?' 'At the hospital, I suppose. Never asked.' That's what she said. 'Not in the hospital. Where in her body, you know, where they're working on her?' 'Yeah.' She knew. I tell you, man, the kid's out of sight. 'They're working on her uterus,' she said. 'On her what? What they call it?' 'They call it a uterus,' she goes. Then she says, 'Don't worry about it none, you ain't got one so you ain't going to get sick there.' And all that time I was walking 'round trying to make sure my kid sister doesn't know what's happening. So I asked her, 'How come you know so much?' So she says, ' 'Cause I talked to the same teacher you did. She even gave me a book to read.' Effie's going to be all right. Someday she's going to be successful, even though she is the daughter of a sick old mother and a father who's just barely staying alive.

"Then there's me. I got the same parents and look at me. David Sindon the nothing. Kind of sad, I'd say, way I'm turning out. I'm sure it makes my old man sad, my old lady, too. I don't know what Effie thinks. Can't think much of me, I'd say. Can't see how anybody'd think too much of me by this time. Most of the time now I don't know whether to blame people for what's happening or just forget them or what. Talking with my old man doesn't help, 'cause no matter how good he sounds when he's talking, I just can't get up the respect for the guy. Like, when he talks to me about being a man, it makes sense, but it'd be a whole lot better if someone else was talking 'cause he ain't much of a man himself. I mean, I'm sitting there, man, and the man's telling me about working and getting jobs and making steady money and having a nice wife and kids, and maybe taking vacations, which is something we never did once in our life. I don't blame him for not having vacations, but what's he talking about all this stuff about living in the middle-class scene, man, when he ain't worked, like, for years, man. There ain't nothing he's done that makes him so much of a man that he can talk like that to me. Just 'cause he's my father? Hell, it ain't nothing to be a father. It's the woman does all the work, not the man. In my family my old man could have done a lot more than he did, too, 'cause he didn't have nothing else to do with himself. Just like me now. We both got all the time in the world on our hands. Neither one of us no better than the other."

David Sindon was fifteen years old when he knifed Jared Alexander in a street fight. Both boys had been drinking. Indeed, the young men who witnessed the fight reported that the two combatants did most of their fighting kneeling and lying down because they were so drunk. Nobody knew what started the fight. David had cajoled a woman into buying liquor for a group of boys. Suddenly David and Jared were fighting. Jared produced a long knife, David broke a bottle and foolishly threw it at Jared, leaving himself without a weapon. But Peter Mixley threw him his knife and the boys wrestled around and crawled and fell over one another. Finally, a gurgling painful sob came from one of the boys and there was Jared Alexander lying doubled up in the street, David's knife stuck in his abdomen. Blood was everywhere and the boys were terrified. At first, David thought of leaving Jared there, but Peter insisted they had to call the police. David argued with him, but their discussion was superfluous as another boy had already run off to get help. Three men appeared and in a matter of minutes the police were present.

David Sindon was charged with manslaughter and put in jail to await trial. His parents were sickened by the news. They visited with him every day, worrying about him, and confused by the long wait before his trial. Because of their financial situation, they were obliged to accept a court-appointed lawyer, who met with David three times in five months.

Victoria Sindon had not responded well to the X-ray treatment and underwent surgery. The cancer had spread to her bowel, a section of which had to be removed. Her son cried when he heard the news of the operation. Effie came to the prison and talked with her brother, but David preferred that she stay away. She was too good and too smart to get messed up by his troubles, he told her. She offered to come and read to him but he refused this, too, even though he loved listening to her. Ignoring his request, she visited with him every week and brought him magazines. She had landed a job with a neighborhood store and spent her money on little gifts for her brother in prison and her mother, who was recuperating at home. Amazingly, Effie Sindon's schoolwork remained steady. Her aunt and her mother's friend, Morane, helped out at home, for everyone wanted to make certain that not all the family's burdens fell on her shoulders. "Effie's going to make it," her father said. "With her brother and her mother and me and every other problem in the world she has to face, the girl's still going to make it."

Friends rallied around the Sindons. Every day one could find someone in their apartment, preparing food, cleaning up. A woman would leave her child in the care of another woman at the Sindons' so that Victoria would not be alone and Effie had time to do her schoolwork. David's friends, too, wanted to help. They washed windows and floors and went on errands for the Sindons. In time, Victoria seemed to be recovering. Much of her strength returned, although she would never be the woman she was. Ollie Sindon became extremely quiet and depressed. No one could lift his spirits, no one could convince him that what he called his collapse as a man hadn't brought down his entire family. He made arrangements to visit with his son every day. Even when David rejected him, he sat alone in the waiting room of the jail. He never read or spoke to anyone; he merely sat, his eyes fixed on the door leading to the cells, hoping his son might change his mind. When visiting hours ended, he rose and walked to the bus stop, waited for the bus, and began the one-and-a-half-hour journey to his home.

Part IV

MATTERS OF DEVIANCE

"The Myth of Being Straight"

SEVEN

Sexual Practices

A friend once recounted this charming, and telling, vignette. She found herself on her way to work, dressed in pantsuit and carrying her briefcase, walking her seven-year-old daughter to the school bus stop. Glancing down at the child, she noticed how the little girl, who had dressed herself, was wearing the epitome of traditional girl's clothing: skirt, blouse, even black patent-leather shoes and white socks. It struck the mother how, in the midst of tremendous change in women's and men's public styles and social roles, her own daughter was "carrying on" in the most "publicly" traditional styles.

This chapter is introduced with this scene to make only one point: In most instances of revolutionary change, one finds the traditional values, indeed a form of conservatism, being underwritten by some of the very people for whom the so-called revolutionary change is intended. Many mothers and fathers of the 1970s, for example, are pushing mightily against the wholly unjust inequalities between the sexes. They teach their children there are no legitimate sociological differences between the sexes, and they act in ways partly to demonstrate an ideal equality or a sharing of responsibility for their children. What is "wrong" with a mother working outside the home and wearing slacks? Then again, what is wrong with her daughter wishing to be seen as a girl in traditional dress?

On matters of childhood sexuality the point of children's occasional conservatism seems especially salient. One frequently finds children even from so-called liberated homes—a term I don't much like—espousing traditional notions, attitudes, and behavior patterns. In the development of the child's identity, it often seems important (to them) to clearly differentiate the boys from the girls. Dangers of exclusiveness aside, the so-called homogenization of peoples required in certain ideologies is often sorely repudiated by the child who seems to prefer discreet notions of what Mommy is and does, and what Daddy is and does. As we know, large-scale social change occurs only when people are prepared, and this means in a social as well as a personal historical sense. In the course of "preparing" people, moreover, one typically finds them holding even more tightly to their accustomed beliefs, perceptions, and styles. It is a perfectly natural response. No one moves easily into new experiential realms. Even in geographical terms, one finds that most people fortunate enough to live in several countries during their childhood or adulthood years almost invariably settle down in the country of their birth.

This is point number one: During periods of extreme pressure for people to recontextualize their values, one finds a retreat to or a reaffirmation of accustomed ways of living and familiar ideologies. Point number two is that people seem to require evidence of traditional values and behavior not only in themselves but in those people from whom they feel their own life-styles are derived. Certainly children make implicit as well as explicit demands on their parents. It is my impression that children prefer to see their parents if not in the idealized terms of perfect deities, then as people leading their lives in the most straightforward, honest, and uncomplicated ways. Children, for example, seem to recoil not only from the sight of a parent drunk or undergoing a fit of rage but from the sight of a parent laughing overly loudly in a public place or acting in the slightest way mischievous. A parent who dresses up for a party in the clothes of the other sex often causes his or her young child distress. It seems ironic, paradoxical even, that children, who can endure the most extreme situations and radical changes, should reveal these displays of conservatism. I recall an eight-year-old girl refusing to let me see her parents' bedroom because she knew the laundry was piled on the bed and prominent in the pile was her father's underwear. Of course I respected her wishes. Her friends, incidentally, found her demand eminently reasonable.

Point number three, still by way of introducing this chapter, is that despite what some "reporters of the scene" tell us, children and adolescents do not necessarily accommodate themselves so easily to the extraordinary changes in values, styles, and behavior connected with sexuality. To be sure, we are shocked to learn that children actually participate in the business of pornography, but the large majority of children remain today not unlike the children of the generations before them. They are still naïve or prudish, or just plain giggly and uncomfortable about sexuality and sexual practices. Some of them act as though many of the bugaboos that haunted me about sexuality persist. Partly this impression saddens me; partly it seems plain all right.

Despite the fact that all sorts of changes in sexual mores, practices, roles, are not only symbolically "in the air" but actually in the home, we still belong to a culture in which many children do not respond quite as readily to their elders' personal evolutions and revolutions as some of these elders would have us believe. Changes or evolutionary steps are often taken by adults, and assessed by adults, with minimal thought given to the impact of that step on a child. In the name of personal growth, development, even liberation, men and women move into all sorts of realms, most of them, ideally, in a positive and progressive direction. In the name of their parents' personal growth and development, many children fall backward, or seek to move backward, almost as a physical response, a counterreaction to changes that they feel ramify too strongly in them, the children. The hydrodynamic model of a family system scares me slightly. I know too little of the laws of physics underwriting such a model, and metaphors in psychology, as I have indicated, often turn out to be precarious even when they are suggestive. Nonetheless, I am tempted to argue that families in part are constituted of a sexual energy, and hence changes in the intensity and direction of sexual energy in one family member ramifies, to certain (physically) accommodating degrees and directions, in other family members. Thus, we find families where when one of the children becomes highly sexual, a second child or a parent suddenly moves away from sexual experiences. We discover cases, too, where it works the other way around, as I alluded to above. As parents find new avenues of sexual exploration and adventure (not to mention new fellow explorers), the children often turn, in response, to the most familiar avenues and partners.

Let me illustrate these points through the accounts of Janie Brierly and Joe Cross, both of whom lived with their respective secrets about a parent, as well as a hope that they were protecting their parents and making it possible to successfully sort out the sexual aspects of their own lives. Before turning to the accounts, however, one final point should be made.

By now, the reader is well versed in the methods and procedures employed in undertaking life study research. On several occasions, for example, I have noted that the subjects of these life study portraits have granted permission for their words to be made public. This aspect of the research is underscored again only to remind us of the courage required in telling a stranger, or relatively new friend, of certain intimate experiences, and particularly when recounting an experience means revealing a secret. But notice in this regard how we might take two varying approaches to this matter of children's secrets about sexual matters. On the one hand, we might argue that if adults were more discreet about their sexuality, if they behaved as they were "meant" to, then their children would not have to undergo the strains of secret keeping. On the other hand, if increasingly more of our sexual perceptions, fantasies, fears, even practices, are openly discussed, correspondingly we should begin to accept these very human aspects of our being, and our children might feel freer to speak about the sexual issues that presently cause them some distress. As will happen, the tension in these two opposing beliefs hinges on an irony: Awareness or recognition of new as well as traditional forms of sexual practice renders the problem for children simultaneously more difficult and easier. "Is a puzzlement," the hero of *The King and I* remarked. His tone, strangely, was not wholly pessimistic.

JANE BRIERLY

When we met, Jane Brierly was thirteen. She was almost sixteen when we began speaking of the secret she had been safeguarding all too long. The second born of three children, and the only daughter, Janie grew up in a middle-class community on the outskirts of a large eastern city. Her father and grandfather were in the lumber business together, and given the fluctuations of the industry and their available capital, they were reconciled to living through a few good times and all too many rough ones. A warm feeling emanated from all the members of Harold Brierly's family. It was said he inherited his optimistic outlook from his own parents, especially his father, with whom he was very close, even away from the business. As Harold was one of five brothers, the older Brierlys accepted their sons' wives with open arms. Harold's wife, Audrey, Janie's mother, was her mother-in-law's favorite. Everyone agreed that Harold and Audrey were a perfect match. More important from the senior Brierly's point of view, Audrey was an ideal addition to the large family. Even-tempered, understanding, respectful of people's feelings, modest, and uncomplaining, Audrey enhanced the lives of the entire Brierly clan. In fact, Mrs. Brierly, Sr., Harold's mother, used to joke with me saying I could forget my research on families and concentrate only on the Brierlys. It was a lifetime's work, she laughed, merely getting to know all their names.

True enough, the family was enormous. Each of the eldest Brierlys had several brothers and sisters, most of whom had children and grandchildren. As relatives abounded and the family kept in surprisingly close contact, a Brierly approaching marriage age was wise to select a mate who would fit easily into this extended family and be able to handle the intrusions of many well-meaning people. The burden, traditionally, of maintaining the family network fell to the women, irrespective of whether they were Brierlys by birth or the wives of Brierly men. The burden, moreover, involved maintaining friendships between some people who had nothing in common but their last name. It was a full-time job. Certainly Audrey, one of the Brierly mainstays, had little time to do much else but keep her own family going and play her part in the ongoing transactions of her relatives. No one in the family, however, questioned the women's role in all of this. The male Brierlys assumed their wives were the keepers of the social calendar, while the women of the older generation watched over the younger women.

In fact, Audrey Brierly rarely complained about her duties as housewife, mother, central agent in the Brierly network. Her friends often remarked on her indefatigable manner, as well as her limitless hospitality. There was no need to notify Audrey Brierly of a visit; you merely popped in and within minutes you were drinking coffee and eating cake with this kind although slightly diffident woman. Perhaps diffident is not the proper word. It was more a feeling of conservatism one felt about her manner. Never openly uncomfortable in my presence, she also never revealed a gregarious side. A hardworking woman with endless responsibilities and obligations, Audrey rarely moaned about her lot or daily duties, no matter how exhausted she might have appeared. She was a woman of strong values that she articulated clearly and unequivocally. "Marriage," she told me, "is an act people ought to perform once and only once in their lives. If one's decision is wrong, then people had best live with it. Families and children aren't able to stand divorce." In response to my question about women finding employment outside the home, she said she believed in it if a woman needed to or wanted to work. A woman, however, who worked outside the home merely to be, as she said, "part of the new generation of women," would receive none of her respect. For the moment, she would make do on her husband's salary. If the lumber business improved, they would do some traveling. If hard times returned, they would find satisfaction with friends and in their own homes. Indeed, finding useful and enlightening activities for children and husbands was also part of the Brierly women's role.

Harold Brierly was as hardworking as his wife. While he spent occasional evenings and weekends doing the endless paper work his business required, he tried not to bring his work home, as they say. He spoke often, and passionately, of the local sporting teams, although he never devoted himself to the sports pages. His political beliefs were boiled down for me as follows: "I'd vote for any politician, Democrat, Republican, *Communist* even, if I honestly believed he gave the slightest damn for the workingman. Until that man or woman comes along, you can have the lot of them!" On social issues, Harold remarked: "The country's going to hell. The whole civilization seems to be going crazy. When families fall apart, society falls apart. The family holds the culture together. That means, in case people forget, a man pulling his share and a woman pulling hers. You break up that cooperation between people and you have exactly what you see happening: a country going crazy with ridiculous ideas and values and everything else. Nobody's going to replace the family with anything. They haven't done it in a thousand years, they won't do it now. And religion, too. Not my religion or the next guy's religion; just religion. I don't care what a man practices or how he practices it, just as long as he practices *something*. You don't have a civilization without it. You have people living together all right, but you don't have a civilization. All you have is primitive people, and don't kid yourself, even people with the kind of technological skill and knowledge we have can be primitive. Look around, you'll see a lot of people you have to call primitive. You hate to say it about yourself or your own kind, but we can be primitive. Like animals!"

Jane Brierly was growing up to be much like her mother, although Audrey insisted she model herself after no one. Surely the Brierly clan was aware of the fact that certain patterns would be broken when the present generation of children grew up. What concerned them was that the family would no longer be held together by the female social calendar guards. It was also doubtful that even one son per family would carry on his father's line of work. College had something to do with this. Most important, however, the family could feel the cracking in previously rock-hard values. Church attendance among some of the clan was falling off; divorce, once an unthinkable eventuality, was no longer a stranger in some of the families, and heaven only knew what the teenagers were doing. Grandparents and parents alike were spending increasingly more time discussing the relaxation in American values and the shocking acts of immorality taking place in every American community. Affairs, divorce, infidelity, were rampant, and little children, they reminded each other, knew all about these matters. It no longer made sense to throw children out of the room when the fateful subjects came up in conversation. Certainly Jane showed sophisticated awareness of these subjects. That some couple married eighteen years was going through a divorce, and an ugly one at that, was something she knew all about. And the story of the woman living right across the street, the woman who had sat in Audrey Brierly's kitchen bemoaning the decline in morality, the woman who had just left her husband and three children to live with a man thirty years older than herself, was also known to Jane Brierly. While her parents kept secrets from her, they nonetheless recognized that America's present teenagers no longer lived in the wake of puritanical Victorian values. Children who saw in their own school ten- and twelve-year-old kids buying and selling heroin would hardly be stunned by the news that Mrs. Colardi across the street had just walked out on her family and was making no effort to conceal her erotic affairs.

The elder Brierlys worried. The depravity and outright sickness of the culture was spreading; no one in their right mind could feel assured that these problems arose only among those certain families living in certain communities of certain cities. Immorality and danger lurked in every neighborhood! "The most moral, decent, clean-cut-looking person in the world might be carrying on in a way that would shock even the most sophisticated among us," Grandmother Brierly, Sr., once counseled me. "Look at Mrs. Colardi. How much closer does it have to happen? These people saw each other every day. Didn't Audrey take those poor Colardi children in every night when that woman walked out and her pathetic husband fell apart! How much closer does it have to be!"

Like many of her generation, Jane Brierly had much to tell her contemporaries, little to say to people my age. Her younger brother Mark seemed far more gregarious. He practically ambushed me when

I visited the Brierly home. Audrey made excuses for him, but the boy was charming, and I enjoyed making my periodic inspections of his room. Jane, in contrast, would nod hello, mutter a few words, and leave me alone with her brother and mother. On a few occasions she joined us in the kitchen for hot chocolate, but mainly she seemed to respect my friendship with Audrey. At least I attributed her aloofness to respect; perhaps it was utter disinterest in our conversations. As is my custom, I had explained to the Brierlys that any conversation would be held in strictest confidence, a word I had to explain several times for Mark. Jane, presumably, construed this to mean that when she saw her mother conversing with me she had to disappear. No matter how often I encouraged her to participate, she never seemed to hear my invitation. "I guess you don't need me" was her standard response.

I never force people, and particularly children, to engage in conversation. In research on families, it is best, I believe, to speak with all members of a family, both alone and in the presence of others. We hardly need be reminded of how we change in different human contexts and in the presence of different people and in various environments. I would have liked to speak with Jane and Audrey Brierly, but the opportunity never arose. It simply won't happen, I mused one March afternoon driving to the Brierlys. Snow was falling heavily from an ominously dark sky when I reached the house. John, the oldest boy, obviously had not yet returned from school as the driveway remained unplowed. Earning one dollar for each shoveling, he prayed for snow as early as October. "White gold, eh, John?" I would tease him. He enjoyed the expression.

As it happened, only Janie was home this one snowy day. Her father was at work, her mother away. Audrey's absence was peculiar as we distinctly had made a date. She had never not been there to meet me. The entire family stressed the importance of being punctual. But of course, I suddenly remembered, my date was for the following afternoon. I had requested this day but Audrey had explained that only Jane would be home. When our conscious wishes cannot make things come to pass, I reflected, our unconscious assumes command. I must have realized I might catch Jane at home by herself. I described these mental flip-flops to her. "It's like a living dream," she replied. "Do you want some coffee?"

"Only if you join me," I answered.

"I hate coffee. But I can make good hot chocolate."

We sat in the small kitchen for an hour sipping hot chocolate, but exchanging only a few words. I asked some questions; she answered them as succinctly as possible. Why is it, I wondered, when all my work is based on interviewing people, I sometimes engage people in such a wretchedly clumsy form? Clumsy or not, Jane Brierly made no gesture to have me leave. She was content, apparently, to have me ask my questions, even if she did respond almost telegraphically. I found the time passing so slowly I would have been delighted to contrive some amicable excuse for departing. I did my best, but I got nowhere. More hot chocolate, more dreary questions, more monosyllabic answers, and three more minutes had limped by; I knew it was three because I watched the sweep of the minute hand on the kitchen clock. It was like being back in grammar school, praying for recess, or a fire drill where we all rush out to the playfields. Interview children? Talk with them, even? Never again. From now on my work would be with adults; loquacious, obsessive-talking American adults, all of whom had just returned from a thirty-year odyssey around the world. And I would be the first English-speaking person they would have met in three decades!

I made a motion to leave. Jane put her hand on the table, as if to stop me. "You know the time you explained the word 'confidential' to Mark?"

"I do," I answered. She would hear some of *my* better monosyllables.

"You think you could explain the word 'nymphomania' to him?"

My shock at her words cannot be described. As the expression goes, I managed to discreetly pick up my insides off the floor without Jane feeling she had just knocked me flat on my back. Slowly I proffered my best definition of nymphomania, as well as its origin. She seemed satisfied. I had passed her second test, for it was now evident that test number one was intended to examine whether I would sit at least one hour with her alone. As she would explain later, she had to discover whether my interest lay in her family or only her mother. Now confident that my visits to her home did not mean, as she once suspected, that I was one of her mother's boyfriends, Jane Brierly revealed to me the following secret:

"It sort of surprises you, doesn't it?" she began, as the snow fell in angry swirls outside. "It would kill my grandparents. Her own mother doesn't know. My father does. He told me so himself. It's like a disease. I've read articles on it. My mother is a sex machine. She goes all the time. She never brings them here. She goes out. It's in the neighborhood, at motels and hotels. She goes out all the time. You know how my mother dresses? She doesn't have anything sexy, does she? You want to look in her hidden drawers up there? She has all the latest sexy underwear. She orders from places she finds in *men's* magazines. She's a machine. You know how she talks about how the country and young people don't have any values, how everyone's immoral? But what's she doing probably right this minute? She's at someone's home, or at a motel. You drive over to the Lyon's Motel on Route 94, you'll see her car. I'll bet you a million dollars. She's there. My father's found her there. I even went over there on my bike once last spring. Six miles. I saw her coming out with some man.

"I don't think she gets paid. She's just a nymphomaniac, a machine. I thought at first you were just one of *them*, except if you were I couldn't see why all you'd do is sit in the kitchen and talk. That's why when you came today and stayed, even when she wasn't here, I decided, maybe you're straight. I'll bet she never let on with you about anything either. Oh, she can control it. It's like she's two different people: Audrey the nice lady, the perfect daughter-in-law, that's what my grandparents think. Then the other person, the machine. I know how hard it is to believe. You can imagine the scene of my father telling me. He was even going to have our doctor explain it. I knew something about it; we have girls in school like that. I mean, they called it an illness; it's not normal. But if she's two people, then so am I. Part of me says it's a disease, the other part says she's a cheap slut, mother or not! Any machine has to have a switch, and if you can't find it, you go to someone who tells you how to turn it off. But the plain fact is my mother *wants* two different lives. She likes being two people. She likes being the nice housewife, and she likes crawling into bed with anyone wearing pants.

"Listen, Dr. Cottle, this isn't just her cheating on my father or having a boyfriend. She's a real machine. I heard her on the phone once, I listened outside her room. I could have picked up the phone but I didn't dare. She wasn't telling the guy how much she loved him; she was telling him how she loved *it*. She can't get enough. She probably does it with two and three guys at once. She'll go for an hour sometimes. Then she'll come back with something from the store for the children, like this secret present so they won't know where she *really* went. Sometimes she's so obvious you'd think she *wants* us to find out. Why would she say she has to run an errand then come back with cookies or potato chips for me or one of my brothers? You go out and you buy stuff for dinner and in addition you get stuff for the kids. She'll come back dressed in her little simple clothes and say, 'Gee, I think I'll take a shower.' Four in the afternoon? Who takes showers at four in the afternoon when you haven't been doing anything all day! She doesn't lock her bedroom door; she locks the *bathroom* door. Her children aren't supposed to see what every man in this city has probably seen. I go to her room. The shower's on in the bathroom and on the bed or the floor are all those underwear specials. Tiny little pants with weird things written on them, or men's names. She came home once with a package that had come in the mail. I found it on the bed. Know what it was? Silk sheets. She took her own sheets. And a little massage machine. She has that, too. Tools of the trade, right? The woman's a machine!

"I used to be angry with her, but no one could be angry with anybody *this* long. Even if she stopped today, if what she's doing now was going to be the absolute last time, I'd still have it on my conscience the rest of my life. She doesn't have it on *her* conscience because she doesn't have a conscience. And I don't mean that I'm *her* conscience. Nobody is anybody else's conscience. You can sit around bitching about how the country's so sick, but the only thing that matters is your own conscience. And when the people you live with and who are supposed to be teaching you the right way to live don't have a conscience, you end up suffering. You aren't their conscience, but what they do sure affects *you*. So I'm not angry anymore, but I'm still not used to it. For a while Mark would twitch in his face. We talked about it at first, then we decided the best thing to do was not remind him of it. He got used to it, and I got used to the old sex machine upstairs; but I can't say I feel sorry for her. She could stop. She could see somebody. Course *I* can't talk to anybody; I have to keep quiet. It sure makes me angry that she gets to do whatever she wants but I can't. I can't even tell her what I'm thinking.

"She told me a couple of months ago, if there were ever any problems I was having with boys I should come to her. She said in families like ours the women have to stick together. What's that mean? That I have to get into the same habits she has? Sometimes I think she doesn't even know about the other person she is. It's really all connected with sex. Sometimes, when you're young, you think about sex, doing things, or when you actually do them it's like it isn't really you doing them. It's you, but it's like it's somebody else, too, since it's not something you do or think about all the time, except if you're my mother. Like, there's the you who does sex and the you who doesn't. Sometimes you want to be one person, sometimes the other. Boys are different. They just want it all the time. That's why they get along with my mother so well. What you have to do when you get older is try to be someone who isn't two different people, when it comes to sex. You can't pretend it's not there, but you know it isn't there *all* the time. It comes and goes, but that doesn't mean you have to be two people about it.

"I'd like to talk to my mother. I'd like to ask her how she was when she was my age. Did she think she was a sex machine then? When did it start? How did she tell Daddy, or did he have to find out like I did? I have to learn some *new* facts of life from her! The birds and the bees and the wild animals. How do I know, maybe I'm abnormal because I don't want to do it all the time. The girls in school talk about nothing else *but* sex. Maybe they're machines, too. Maybe that's the way you're supposed to feel. I'll never be happy about sex. I'll never just have everyday old feelings about it. It isn't so important what's going on, like my parents with their feeling that everybody's being immoral. I don't care about dirty movies and dirty books and dirty Mommy; I care about *me!*

"I don't know how to say it; she's just in the way. I can't see myself getting past her. I'm this little car, you know, and I'm going along on this highway. There's all kind of room. Then all of a sudden there's this big truck, standing right in the middle of the road. It's blocking all the lanes. That's her. So you get out of your car, and you go to talk to the driver to tell him to move over, but there's nobody in the truck. It's the same way with my mother. I *want* to talk to her about *it*, but I can't. I used to listen to your conversations. I thought you'd talk about it. But if *you* can't talk about it, how can I? I'm stuck. I guess a part of me hates her for my being stuck.

"I have this way of looking at things. A little child has to do whatever it's told, no matter what its parents say, that's how the child must behave. The adult has to behave right, because it's the adult who teaches the child. But in between is me and people my age. We have the right to misbehave just so we can see how different things feel. That's why my parents say you should date a lot of boys so you can see what different kinds of people there are in the world. Talk about playing the field! But all that's what *I'm* supposed to do. *They're* supposed to be like a mother and father. They're supposed to be moral, otherwise they don't deserve to keep us.

"I think my mother doesn't deserve to be my mother anymore. I don't need her, so one of us should move out and I don't see why it has to be me. Maybe I'll become a nun; that would put her in the grave, even with all her talk about how people should be moral and go to church. That's another thing: How can she sit in church letting on she's so pure. Children want their parents to be pure. I don't want them doing *anything*. Daddy jokes about going to a disco. I think I'd die if I saw them in a disco. If they want to go to a disco, there should be a parents-only disco. It's hard to think of my parents doing sexual things. I mean, you know they do, or they did. I mean, they don't come to the breakfast table and announce what they did. One of my girl friends said the day you *really* aren't a virgin anymore is when you can accept the fact your parents do it, maybe even a lot, maybe even more than you do. My mother probably does it more than anyone in my high school. You know, you wonder, is any boy too young for her? You think she'd go to bed with a boy in *my* class? When you're a machine does anything in your brain work anymore? What I'm saying is what she does is immoral, really gross. You can say it's a sickness, but it's still immoral. It's like, if I killed you they could say I was insane, but it's still immoral. What she does stinks it's so immoral. Maybe she really *is* two different people, but it's still immoral, because she *is* making choices. When she says to herself, no I couldn't do *that* or go out with *him*, she's making decisions. That means she's *decided* there are things she can and can't do. So she *isn't* insane, and she isn't sick; she's immoral!

"It's really disgusting to think about it. And keeping it a secret doesn't help in the slightest. It may help *her*, but it doesn't help *me*. I try to imagine what she's doing and it's like I'm going to throw up. I get frightened. I can think about dying and it doesn't bother me. I used to think about my parents dying and it made me frightened, too. Now I think if she died it might be the best thing. What would probably happen is that she'd die with some guy and all of us would have another secret to keep from that dirty, immoral world out there. I think I want her dead. I want her to be punished just like they say in the Bible, because of all her sins. One of her worst sins is that she doesn't let *me* commit any sins. I mean, I'm terrified of doing anything because I don't know if I have the same machine stuff in my blood. I think she'll have to die before I can get on with the sort of life I'd like to live.

"Sex is something special. Everyone wants to think they're really experienced with it. Nobody likes to say, I don't know what to do or what to say. You only joke about it when you think you know what's going on. There's all kinds of secrets with sex. You aren't supposed to talk about it that much, but that's my choice. The kids who talk about it, I don't believe them. They say it's the quiet ones who do all the action. I don't know if that's true; it's another one of the little secrets about sex. Anyway, I can't explore it by myself, and I can't be dumb about it. My mother's made that impossible for me. It's like, when it comes to sex, I've been through college before I even started

high school. The wrong things are secrets for me. I imagine anything
I do will be talked about all over the school. *I'm* the one who's afraid
of my reputation. And I don't care that people say how reputations
don't matter anymore since everybody's doing it. That's so wrong I
could laugh. People spend all their time talking about it so they
don't have to *do* any of it. They *do* ruin a girl's reputation if they
talk about her doing this or that. You know what they say if
they find out you don't do it? They say you're frigid. And if you do it
they call you the school nympho. You can't keep *everything* about it
secret, unless you become a nun. It's the big secret game. They got
you any way you turn. The only thing to do is keep on doing what
you feel comfortable with. But in my case I'm blocked any way I
turn by the big machine out there in the road. The big truck.

"Some people teach their kids to think sex is like a crime. It's this
horrible, nasty thing people do to each other, or by themselves, that's
supposed to be the worst crime, too. That's what they say is part of
becoming mature: Learning it isn't a crime. Too many people think
that sex is evil. It's bad to think that, right? But how can I get my
mother out of my head and not think if I don't watch myself closely
I'll end up a criminal like she is? She might be pleasing herself but
isn't she hurting a lot of other people? Sometimes when you have an
animal that's really gone wild, the only thing to do to stop it is to
kill it!

"I imagine walking in on her and finding her in bed with this
slimy old guy, lying there under my mother's silk sheets which she
brings to the motel with her. I wonder what she'd say. 'Well, take
your clothes off and get in with us.' She couldn't pretend to be embarrassed. No one who walks around in that collection of underwear could ever pretend to be embarrassed. She'd invite me to do it.
Sitting here with you, she'd say the whole country's acting immoral,
but under her silk sheets that she paid for herself, she'd say, get in.
That'd be the generous thing to do, share whatever you have with
your daughter. God, it's all so sick. But if I did go there, I'd go with
a gun. I'd kill them both. At least I imagine I would. Really I'd
never go there. I'd never do anything; I'd never even tell anybody
about this, except people I know won't do anything to hurt us. I'd
like to kill her but I know I wouldn't. I'd like to see her doing sex, I
really would. Like she'd be this great teacher or something. How's
that for being sick!

"Parents are supposed to teach their children everything, but no
parents I know tell their children *anything* about sex. Even when the
children ask, parents act like they're keeping this big secret. So my

mother can become my famous professor of sex. But I'll never watch her, or talk to her. And I also won't do much with boys, but it isn't because I'm too young. It's because I have the same scary feeling all my friends have about sex, whether they admit it or not. I'm also afraid that someday I could find another person in me. A really sick, screwed-up sex machine. That's *my* big sex secret, but it doesn't do much good talking about it till she breaks down and talks about *her* big sex secret. She's the freak; I'm only the kid on the scooter trying to scoot by. Maybe you don't believe in this. People have weird ideas when it comes to sex. But it's true. I don't know where she is now, but if you can drive in that snow out there, go over to the motel, you'll see her car in the parking lot. You'll see it, the light blue Chevy. And if it's there, just imagine that little car carries that big truck of a machine inside it. You can call your book on us, *The Nymphomaniac and the Nun.*"

Of course I believed what Jane Brierly had said. And of course I was stunned by it. It was hardly the rambling of a girl whose sexual terrors distorted her perceptions of reality. Her speech, naturally, wasn't perfectly coherent, but who of us *is* coherent when such feelings are being expressed! I didn't question Jane's secret; I doubted not one item of her account. Yet I found myself driving in a heavy blizzard, going out of my way to pass the parking lot of the Lyon's Motel near Route 94. Perhaps I justified the detour by reasoning that the roads bordering the highway would be the first to be cleared of snow. In fact, the giant snow-clearing machinery would not hit the streets for another two hours.

Fewer than twenty cars were parked in front of the motel. Audrey Brierly's light blue Chevrolet was in the slot closest to the driveway.

JOE CROSS

One does best, I repeatedly tell myself, not to make comparisons between children. No matter how similar children may be, ultimately they remain incomparable. But that I even write these lines confirms my perpetual temptation to make comparisons. I was tempted, for example, to compare Joe Cross with Jane Brierly. At sixteen, Joe Cross was one angry young man. Tall, with an angular face, deep-set brown eyes, and low hairline, stooped-shouldered Joe Cross was just plain hard. He was hard to talk to, hard to get to know, hard on people, and physically hard as the proverbial rock. Three hundred and sixty-five days a year he spent at least one hour lifting weights, squeezing levers, or pulling at springs to tighten one muscle or another. He worked out at three different gymnasiums and had a cabinet in his bedroom filled with muscle-strengthening devices. An expensive rowing machine was the first thing he would buy, he said, if he ever had money.

The son of a bank manager father and secretary mother, Joe Cross was an anathema to his parents. That a boy chose to become interested in developing his body was acceptable to them, but the activity had become a religion, according to his parents. His preoccupation with it, moreover, stood in the way of his doing almost anything else. Body building was more than a hobby; it was the inevitable excuse for Joe not having time to study, make friends, go places. What did Joe Cross say about that? "I say if you don't like the way your son is acting, either throw him out of the house or stop bugging him. A man does what he does. It's a right. That's it pure and simple. You don't like body building, hey, I got no gripe. You don't hear me asking *you* what you get *your* kicks out of. You want to sit in front of the TV and watch twenty-two giants bang their heads together on Sunday afternoon, that's your privilege. They're doing it for you. They can't do it without an audience. Me, I don't need no audience, I don't want no comment on what I do. When I break a law, everybody can give me their comments. But I ain't breaking no law. I'm only making strong what God wanted me to have. Okay? That's the end of the song."

For a host of reasons I was fascinated by Joe Cross. Many people are consumed by an interest in one activity. For some people it's fishing, for others gardening, golf, making money. I had met many young men obsessed with body building, but no one like Joe. The quality that set him apart from the others was his need to convince people that not a single thought ever crossed his mind. Whereas some body builders want to learn whether one upholds the prejudice that only morons become involved with weight lifting, Joe Cross seemed dead set on convincing me his head was empty of everything but the names of muscles and every vitamin, drug, or steroid that might enhance a man's effort to become superhumanly strong. And he *was* strong. He was also intelligent. Both facts were easily noted. What I didn't note at first, however, was that he was being consumed with something far more important than body strength.

I pass over many hours of conversation with this young man when

I say that our friendship went through innumerable transformations before he revealed to me what, as he himself remarked almost good-naturedly, all his muscles and hardness were meant to hide.

"All right, let's get it out," he said one afternoon in his inimitable way when he felt we had walked far enough from one of his favorite gyms. He made certain to notice nobody was around. "All right, I'm walking here, you're walking there, nobody sees us. You got your clothes on, I got my clothes on. Nobody sees us now can tell who's the strong one, who's the weak one. We're all hidden up in our clothes. My secret is I got this hard body; your secret, I don't know what your secret is. So the clothes hide the body, and with me the body hides the mind. All right? You want it? Here it is, man.

"I got a father, right? He's queer, all right? You got it? My father's a crooked queer. You hide your goods, I hide my goods; his goods, man, are crooked. The man who is my father, made me *alive*, he's a homo, baby. All the way. That's my song. We keep walking or you want to rest?

"You're thinking, oh, so *that's* the reason this guy's so hung up with his body. So afraid he may end up crooked like his father he's got to show everybody he's all male, straight. You don't think I haven't thought of that? Kid wakes up one day, like, learns his old man's queer as a three-dollar bill, tells himself, hey, I gotta prove to the world I'm straight, right? So what'll I do? I'll build up my body, be Mr. He-man 'stead of Mr. *She*-man, right? That ain't it at all. Guys go through a stage where they think they're queer. Everybody does. They don't talk about it; it's their big secret. Girls' secret is they either are or are not a virgin. Boys got a secret: Either they are or are not queer. Girl's got an advantage 'cause she knows, but the boy, he don't know straight from queer. How's he know? 'Cause he made it with some chick? What's that prove? Say he breaks off with some chick, tells her he don't want to get it on with her 'cause he's afraid it would, like, ruin her reputation. Maybe he's old-fashioned. Maybe he thinks, hey, I don't want to sleep with this girl. If she wants to that's her business, but I got my morals, too. So what happens? Guy goes home feeling good about himself, and the girl tells her friends the guy's queer with a capital Q.

"That's the big secret: Am I or am I not? Me, I'm pretty sure I'm straight. I got my hang-ups but none of them are about *that*. Still, like I say, sex comes with secrets; you don't get around it no matter how hard you squirm, and baby, I know lots of people spending their life squirming when it comes to sex. Men, women, boys, girls, squirming like they're drowning, the bunch of 'em like little babies.

Squirming around with sex, trying it out, figuring out who you are and, like, what your body means to you. You got to read between the lines about sex, you know. Not too many people tell you straight out about any of it. Guy drops a line, you got to pick up on it, try it out. You got to figure out from all the crap people drop, what's this guy doing and what's that guy doing, right? No one's going to tell you he's no good, or he can't do it. Everybody's a pro, right, a champion!

"But here's the sixty-four-thousand-dollar question: If nobody tells nobody and everybody's bobbing up and down with their secrets, how come everybody finds out what they're supposed to? How come practically nobody drowns at all? *That's* what you want to know. And the answer is, your parents. Say what you like, you can tell yourself you're growing up, you know, doing all these things nobody else has done, only someday you gotta come to the conclusion, hey, what am I talking about? My parents didn't go through all this? Or a boy thinks, my father didn't try this and that? He ain't a man? That's what, like, gives you confidence; *he* made it, *you'll* make it. What the hell else he been telling you all these years? You'll make it. I grew up with guys, these guys are going to end up in jail. Fifteen years old, they been arrested more times than you could count. It's their life, being in and out of jail. What do they get out of that kind of a life? They don't *get* anything. They just don't have nothing else. They never had a father around, so their lives go to hell. A father may not show you the way. Hey, there usually isn't even *a* way. But knowing he's there, *that's* what makes it possible for you to do all this secret squirming and know you ain't going to drown. He's there, doing it the straight way, the I-guarantee-you-won't-drown way. You might not like the guy but you ain't gonna drown. These guys in jail, doing drugs, letting their bodies run down, they're all finished squirming; they drowned a long time ago.

"You got two kinds of secrets. You got the kind you know you got, and the kind you don't know you got. The kind you know you got, those are the ones you squirm over. I'm not getting enough sex, maybe I'm queer, stuff like that. Secrets you don't know about, and don't ask me how they get there, those are the tricky ones 'cause you don't even know they're there till something happens to bring 'em up. All right, my mother sits me down and tells me the birds and bees around our house are painted violet. I got an old man who I thought was staying out doing business, instead he's hanging around queer bars. He told her. She told me. *He* can't tell me. I don't even want to hear it from him. Other than that, she says, he's a decent sort of a guy. Other than that, I'm thinking, what the hell is left over after *that?* How come you call a guy decent? 'Cause he didn't stick a knife in the fifteen-year-old boy he just made love to? I mean, what's your basic definition of decent? Anyway, my mother told me, and suddenly all those other secrets you don't know are there start popping up all over the place. For a while there, I was the one didn't know which end was up. Like they put you on your head and tell you, go ahead walk. What's the matter with you, how come you can't walk? Your insides are popping all over.

"I told myself, look, you got your mind and you got your body. Nobody messes up your body. You're the king there. Let yourself get weak, that's nobody's business. But not your mind. Anybody can mess with your mind. Any day you can get some news, and boom, there goes your mind. A guy gets in a car accident, breaks his neck, his body goes to hell 'cause his mind ain't working. That's what it was like when my mother hit me with the news. My father's a queer. Hey, that's terrific, man. Get the number of that truck; I think my mind just went dead. Maybe you could say I'm dying inside my head. So I keep my body up so I don't have to keep thinking about the other stuff. Maybe my body's keeping me from thinking about all the stuff in my mind that ain't secret no more. I ain't got no problem about telling people about my father. He goes and destroys his life, I ain't about to add to his misery. Nobody'll find out, although these queers have a way of making sure everybody does find out. Seems they have to advertise it. But I'll look out for him. Hey, he's been looking out for me. What I got to do is keep all them little secrets inside me from becoming big-time explosions.

"I'm sitting on dynamite, my man. It's making new secrets for me. You got little bacteria in your gut, live ones, don't you? You need 'em so you don't try to get rid of them. How do we know the brain and the mind don't have bacteria, too? Little sex boogeymen running around up in there, not doing anybody harm till you do harm to them. Okay, I know there's nothing wrong with me physically just 'cause my father turns out to be queer. Maybe he was straight when they got married and had me. Maybe he only went queer two hours before my mother told me about him. How do I know? How do I know what that information does to all those little boogey people? You don't know what the hell's going on inside you when it comes to sex. Lots of mysteries, lots of secrets. Lots of stuff maybe the body ain't supposed to know about. Maybe it's all those little boogey people making you feel angry or sad, or turned on. You tell me why a guy's walking down the street feeling absolutely nothing, then out of nowhere he's turned on and he ain't even seen anybody. No one, man. Maybe it's one of the boogey people. Maybe they're up there in my head laughing at me right now, playing little games with me. They can do it now, see what I mean, 'cause *they* found out about my father, too, right? I might be the only one my mother told out loud, but if I hear it it means my mind heard it, too. Boogey people up there right now laughing away at the kid's bad news.

"Maybe all this is just a lot of words. Maybe I don't like words, especially the ones my mother told me. Words and sex seem to be all tied up together like sticky caramel. You get people telling each other this and that, as though what they were doing is talking about sex, or having sex just so they can talk about it. My father's the same man now as he was when he left home the morning my mother told me. All right? Then all of a sudden comes a bunch of words from her to me and now he's different. You work on your body you don't get caught up with words. You move away from words and thinking about words. Be nice and sweet if you could have your old body secrets back instead of those boogey people secrets. What a blow, eh? I tell myself, hey, what's a big man like you falling to pieces over this kind of news? What could be worse news! It ain't like I wish he could be like he was before the accident. Wasn't no accident. I can't come up with the right way to say any of this. Everybody's got these boogey people. They keep quiet for you some of the time, and they make a helluva racket on you other times. My dad's been going about his life, his queer life pretty quiet; now there's all kind of noise going on in my head. I keep it quiet when I work out at the gym, but you can't work out twenty-four hours a day. And I sure as hell can't work out the rest of my life.

"I'm embarrassed for the sonofabitch. The man's walking around with his fly open and nobody can tell him nothing. He's making a fool of himself. Everybody's hanging on his secret, for all I know. All my mother and father's friends. What about *them?* Christ, that sort of news could blow him right out of the water. What gets me is how I got to clean up for the guy. I gotta clean up his mess, change his diapers, like. I got to live with all his shit while he walks around making everybody think he's living the good, clean life. What kind of crap is that? It's like these high-powered generals start wars and the punks of the world have to fight 'em. How's he expect me to amount to anything with him going around queer? What am *I* supposed to feel? Not the boogeymen, *me?* You live long enough with lies they'll start eating up your body *and* your mind. You could be three hundred pounds, and news like that will eat you down to fifty pounds.

It'll shrink you! Every time someone says the word 'father' all I'll ever be able to think is queer!

"Think of the guy. Going out, sticking it into some kid's ass. You got to be kidding. My *father*, wearing that gray suit of his and the tie with the little yellow butterflies, nice-looking clothes, all right? There he is, can you see him, standing in some dark hotel room with this kid, this pale white kid with arms the size of your goddamn fingers, and the kid's kneeling down in front of him, playing with my father. My father, all right? I ain't talking about no movie I saw. That's it, baby, right there. Your mother sits down and tells you what she told me, and all those secrets you didn't know about are suddenly going off in your body and your mind, 'cause what's happening is that everything you were afraid to find out, everything you hated to think about the most, turned out to be true. True and in living color, my man. You don't separate a kid from his father. That's what being a kid is. You're practically the same guy, in your head. News like this doesn't change one little bit of it neither. It's only in my body now, 'cause I worked on myself, so I know I ain't him, or anything like him. But it's never going to go away. His queer streak? It's running all over me right this minute, and I can't do nothing to stop it. Don't worry, it ain't catching, like some disease. *You're* safe. This kind of disease only goes between fathers and sons, all right? They're the only boogey people."

In an age that associates young people with the most Dionysian sorts of sexual practices and rituals, an age in which narcissism is blessed by the gods, and constraint and control are viewed as actions of the devil, I find it peculiar that so many young people maintain the sort of outlook evinced by both Jane Brierly and Joe Cross. While their accounts cannot be neatly tied together, both young people seem committed to moral though not prudish behavior, and social order at all costs. Both seem concerned with the possible disintegration of family life, which means for them the dissolution of viable relationships between parents and children. Both seem only the slightest uncomfortable, moreover, with the notion that formal religion might serve to integrate people, solidify their attachments, and help to make morality a more understandable commodity. If nothing else, religion offers positive values, which stand in contrast to cultural chaos.

One sees, too, in these accounts, a series of tensions, antinomies, forces upon which, clearly, both young people have reflected. The civilized world versus the primitive one is perhaps the first of these tensions, and sexuality, significantly, seems able to lodge in either extreme. Without proper control, sexuality emerges as the force causing things to remain primitive, or perhaps return to some earlier primitive state. Under proper control, sexuality becomes a fundamental part of a civilized social order, a culture honoring both free expression and necessary restraint. More relevant for both young people, control of erotic feelings is most essential between family members. In this regard, interestingly enough, both Janie and Joe contend that it must be parents who demonstrate constraint. Without parental (self) control, children seem doomed to remain at a primitive (sexual) level of development.

Linked to this first tension is the tension between impulse control and expression. Both children's accounts are filled with references to this issue, as they struggle to find a congenial vocabulary to describe their feelings. One moment sexual urges take the form of microbes or bacteria; the next moment they are reduced to boogey people, literal personifications of inexplicable sensation. Related to these tensions is a third tension; namely, the struggle between anger with parents on the one hand and guilt stemming from parents' sexual behavior (or misbehavior) on the other. It goes without saying that no one can easily disentangle these themes which invariably play a role, or appear as impediments, in the sexual evolution of young people. Still, we might offer a few comments on these accounts, keeping our eye, as always, on the secretive aspects of this sexual evolution.

Let us draw a connection first between the secrets kept by these two young people and the secretive nature of sexuality generally. Granted, not all children encounter the extraordinary problems extant in the lives of Jane Brierly and Joe Cross. Nonetheless, all people do contend with their sexual moods, appetites, values, meanderings, most of which, despite our contemporary impressions, remain as secrets. Furthermore, as secrets, our sexual musings often become distorted, even grotesque. Perversion substitutes for normality, and the mind becomes filled with ludicrous, scary, amusing, terrifying conceptions and misconceptions of what sexuality is, and is not, and what should come forth as normal or abnormal thoughts and behavior. But if the mind is filled with strange new sounds and images of sexuality, then the body, too, is filled with new sensations, which also demand attention for the sake of the person finding gratification, or reducing frustration, as well as for the person comprehending just what these evolutionary changes may mean. More precisely, both the mind and the body may be said to experience sexual energy. Both are susceptible to external as well as internal stimulation. Society provokes us, people touch us, our minds arc capable of evoking any and all sensation, from ecstasy to despair. All of this happens naturally and secretively. We tell others some of our experiences, but relative to what we realize is happening to and in us, the amount of communicated interaction is minuscule. This is what is meant when we say that much of our sexual ruminations go on privately, secretively, and hence sexuality itself, getting a large boost from societal values, customs, and conventions, becomes associated with secretiveness. Joe Cross's allusion to clothes symbolizing sexual concealment (and containment), and nakedness symbolizing revelation (and expression), makes this point in more graphic detail.

If we read back over these last few thoughts *and* the accounts, we note a rather old and precarious philosophical bugaboo emerging in our discussion. Are we actually suggesting that the mind and body are split? Are they wholly detached organisms to be joined, presumably, by some overarching force, say, an ego, a self? Philosophers and psychologists alike would have much to say about this direction in our thinking, but if we examine the accounts closely, we notice a differentiation of mind from body that both young people seem willing to present. Perhaps I would do more justice to the accounts by asserting that both children feel that bodies get in the way of minds, or, in Joe Cross's words, that either can go dead from the behavior or action of the other. What, then, is the disassociation between mind and body that appears in both accounts? What might this struggle between mind and body symbolize, assuming of course that in reality both young people would admit that a separation of the mind and body is merely a figure of speech?

My own answer to these questions is that the accounts reveal children who, in the midst of their sexual evolution, which means not only their psychological and somatic development but their cognitive attempt to comprehend this evolution, find themselves inextricably entwined with their same-sex parent. The anger and guilt both people feel in relation to their stated anomalous parents reveal some of this entwining involvement. The anger, for example, seems to reflect some of the *differentiation* of child from parent, while the guilt reflects, in part, the *fusing* of the child with the parent. Are not both young people expressing a felt conflict over being the living conscience of their parents? Whereas the parent evinces his or her animalistic, primitive, uncivilized needs, the child supplies the control, while simultaneously experiencing the retribution of the parent's reprehensible deed? Put differently, the children fear that their parents' sins have already returned to haunt them in the form of blocking their own sexual development. But how is it that a parent's "misbe-havior" would obstruct the sort of sexual and developmental progress to which both young people refer? I would suggest again that it is not precisely the truck that blocks the car, as Janie alleged, but the fact that the truck and car are one, driven by the same motors, fueled by the same passions. (It might also be mentioned that her metaphor speaks to the depersonalization of sexuality.) Furthermore, if the truck obstructs the car, it means only that both Jane and Joe retain a sense of their sexual destiny, and more precisely, an intuition that they cannot mature as long as they remain linked to their parents, which they are by dint of the parents' seeming psychopathology.

In this context of parent and child being fused, we recall Jane's ref-erence to her mother's sexuality as being simultaneously invisible and all-consuming. Is this impression formed from her being so close to her mother psychically that psychological differentiation is made im-possible? Does it relate, moreover, to her need to control her mother's sexual impulses, her desire to "watch" and "learn" from her mother, and her rather surprising though abject assertion that nym-phomania may be normal? Clearly, both of these people have reflected long and hard on a topic so delicate and complex one barely finds words to describe it. Indeed, in reflecting on sexuality, images often substitute for words, if people, as Joe suggested, do not turn against words altogether. But here, with words, we find still another clue to the secret of sexuality and to this alleged fusing of children with parents, a fusing that seems to make normal sexual develop-ment cumbersome, if not implausible.

If, in cultural terms, sexuality remains secretive, then in the mind sexuality and secrets become married. The secret, therefore, *is* the sexual act, and people, as we know from reading clinical literature, suffer guilts over sexual acts committed purely in their minds. We also begin to see how children may derive those proverbial pangs of guilt not only from their own sexual ruminations but from the per-ceived immorality of their parents. Guilt, therefore, may become the glue of the parent-child fusion. Guilt, conscience, sin, immorality, all the ingredients of a complicated intimacy, the type of which both Jane and Joe would happily have forfeited. But underlying these in-gredients and the glue of a parent-child fusion was the need to keep their parents' behavior and their own reactions to it secret. To tell the secret was to destroy the parent, which both young people believed may have been the only way they would ever extricate them-selves from their respective parents and their parents' illnesses. Yet, because of the aforementioned relationship of secrets and sexuality, to tell the secret would be likened, psychically, to having sex. Thus, confessing their parents' illicit sexual practices is essentially identical to participating in the illicit sexual practices, which in turn reiterates the fusion of child with parent. Not surprisingly, then, both young people make a conglomeration of sexuality, confession, mental and physical illness. If sexuality is illness, then so is the secret, although both children remain unconvinced that in telling their secret they will be cleansed, cured, liberated.

Finally, in their attempts to differentiate themselves in the most primitive and yet sophisticated fashion from their parents, both Jane Brierly and Joe Cross revealed a desire to differentiate aspects of their own self, their own person. One might say that their sexual excursions, physical or psychic, required them to put their personal house in order. To do this, it would seem that their own normal sexual advancement demanded that they be allowed to try or at least contemplate sexual perversions, pathologies, pranks, if you will, if only to discern for themselves the comfortable bonds of normality, morality, and health. The so-called trucks that stood in their way were precisely their respective parents' misadventures, misadventures that precluded sexual travels of their own, a fact that made them feel angry, guilty, and utterly sad. Misbehaving, even when kept at secretive levels, remains a bit like child's play. We are entitled to psychological misadventures and misdeeds, particularly in the realm of sexuality. Our protection in all of this is the secret itself, or more exactly, the nature of secrecy. How often we recall that familiar phrase: "Oh, if one could be arrested for one's thoughts." When the very notion of secret is made counterfeit, evil, sinful, immoral, or illicit, as it is in the accounts heard in this chapter, then sexuality will suffer. It will suffer in the body as well as in the mind, and while the children will hold tightly to the secrets that have caused them pain, the evidence of their pain will remain no secret to anyone even remotely close to them.

Part V

MENTAL ILLNESS

"The Myth of Normalcy"

EIGHT

Alcoholism and Drug Taking

While a more general discussion of family secrets is reserved for the final chapter, a few points about secrets are offered at this time.

Let us note first that it is not too great a leap from the actual secret a young person is preserving to some primitive set of feelings that the child—all children really—must be experiencing. These feelings, importantly, are a natural part of the normal development of children. The recognition that one's father is a homosexual, has gone bankrupt, or has physically assaulted a member of the family hardly represents the first occasion of sexuality, immorality, or violence. Whatever words one prefers, each of us realizes that children experience sexual and violent feelings, and each day of their lives come to terms with new and still newer senses of what their family and their society define as moral, immoral, and amoral acts. Much of this development is intellectual and cognitive; some of it is emotional. But again, secrets are intimately bound up in the development of children's private and public definitions of themselves.

A second point we wish to consider comes directly from the accounts heard throughout this book. It has to do with children needing their parents to be the "straight," traditional, almost conservative background against which they may experiment with their own "twists" of behavior. "Twists," in this context, is not a wholly capricious term. We say, for example, that someone has a "twisted mind" or that one's thoughts or emotions regarding a particular matter are "twisted." Carrying the metaphor one step further, it would seem that "making" a person "normal" involves helping him "untwist" his mind. The words, surely, are clumsy, but isn't it true that most children feel something about themselves is twisted? Granted, our overly psychologized society has made everybody question whether or not he or she is "sane." But apart from the often confusing influence of professional psychology and psychiatry upon us, a normal aspect of childhood involves the wrestling with ourselves over whether or not we have twisted something up in our minds, something that ultimately must be untwisted. Essentially we may twist up something in the public realm, perhaps an event that we have witnessed or heard about. We may also twist up our feelings, drives, and impulses; that is, misunderstand or "misfeel" them in some way. Thus, the twisting involves both intellectual and emotional processes. We might mislabel some event or experience, moreover, just as we may manipulate events or feelings in our imaginations. We may twist some matter so as to make it less painful, or more comical or outrageous, but typically the twisting results in the diminution of tension. Much of humor is dependent on this twisting of fact and feeling, intellect and effect. Indeed, a good measure of children's gratification in comprehending a joke is based on the realization that the twisting of items within the joke is reminiscent of the mental twisting children often make on their own.

The important feature of "psychological twisting" is that in the main, it goes on in one's mind. Its products—images, fantasies, distortions, misreadings—may emerge in publicly shared forms, as in a story, picture, or in the recounting of dreams, but the *act* of twisting remains private. Twisting represents a bit of internal communication with oneself. Essentially, it is not for public consumption, especially when one is young. Some of it, moreover, is accomplished verbally, while some of it appears to remain at an unspoken or imagined level. Even if we wished to share some of our psychological twists, our mental secrets, we could not, for we would need to make a movie if the other person is to receive the full impact of our words and images.

To repeat, the acts of psychological twisting are one of the primitive, or let us call them early, secrets in which children engage. But note that whereas part of the mind sets to work on the twisting and untwisting, another part of the mind merely observes the first part.

This process, too, the emergence of what we might call internal self-consciousness, also begins to take the form of a secret. (We discussed this matter in Chapter Seven.) The child, in other words, attempts to untwist some feeling or piece of reality, something he or she feels requires untwisting. This need to untwist, or more precisely, the work of untwisting, constitutes a mental act; it also constitutes an early form of secret. But secret number two is the child's realization that he or she in fact is engaged in the act. We call this latter act an act of *internal self-consciousness* not for the purpose of advancing professional jargon, but to differentiate this *private* form of mental activity from children's *public* self-consciousness that arises when they discover they are not their mother or father. While this act of differentiation also qualifies as a mental one, it is of a qualitatively different nature.

We have before us, then, two basic notions. First, the child *works privately* at twisting and untwisting perceptions, thoughts, feelings, while simultaneously recognizing that he or she is doing just that. Second, the child seems to require a belief in the security, constancy, predictability or calculability of the parents' *public* behavior in order not to feel terror in "working" on these secret twistings and untwistings. The calculability or "knowability" of one's parents on a public level supports the child in these private, secret quests. To repeat, by linking these mental acts to the concept of secret, I am suggesting that much of the twisting and untwisting work evolves on a *conscious* level. Presumably, the work goes on simultaneously at unconscious levels. As certain psychological problems are "born" unconsciously, so are they dealt with unconsciously. Nonetheless, by using secrets in this context, we are implying conscious, even rational, though secretive mental activity and mental acts.

It is not the case, therefore, that children cannot articulate their twistings and untwistings. It is not that they *sense* something is amiss but have no idea of the source or meaning of their distress or malaise. It is not, in other words, something children can barely put into words. On the contrary. Many of these psychological twistings, as well as the recognition that one engages (if not indulges) in the work of psychological twisting, could very well be articulated, as they are from time to time. Confession or admission of one's twistings and untwistings also are a normal part of childhood, a part, not so incidentally, that children typically reveal not to their parents, teachers, ministers, psychiatrists, and somewhat intrusive researchers like myself, but to other children. The confirmation of one another's secrets is captured in the phrase "My God, so do I." The phrase bespeaks the "release" of burdensome secrets. Do we not resonate to the image of the child sleeping at a friend's home and, in the darkness, broaching some deeply personal secret to the other child. Is it not true that the confessing child has wrestled with this particular intellectual or emotional twisting and now, finally, wishes to know whether someone else has wrestled with it? Are not these matters precisely the sort of things children only infer in conversation with their parents? What relief, what joy to learn that another human being, developing totally independent from oneself, has struggled with these same issues, even if he or she has not reached the same conclusions about the matter, or about oneself.

One could add to this thought the significance of feeling affirmed by one's listener, although learning that another person has dealt with the same twistings as we does more than merely affirm us. It *connects* us to our listener, as well as lessens the mysterious quality of the secret we have been keeping. That another person recognizes himself or herself in us, or in our secrets, means that we are not utterly different from other people; which in turn means that we are doing things, in our mind, that we are "meant" to do. In the end, the affirmation of another becomes a test of *normalcy*. How else might one take an inventory of one's private stock, so to speak, without testing "one's data" on someone else, even if this means putting oneself into psychological jeopardy. What if the other person hasn't wrestled with these same twistings? Will they see us as crazy! Is not our desire, then, to share our secrets based in part by a need to confirm our sanity. One of the child's fundamental definitions of insanity is to be different. While children might *appear* and *act* like others their age (as public institutions demand that they do) children nonetheless wonder about those internal unconfessed secrets, the twistings and untwistings that continue to intrigue and haunt them. No amount of mirror gazing will assist children in fully comprehending the significance of their secrets. Only in the telling of secrets and the hearing of others' responses (and secrets) will answers be forthcoming to the questions of differentness and insanity.

While the usage of words like "differentness" and "insanity" may seem rather inappropriate or excessive in the context of children's secrets, let us not overlook one obvious point: The child perceives and experiences a host of stimuli, some located externally, others internally. He or she witnesses an automobile accident or awakens one morning with an earache. Intellectual and emotional sense now must be made of these experiences. The earache is hardly funny, but the accident may seem so. Perhaps one is supposed to laugh at the sight of cars colliding. Eventually, the child will learn how to distinguish between serious accidents, where people are injured, and pretend accidents of clowns or cartoon characters. Yet again, one is constantly seeking to make sense of these sights and events, while feeling their impact, an impact that may or may not be conveyed to other people. Let us also not overlook the fact that these same mental activities take place in the minds of preverbal children. In their first years of life, babies, too, attempt to "work out" (or play out) the intellectual and affectual meanings of human experiences, only a bit of which get communicated. The process never stops; the secrets never recede.

In general terms, each phase of life demands that we work at the psychological twistings and untwistings indigenous to that particular phase. What does one think about graduating college, getting married, burying a parent, giving birth to a child? Privately, in our minds, we work on the meanings of these experiences, and the attendant feelings, occasionally sharing some of our results with trusted friends or professional listeners. But as our focus in this study is on children and adolescents, we underscore the natural (life) processes that young people are obliged to deal with and keep, for a time, as secrets. These processes constitute all emerging experiences, be they natural or traumatic. The rise of sexual feelings, the desire to kill, the need to do something one knows one is not supposed to do, or think, represent a few of the significant matters young people eventually must confront. The popular phrase "*coping* with experiences" implies intellectual as well as emotional *work*. It also implies some adjustment in one's behavior. One *learns* to *cope* with the death of a parent. Yet coping strategies often reveal that secretly the child has been "working" on the particular problem ever since it was first conceived. Children lie in bed thinking about death (which often is associated with sleep), or they wonder about those strange new feelings in their bodies, some of which are frighteningly pleasing. The questions asked by children reveal the shape of their inner working (not only workings). More precisely, they reveal that children are at work on psychological twistings and untwistings, although probably they will not yet reveal the contents and results of their labor. Some of these results, however, will emerge when they are older. The ten-year-old says, and not without a certain smugness, "When I was little I used to think . . ." The pain of the early secret struggles, the formerly held secret definitions and resolutions of problems have disappeared. Whereas adolescents may speak to friends about their inner world, much of this communication is not yet developmentally possible for the young child. Young children may confide in a parent or friend, but usually their confessed secret has more to do with a physical act than with a rumination or piece of wonderment.

Let me now place this discussion in the context of the present chapter.

It seems appropriate that we explore the idea of psychological twistings and untwistings in a section entitled "The Myth of Normalcy." The term "myth" has two meanings or two referents within the context of this discussion.

The first referent is to the individual or family attempting to give the appearance of being normal, or acting normally. The second referent is to the psychological or secretive aspect of musing; that is, the constellation of the child's mental acts. Children and adolescents are keen observers of themselves and their private and public situations. Much of adolescence is devoted to shaping these so-called skills of self-consciousness, even when they assume the form of exhibitionism and, admittedly, rather tiresome self-interest. But adolescence is most definitely a period of learning about the self, even if some of this learning is inadequate or seems primitive because much of what one learns is not properly articulated according to standards set down by adults and authority generally. In point of fact, adolescence is a time when people *normally* deal "straight on" with matters of sanity and insanity, differentness and similarity. Adolescents learn to make intellectual and emotional sense of external and internal experience, just as they learn how to articulate experiences, if only to themselves. Only naturally, then, we discover adolescents dealing with these matters openly and secretly, clumsily and eloquently.

The shorthand style in which adolescents communicate some of their "findings," as observed in adolescent "cult" songs and poems, might well express the fact that adolescents do not wish to dwell overly long on some of the issues they are obliged to encounter. I prefer to believe, however, that the shorthand style, captured in the belabored phrase "Well, like, you know," is actually a codified form of communicating: "I've thought about this, haven't you, too?" A few key words are uttered, and then follows that phrase, "Like, you know." The response is affirmative. The other person *has* dwelled secretly on these same issues. One reveals, in other words, only the fact that one has been ruminating on a topic. The substance of the rumination may never be told, but the substance of the secret is not the point. Instead, the point is to make certain that one is not different, singular, or crazy. One must be like the others, for private as well as public *identicality* proves sanity. Adolescents, then, have a huge stake in the myth of normalcy. For them it relates not only to questions of sanity and insanity but to matters of individuality. Whereas both the child and adolescent work out the intellectual and emotional meanings of incoming and internally generated experiences and images, the adolescent in addition must learn to place these ruminations in a social psychological context. That is, they must deal with experiences in terms of what these experiences mean to them personally, as well as how these meanings might affect their position in the network (and hierarchy) of friendships and associations. On the basis of a particular untwisting, an adolescent may decide he or she is not crazy, but what might someone else believe if the secret rumination were ever divulged?

In offering these remarks, we have fixated on the metaphoric terms psychological "twistings" and "untwistings." We have chosen these terms not only because they describe, somewhat, the way people privately "solve" personal problems or deal with new experiences but also because of the familiar association of the words "twisted" and "crazy." Any new or extreme feeling may cause one to believe something is wrong, or indeed, especially right. The painful or ecstatic feeling, like the still unresolved or recently solved problem, looms as a potential secret. Some people allege that adolescents know gratification from an experience only after they have broadcast the experience. In some instances, presumably, the allegation seems fair, although people of all ages find almost as much pleasure in recounting an experience as they found in living through the experience in the first place. I think it fair to say that during adolescence, people recognize that their private ruminations begin to accumulate as secrets. I think it also true that adolescence is a time when people learn that these personal ruminations have great significance for establishing private *and* public identities which require adolescents, paradoxically, to be identical to and wholly unlike their special friends. These facts, too, begin to accumulate as secrets.

Secret material, then, constitutes young people's store of information about their normality or possible abnormality. Furthermore, normality and abnormality, along with their attendant myths, are personally as well as collectively defined. Thus, adolescents' decisions about whether or not they are normal automatically become linked to the decisions and determinations regarding abnormality of one's peers and authority figures. Secrets, therefore, contain clues to one's own actual or potential madness or, less extremely, abnormal development. In this regard, we might point to the strictness of adolescent moral codes, even though these codes may differ in substance and form from adult codes of morality. The phrase "honor among thieves" is no hollow directive. The so-called deviant in adolescent society pays an enormous personal price; and many who are publicly accepted, even acclaimed, wonder privately whether they are more disturbed or deranged than their closest friends could ever recognize.

Children and adolescents wonder about their private and public development, just as they wonder whether they have overlooked some significant point, twisted some message, or indeed, "have come out twisted." They want their privacy and individuality preserved, just as they wish to have others believe they keep no secrets. This paradox, experienced partly as indecision, partly as deceit, also emerges as an adolescent secret. Still another matter adolescents wonder about is their own normality or abnormality. The concept of and concern with madness are no strangers to the adolescent mind. The mystery of the mind, adolescents discover, is at times exhilarating, even entertaining, at times terrifying. The stuff of the mind often presents itself much like the ghost story or horror movie. It tantalizes, intrigues, frightens, occasionally overwhelms the person. In contemplating one's fears, anxieties, perversities, one grapples with extreme forms of normal events and emotions. One deals, moreover, with commonly shared, even culturally determined, mental representations and psychological symbols. We desire to murder a parent. The thought terrifies us. So, as if by magic, we "find ourselves" imagining a scene in which a small bird pecks away at a ferocious beast. But notice, our emphasis in this example is not on the symbolism, but rather on the secret wish to murder, the child's fear that the wish or the image of the bird pecking at the beast makes him or her somehow abnormal. How do children find out they are not crazy, as most all of them do, thankfully, without the help of professional mind experts and dream interpreters?

While the secret twistings and untwistings of experiences in children's minds raise the question of their normality, what keeps children from reaching a state of panic is, again, the constancy, predictability—really "knowability"—of the parents' public world. It is the perceived social order and normalcy of parents, both as individuals and as a partnership, that lend support and security to children as they deal with their secret musings. No one denies that the children's earliest impressions of what they will become, even look like, derive from their identification with parents. Parents, in other words, are the first imagined peek into one's personal future. I will be a doctor or mechanic like my father, is an all too familiar childhood utterance, but in saying this, children are simultaneously making another calculation: If my parents are normal, then I will be normal, too. In fact, parents communicate this message to children both verbally and through their individual and collective actions. Granted, children gain new models of adults (and adulthood) over time, just as they will make wholly new determinations for and about themselves. Still, children's involvement with their parents remains their first encounter with adulthood and future possibility. The initial human foundations of a social order and a sane personality are established by parents. The myth of normalcy, therefore, is a far more weighty concept than one might assume at first glance. The "myth" of parents as normal human beings enhances the child's development and makes less frightening the work of twisting and untwisting human experience which underlies the child's (normal) involvement and fascination with secrets.

We have elucidated the matter of psychological twisting at this point because our concern in this chapter is with children's secrets in the context of mental health. In this and the following chapter we examine the accounts of four young people, all of whom safeguard their special secrets about the mental health of various family members. Whereas many of the children encountered in the previous chapters were obliged, if not outrightly compelled to keep their secrets, not all the children we are about to hear experienced this same obligation. In some cases, children are told not to reveal the psychological problems of a relative. In other cases, however, it is merely assumed that the child will reveal nothing, although neither parent has demanded secrecy. In still other cases, parents encourage their children to speak to someone, a minister, therapist, school counselor, about the problem, only to have children refuse. We must be clear on the issue that many vows of silence are self-imposed. And if the phrase "vows of silence" rings with a monastic sound, then it is an apt description. For many children, themselves practically stricken by the mental illness of a parent, have chosen to live an almost monastic existence. Quiet, abstemious, austere, they lead their lives in a manner that distresses their family, who obviously recognize the source of the child's disturbance. Children's loyalty to parents, taking, as it does, many forms, often seems remarkable.

MICHAEL JENKINS

The sad irony of Michael Jenkins' story was that everyone, well, a great many people, knew of his father's unrelenting need to drink. I always refrained from calling Mylo Jenkins an alcoholic because his fourteen-year-old son, Michael, hated the word. It rarely came up in our conversations. While some might argue that had the boy been able to say it, he might have been better able to deal with his father's problem, I remain unconvinced. Michael faced only too directly the agony felt by his father, as well as his mother and three sisters. The entire Jenkins family suffered with the once happy-go-lucky, but now depressed and enervated head of their home, the man whom they had watched gradually disintegrate over the last years.

As in many of the preceding accounts, the "story" of the Jenkins family seems somewhat familiar. But herein lies one of the potential dangers for those of us researching family histories and experiences. After hearing a few fragments of a family's biography one begins to (believe they) have a relatively accurate sense of the family's fundamental characteristics. The pieces, as we say, of one family fall together much as they did for other families. "It's the usual story," one colleague will tell another, referring to the problems of some family. "Father does all right, makes some money, nice wife, nice kids, suddenly the business falls apart, money disappears, and, well, the usual. Father starts drinking, coming home late, Mother gets angry, kids grow frightened, family falls apart, social workers snoop around, a daughter becomes pregnant, a son flirts with some delinquent activity. You know, the usual . . ."

The danger for researchers in these "instances of familiarity" is that they stop listening to families recount their stories. As soon as the familiar themes are heard, the substance and fabric of the family seem to become less salient and discrete. What difference if one loses a few sentences here or there? What one misses with the Jenkinses, one can always fill in with the Smiths or Browns. I caught myself in these lapses when speaking to Michael Jenkins. His manner of describing his secret almost seduced me into not listening to him. Repeatedly he used phrases like "It's the typical problem," or "I'm sure you've heard of lots of families like ours," or "It's the usual sob story." Of course it became evident that he was challenging me to attend to something he knew from movies, books, and television. It *was* all too familiar to me. His phrases also suggested that he was concerned, only naturally, with the matter of his public image and private sense of self. Outwardly, he desired to give the impression of being a member of that anonymous cadre of people known as sons of drunk fathers. I don't want anybody feeling sorry for me, he seemed to be saying; there are millions more like me in the world. Inwardly, however, he was engaged in the work of psychological twisting and untwisting, and evidently he was distressed by the fear that his father's problem had left him isolated in the world. I hope that is a fair assessment of his state: Michael Jenkins seemed utterly detached from people and things. To listen to him was to believe he was about to lose touch with what he himself called reality. These are his words:

"Everybody has nightmares. Not just dreams, the scariest of the scary. Everybody must have them, not only children. Something horrible is happening or is just about to happen when all of a sudden you wake up and you're happy it's only a nightmare, although you don't start laughing right away because it seemed so real while it was going on. For the last couple of years, my nightmare is real. Nothing I can dream is worse than what I have to see all the time.

"I get home from school early. I don't like hanging 'round on the street, wasting time with other guys. They don't do anything. So I come home and try to do things but I can't. I'm really killing time. I'd like to watch television but my mother says no television in the day. I tell her it would calm me down. I could just sit there, I wouldn't get into trouble. And there's lots of chances around here to get into trouble. But she says no TV. I could watch when she's not around, but I'm sort of afraid to. Probably what I imagine she'd do is worse than what she really would do. But you don't know. Like I say, with my father, things are worse in real life than they are in my head.

"Anyway, I kill time. I used to like to read but I don't do that anymore. I can't get myself to concentrate, not even on the sports pages. I can read, like, who won the games, but no more. I start but I quit after two sentences. In school it's worse. All I do is nod my head every time the teacher looks at me. She doesn't know if I'm listening to her. And she sure can't tell whether I understand what's going on. So I just nod, nod, nod, nod. Then comes dinner, which is a surprise party most of the time. I call it the big quiz show 'cause you get to guess whether *he'll* be there or not. He shows up most of the time, but lots of times he's out somewhere. Where is he? He's out there with the bottle, drinking the cheapest white wine you can find. Sometimes when he comes home the smell's so bad you can't even talk to him. I got to move away. 'You don't like me, do you, Michael?' he goes. 'I *do* like you,' I go. 'If you like me, how come you walk away when I come home?' 'I was just walking out when you came in. Really.' I'm lying to him, but I can't tell if he knows whether I'm telling the truth or not. You can't see what he knows from looking at his face. There isn't anything on his face anymore. Before you could tell what he was thinking and what kind of a mood he was in just by looking at him. Now he always looks the same, like his face has gone dead. Something inside him is dead, so I guess his face went with it. Pretty soon it'll be his body, too, then they can come and take him away. Can't be too long with a man who puts away all that liquor and never touches food. My mother practically has to feed him like a baby. He wouldn't eat if she didn't make him. And that isn't even the beginning of the nightmare.

"You start to talk with him and it's like he's not even there. I'll ask him a question and he'll say, 'You don't like me, Michael. I know. I can tell.' I just asked him a simple question, like, how do you feel or something, and he's saying, 'You don't like me.' You *know* he's the problem, but you ask yourself, is it me? Did I think one thing and ask another thing? Maybe I can't even hear myself think or talk anymore. Then he'll walk, when he's in a bad way, I mean. That's the hard part because then it really *is* like he's a baby. Not a cripple. People like my Aunt Florence say I have to think of my father like he's an invalid. But she's wrong. He's a baby. An invalid is someone who was born wrong or had something horrible happen to him. When the problem first began I got scared because I pretended he was a soldier. Every night he came home I pretended he was wounded and we took turns taking care of him. It was easier to make sense of what was going on like that. But I don't pretend anymore, especially when he's trying to walk. I'll be sitting in my room and suddenly there's this big crash. I know what it is but I'm not moving out of my seat. I used to run in like a jerk but not anymore. Then I hear my mother. She's in the kitchen. She knows what's happened, only she isn't going to help either. 'Michael,' she's yelling. 'Get in here and pick up your father.' Boy is she angry. She doesn't mind doing the housework, she had to do that before, too, but when he falls down that's the end of her. So I go in and pick him up. And he's heavy, too, let me tell you. He used to be fat, now he's thin, but it's all dead weight. We had a fire drill like thing at school once and they showed a movie where firemen were picking up people. That's where I learned how to pick him up. I put him over my shoulder and carry him to his bedroom. My parents don't sleep in the same room anymore. My mother sleeps in the living room. At first she said it was because she couldn't stand him snoring. Now she admits what it is. She says she won't get a divorce because you can't divorce a baby. When I have to carry him I really like what she says: He *is* like a baby. You can't stand doing it, but you don't have a choice. He needs all of us. If we walked out on him he'd go out on the street and die. Maybe that's only what I imagine would happen, but it could. That could be the end of my nightmare.

"So there I am, the fireman, carrying my father to bed. I practically have to throw up when I'm done 'cause he stinks so bad. He doesn't even take a bath anymore. I'd like to drop him like a sack, but I'd be afraid to, even though he might not even know the difference. He seems to be asleep half the time anyway. Then the horrible part, undressing him. *That's* what my mother refuses to do. She'll take off his shoes but nothing else. I have to do the rest. My sisters do work around the house but they don't have to do this part. I hate it. His clothes are filthy, and there's usually dirty sheets and blankets on the bed. My mother says what's the use of putting clean sheets on a bed for a filthy man. So I undress the little baby and put him to bed. He doesn't move. I have to pick up each arm, and each leg, and his head. It takes forever. Sometimes I don't do all of it. Just the top. She checks up to see if I did it. But I can't stand to take off his pants. So I put the tops of his pajamas on. He doesn't know the difference so who cares, and anyway, tomorrow he's just going to go out and do the same nothing he did today, right? Then I finish and look at him lying there; it's an ugly sight. Sometimes when I look at him, he's so still you think you're working in a funeral parlor, but I see he's crying. Not a lot of tears, like a baby will cry. Little tears, and not very many of them. He's not looking at anything; sometimes his eyes aren't even open but the tears are coming out all the same.

"That's what goes on every day, and that's usually the last thing I see before I go to bed: my father lying in that smelly bed, which I put him into, in his dirty, smelly pajamas, which I put him into, looking like he's two hundred years old, and he's not fifty yet. We used to have birthday parties for him. My mother made a cake and we had games. He wanted that. Just the family. Now we don't have birthday parties and I don't even know anymore how old he is. I know my mother's forty-six. Anyway, the last thing I think about before I go to bed is how I'm working in a funeral parlor. Every night I get to put the same corpse in the same coffin. Nobody says anything about it, but that's what it's like, although it wouldn't be better if he did. It will be worse when he dies. My mother's going to be very guilty. She says no but you'll see. She stopped helping him too soon. If I didn't pick him up and put him in bed he'd stay on the living room floor, and it isn't only because she can't lift him up. She quit. She was on his side when he was making money, but when he went down she sort of walked away. She moved out of their bedroom, didn't she?

"He tells me her quitting on him is the saddest thing of all. If she helped him he could make it back. I told her once. She goes, 'Don't you ever repeat the words of that filthy man. When he can stay sober, stand up when he's supposed to, and sit at the dinner table and earn a living like every other man in this country, then he can tell me how I quit too early on him!' My sisters heard her say it. They said they didn't agree with her so she told them, 'If it's so damn easy, *you* be his wife. I agreed to be the man's *wife*, not his *nurse*.' She wasn't going to change her mind, no matter what we said. But I still feel she didn't do all she could.

"There's something else my mother does I really don't like. I don't like the way it's going on, you know, and she knows I'm upset by it. Every day and every night it's the same thing. With people like my father nothing changes. So you think, God, maybe I'll be doing the same thing with him the rest of his life, or the rest of *my* life. But then she goes, 'If you're feeling bad about it, maybe you could talk to someone. I don't care who you tell. You can tell the television reporters for all I care.' She knows I can't tell anybody. It's one thing not to want to change his pants, but you wouldn't walk out on the guy when he's crying, or go down the street telling everybody you meet, hey, my father's a drunk. You want to come up to my house and see him? And smell him? I'm not going to my school counselor; it's none of her business. She'd probably say, 'What are you telling *me* for?' It's true. I wouldn't be telling her for *my* reasons. She can't do anything about my nightmares.

"This is a family secret; it's my job not to tell people. I don't even talk about it to my relatives. They always ask me, 'How's your father, Michael?' 'He's fine, Uncle Ralph.' That's my mother's brother. He knows everything. She tells him. But just 'cause *she* does doesn't mean *I* have to. My father makes a bowel movement in his pants, his pants, for real, 'cause he doesn't always wear underwear. You don't have to tell people that. My mother would like to pretend it doesn't happen. He does it and it smells, but you don't have to say anything; people know. But I'm not going to blab off about his problems. I wouldn't want my sisters going around telling anybody their brother's having some mental problem. So my mother can go on how she wants me to tell anybody and everybody. I think there are things you keep secret, especially when they have to do with bad news about your father. If you don't go out asking for help, then you don't go telling the whole world your problems. Telling people doesn't help anyway. She's told enough people already, and I don't see where it's helped us any so far. All people say is, that's too bad. So now they think my father's a bum. And *he* doesn't need that. If he didn't think the same thing, he wouldn't cry at night when I put him to sleep. If you watch him, like I watch him, drunk as he is most of the time, you know you don't need to tell him about his problem. You also can tell he doesn't want you telling a lot of people what's happening. My father knows I wouldn't say anything to hurt him. I only wish sometime he could get well enough to see how *I* feel about the whole thing. I mean, if he could *see* me he'd know I wouldn't tell anyone. I'd like him to know I cry, too. Maybe not as much as he does but I cry, not that I'd want *him* telling that to a lot of people. I cry when I go to sleep, too, but no one's around to watch then. Maybe I wouldn't cry if somebody was there. But maybe I would if I was drunk and had his sort of problems. Yeah, I'd cry then, no matter what my mother told me to do, or not do."

I have purposely omitted the social background of the Jenkins family. Given the familiar threads of the account, I thought in this one case the reader might prefer to hear the words of this boy without being prejudiced by the familiar sociological clues. It may be stated now that the Jenkins family is white, and is best described as middle class. They live in a two-story two-family house. The other tenants, once fairly close friends, now avoid the Jenkinses, presumably because they feel self-conscious about Mylo Jenkins' "problem."

The Jenkins children attend public school and speak of the possibility of attending college, if there is money available. Before he became ill, Mylo Jenkins took his family every summer on two-week holidays. The children swam, picnicked, camped, and tried their hand at fishing. There was always talk of purchasing a small trailer, an idea that delighted Michael. Needless to say, the trailer never became a reality. Neither Mylo nor Roseanne Jenkins was ambitious or greedy. They believed that whereas America was a place in which to grow rich, too many hardships came with wealth. It was better, they agreed, to wind up somewhere near the middle. Furthermore, people liked you better when you didn't stand out too much. So the Jenkins family led their life in a quiet way, remaining loyal to old friends, and a trifle hesitant about making new ones. I was never made to feel uncomfortable in their home, which must be seen as a significant gesture on the part of people for whom psychological research seemed a rather peculiar enterprise. Or perhaps what they wished to communicate was that my research was not unlike the problem of alcoholism: something meant for families other than their own.

In some of the accounts, I have gone beyond the words of the young people and provided a glimpse of how the child has fared over time. Often it strikes me that the children actually remain relatively unchanged; their burdens have not been lifted, the weight of the past, in Kafka's words, continues to influence their behavior and outlook. In other instances, the children appeared to take noticeable turns for the better. It is difficult to determine just why it was that the tension, sadness, or anger associated with their secrets slowly abated. One might suggest that time healed even these special wounds, and the children, with or without their parents, went on their way.

Some outcomes, however, are not as pleasant. The case of Michael Jenkins, for example, represents one such bitter ending. A great deal of psychiatric help was offered to the Jenkins family, as the problem stemming from Mylo's alcoholism continued. In time, the family saw the father's problem as being a systemic family problem; they were all involved. But they were losing strength merely in keeping their heads above water. One saw slightly less anguish in the two younger girls, Martha and Alicia, who rarely revealed their feelings to anyone. Nonetheless, they, too, presumably, were holding tightly to secrets. One heard a bit more from the oldest daughter, Kathleen, whose account sounded not unlike the one her brother had presented to me. In fact, the two children, Kathleen and Michael, were similar in temperament, except that Kathleen turned out to be the stronger of the two. For shortly after his fifteenth birthday, Michael Jenkins took his life.

Throughout the previous chapters, I have remarked on the racial, ethnic, and social class characteristics of the various families. I have mentioned, too, that while one prefers to have this type of sociological information at one's disposal, social characteristics often loom as misleading signposts, if not empty messages. One is advised that a particular family is middle class. Fair enough, but what precisely is one to draw from that infamous catchword? Or a family is designated as being black or white. Again, while curiosity would urge one to want to know a family's race or ethnicity, the reader only naturally suspects that the reporter, in listing the family's race, intends some further implication.

Personally, I find the familiar social and sociological designations helpful, if only as guideposts. Our concern in this book is with secrets, their substance, meaning, and most especially the impact on children of keeping family secrets. Too often in our culture, however, the sorts of social and psychological problems we have been examining are automatically associated with working-class, poor, and minority families. Unemployment typically is thought of as a problem befalling only poor families; statistics, of course, support this impression. But incest, sexual, and criminal problems also turn up primarily in the accounts of poor and minority families, when in fact all families are susceptible to these problems. That the rich are somewhat better protected from researchers and journalists, and hence better able to keep their secrets, does not mean that they are free of problems. One of the "rewards" of being a member of a minority or poor family is the increased likelihood that the conditions of one's life will be exposed to the public, lending support to the impression that *only* poor and minority families sustain the sort of secret difficulties we have been recounting.

I again raise these matters before embarking on an account of a child whose parents were drug addicts, for I fear that some people may be tempted to overgeneralize from this one account. That the Morgans happen to be poor and black hardly means that all, or even a great many, poor or black families suffer with the problem of drug addiction. Similarly, I did not present Michael Jenkins' account so that readers would reach the conclusion that *all* middle-class white families conceal an alcoholic. Nor do I wish to conclude that wherever one finds an alcoholic, one also finds a potentially suicidal child. The main point to be stressed is this: The poorer the family under study, the greater the likelihood people will generalize the findings on that family to large groups of people. The rich alcoholic is an anomaly, if not an anathema; the poor or minority alcoholic is a piece of the expected and usual. The problems of the rich go against the grain of our expectations and fantasies; the problems of the poor document our preconceptions. The devil owns the "inner city"; heaven is synonymous with suburbs, which makes children of the rich God's own angels.

TYRONE MORGAN

Tyrone Morgan rarely smiled, at least he never did in my company. Thirteen years old, one of four children, each one so different from the others it was hard to believe they came from the same womb, Tyrone Morgan found nothing charming or pretty about his life. My own environment, however, enticed him. He would make me drive him to my home so that he could look around, but he invariably refused to see the inside of the house and meet my family. "Just checking it out," he always said, as if he wanted to smile. "Just what I expected. All right, my man, we can go home now."

After knowing him a while, Tyrone spoke a bit about his aspirations, which we agreed were high but realistic. He wanted to become a doctor. A general doctor, he explained, not someone "who specializes in the left arm." His intention was to care for people in neighborhoods like his own. He had read about medical training and college admissions policies, and, as they say, he was resolutely looking forward to his future. He also made it clear that he understood how America felt about poor black students imagining they can just amble into swanky medical colleges. "We're meant to be ambulance drivers," he said once. "That's as close as we're meant to get to hospitals. But that ain't for me." I made some passing remark, something about how he had brought together a large store of information about medical schools. The remark was meant only to suggest that he knew what he was talking about. "I know a lot about a lot," he said. "My mind's *always* working."

Certain is the word I would use to describe Tyrone Morgan. He was a boat dead set on its course; nothing would veer him a single degree in the wrong direction. Guy's all right, I would tell myself, musing on his almost flight plan approach to life. Perhaps his future does seem rather "overorganized" and blueprinted, but no building of any significance was ever constructed without a detailed set of drawings. Then again, a voice inside me protested, a personality doesn't require architectural blueprints. Well, perhaps a medical career did.

In time I came to know several of Tyrone's teachers. All of them believed he was college and probably medical school material, even though that latter phase was years away. His grades were excellent, his study habits impeccable, his behavior perfect. He was an ideal student who surely would enroll at a good college, a college that would enhance his chances for admission to medical school. The same teachers, however, also added that it might be a good idea if somewhere along the line the boy learned how to relax. They characterized him with expressions like "tight as a drum," "wound up like a corkscrew," "inflexible" and "unbudgeable." One stated emphatically, "The boy has to realize all life isn't gotten from reading books." Another commented, and not without compassion, "I'm sure he can make any goal he sets for himself. What I fear is that he'll crack before he makes it halfway there."

I remember this last phrase primarily because the word "crack" is one I, too, had used when reflecting on this kind, intelligent but somehow excessively serious young man. Perhaps he was brittle, perhaps something had scared him and in response he felt obliged to protect himself from future accidents. Whatever it was, I, too, felt he could crack. He was so serious I never dreamed of saying to him: "Hey, Tyrone, don't you *ever* relax? Don'tcha wanna just flake out once in a while?" One didn't speak this way to Tyrone Morgan. No one joked with him, no one raised the subject of relaxing with him, because Tyrone Morgan was an intelligent young man who spent a lot of time not only planning his future but honestly and painfully assessing his chances of attaining his goals. He had made himself "the thing he was researching. We're working together," he told me. "The both of us interested in the same thing: me!" And did he feel he might crack? He believed it as strongly as he believed in himself. After two years of friendship, he let me know a bit about that well-organized personality of his.

"*You* see the good parts, only the good parts. Bad parts they tuck away from me, and I tuck away from you. Hide 'em away from all of us like children's presents. I'll unwrap a few for you. Let me tell you something, though. You're a psychologist so you study all these things. But most people, they don't study psychology. They don't sit down with their teachers and talk about their mind. Your mind, my mind, anybody's mind. What's going on good up there, and what's going on that can make you sick, nobody tells you about. You got to figure it out all by your lonesome. But you aren't going to find lots of folks facing up to themselves. Folks say, look at yourself in the mirror, really *see* yourself. That ain't what I'm talking about. I can't see my face better than anybody else; folks don't see their own faces. I see *your* face, not my face. But I see my mind. I can look 'round the inside of my mind. Can you follow what I'm saying? Ain't something you see, it's something you got to work with. Trick is, you got to use your mind to get to work on your mind. You got to sort of turn your mind inside out so it can look at itself. You twist it, like you were rolling up all these rolls of clay. You make yourself feel different inside than what folks think you're feeling, but nobody in the world knows what you're up to. It's the secret world you got to play with in there.

"Teacher say, Tyrone, why you sitting there looking so sad? She say, *looking*, but she couldn't know how Tyrone's feeling on the inside. He could be laughing his head off on the inside for all she knows; could be crying, too, to the point where maybe he thinks it'd be a whole lot better if he was dead. You got two very different lives you got to work with at the same time, and nobody but you can say which is the best one, or which is the real one. I'm not saying the life everybody sees isn't important; it just isn't the only one. But just 'cause folks see, or *think* they see it, don't mean they know about it for sure. Could be part of your secret, too. You got to, like, control these two lives, 'specially the one on the inside before it turns inside out and you don't know whether your inside one is the real one and the outside one is just you faking your life to everybody. Like, nobody knows for sure whether you're telling 'em the truth. You say, I got a secret. I'm going to keep a secret from you. Now I tell you, hey, Tom, I'm going to keep a secret from you. Now I tell you, hey, Tom, I'm going to let you in on a secret. All right? Now, how do you know what I'm telling you is true? How do you know that's the secret I wanted to tell you? How do you know for sure there even *was* a secret? Man told me once, there's nothing you can *ever* know for sure, 'cept you're going to die. I told him, how do I know *that*? I don't even know what dying means. For all I know dying could mean everything that was real isn't real no more, but that doesn't mean things *aren't* no more. Nobody can tell me there's only one thing I *know* for *sure*.

"Man told me I'm going to die, but he also told me nobody can tell nobody what dying's all about, what it feels like. You aren't a real human if you don't think about dying. You *have* to think about dying and ask yourself some questions you aren't never going to ask nobody else. Okay? Now, how does anybody know all those things you think about death isn't what death is in the first place? Maybe those two lives you have are put there so if you're living life, the part everybody else sees dies, then you end up with the other part, the kind of living-dead life. That's the part nobody sees while you're alive; nobody's ever going to see either. I didn't ask the man, but I'd like to hear him answer *that* question. You have two eyes in case one goes bad, and two ears, two hands, two legs. Maybe you have two lives, only *you're* the only person who can see them both or feel them both.

"Here's another reason I feel it could be this way. When I was little, I got up one night. Maybe I was having a dream. I got up but I didn't call for my mother, which is what most kids do. She was getting tired of me doing it so I taught myself to get up and think about what was wrong and not bother anybody. But this time I got up and heard my parents talking over something with this man. They were fighting over money. He was telling them, 'You pay up or else,' and they were begging him to keep coming to them. My father was angry and my mother was crying, and this man, he was telling them they had too many times on him, and he was finished with them 'cause they didn't keep their word. I was scared, but I wanted to see what the hell was going on. It was late, too, everybody should have been sleeping. I remember it was cold. I was freezing. I saw my parents. They were freezing, too, but they didn't have a lot of clothes on. I opened my door and looked down our hall, you know, and I saw them, but I didn't really know what I was seeing 'cause you can't always see that good when you're sleepy. Then I saw all this stuff on the floor and I sort of got the picture. They sure didn't explain it to me, but I got it. They had a man come sell 'em heroin they could stick in their blood. When they couldn't pay, he told them good-bye. They told him they'd die without it. He told them, ain't his business what happened to them. They told me *none* of it was my business. I told them nothing. I knew about folks doing that stuff, but up to then I didn't know it was going on right next door. They did one helluva good job hiding it from me, and both of them, you understand what I'm saying, had the habit. He got it for her, she got it for him. I figured, hey, I'm not going to mess them up no more asking them questions. If I'd been sleeping through the night like folks supposed to, I wouldn't have found out. I respected them for not saying a word and going on pretending we was just another family. Till that time that's what I thought, too. Just another family.

"But see, that's what I'm trying to get across to you: Nobody can *tell* you what's going on. You see faces, like I saw my parents', but you don't know what's happening. I was living 'longside two addicts. Fact, you can make that three, 'cause when I told my sister she told me she was doing it, too. You think I let her know I was surprised? All these folks living in the same house, one after the other letting the cat out of the bag; I ain't going to look surprised for *their* benefit. But you better believe I wasn't going to ask no more folks what they're doing when I'm not looking. I told myself, you just go mind your business. Don't go looking into folks' problems. Folks tell you something, that's one thing, but don't go looking for their inside life. You know what you get when you go looking inside? You get the dead-life, ugly stuff folks don't want nobody to find out. You think my mother wanted me to know she was putting a needle to herself couple, three times a day? Hell she does. If she did she'd be talking about it now, but she's keeping her secret and I'm keeping mine.

"What you got to do is take stuff like that and *right* away stick it inside you. Stuff goes straight to your mind. Your eyes see it, your ears hear it, then they send it to your mind. Take it right out of one life and put it in the other life. Man comes home and tells everybody, 'You know what? I just got me a big raise. Making *twice* the money I was making when I went to work this morning.' Now *that* stuff's for the outside. That's living life stuff. Both my folks being on the line, that's for my inside. That means your mind's got to work with words nobody's going to hear. Can't talk it out with yourself. Can't use the same words you use in your other life. Got to find all new things—don't even know *what* to call 'em. All I know is you got to think over again, in all different ways. Boy goes out of his room at night and 'stead of it being dark and scary in his house like he's expecting it's going to be, it's all lit up, and scarier than he ever thought it *could* be. But that isn't the end to it, 'cause you got to go on living and not saying a word to no one. You got to watch yourself pretend every time you talk to your old man or old lady. Every time they say, 'Hello,' you're thinking, go pretend now, Tyrone, and don't mind that pretending's a little like coming right out and lying 'tween your teeth. You pretend in the life side; don't pretend in the dead-life. No way you could. Who'd you be pretending *to*? Folks don't keep no secrets from themselves. I might not tell you a secret, but I'll tell *me*; I have to. Little kids, you know how they'll close their eyes and play they're dead? That ain't the dead-life side doing that. You don't play no games like that on the inside; your mind wouldn't never allow it.

"Folks say, deep inside, what you *really* think about this or that? That's when they want to talk about the dead-life inside. They know you got one 'cause everybody has. You can't tell folks exactly, but you kind of know what they want you to talk about. But you take like my mother, she can't go asking me no more, 'how you feel?' She can't ask me nothing anymore 'cause she's afraid something from my inside might pop out and she don't want to know what it is. She's afraid I could let something out of the bag same as her. She don't want to ask me no questions about *nothing!* And I'm not fixing to ask *her* anything either. Her mind is working the way she wants it to work, and my mind is working the way *I* want it to work, so we keep away from each other. Same way with my father. He don't show me nothing like what he's got inside, so I don't let him know nothing about what I'm thinking.

"Course, the way it goes, nobody wants to let nobody hear about the inside part 'cause they'd think for sure the other person just went crazy. You let folks see that mishmash inside and they're going to put you away for the rest of your life. It's like you go visit where some guy's working on something. You don't know what he's doing. Stuff crowded all over the place, things piled up, man can't even find a place to do his work. All of a sudden something comes out, like a beautiful painting or something. All that is is the mind working. All that mumbo jumbo, ain't no one able to say what they're working on till they're done working on it. 'Course you die before you can tell anybody about what your mind's been working on. But like that guy, every once in a while something comes out and sort of, like, makes sense to you. Here's what I'm doing, little present from my mind. Folks got to make these little presents, otherwise they're going to end up crazy. You got to make sense of *some* things. I figure, you got to tell folks *some* things about the inside just to make sure you still feel all right; I mean, so you know you aren't crazy. When you can't say *nothing* about the inside, you are *all* the way gone. So you tell. And that's like telling one of your secrets. You *got* to tell a few secrets so you know you're doing all right on the outside *and* the inside. My old lady and old man, they can't tell me nothing no more, and I can't tell them nothing. So, where's that leave us? If they can't tell no secrets, and I can't tell no secrets, we both got to end up going the wrong way. You can keep it inside, but sure as hell old death going to come and gobble it up like some big vacuum cleaner. You *got* to tell some of your secrets. Working on your secrets for too long and you sure as hell will crack. Right in two. Right in two."

Two years after this meeting with Tyrone Morgan, his mother became seriously ill. At first, nobody seemed able to diagnose the illness. Finally it was discovered that her liver and spleen were infected. In the hospital, she made slow but steady progress until the doctors decided she would be better off at home. Learning of her addiction, they recommended a methadone program of rehabilitation.

Plans were made for her to enter the program, but after a month at home she again became sick and was readmitted to the hospital, where she died. She was not yet forty years old.

Tyrone's father, in the meanwhile, had been involved in a heroin rehabilitation program where he had met a woman with whom he lived after his wife's death. He is himself a man in frail health, although recently he has reported feeling stronger.

With his mother dead and his father living with a new woman friend, Tyrone and one sister went to live with an aunt. They were selected because their aunt's home was located near the school the Morgan children attended. As she could house only two children, it was felt that the two smartest ones should be chosen so their school-work would not suffer. The other Morgan children were sent to live with their mother's brother in Mississippi. At my suggestion, Tyrone promised to consider consulting someone if he ever wanted to talk about that "inner dead-life" of his. He said his decision rested on whether or not in good faith he could reveal his secrets to anyone. After all, he reminded me, it was learning his parents' secrets that had "sent him to work" on his own mind in the first place. I understood his dilemma; naturally there was no way I would force him to do anything. Even when a teacher contacted me to report that Tyrone was "just not right" and his academic work was suffering—this was nine months after his mother's death—my words had minimal effect on Tyrone. I settled for short visits with him now and again and occasional telephone calls. He saw through my casualness: "You're still waiting to see whether old Tyrone's ready to let his cat out of the bag," he would say. Then he would laugh, in a disingenuous manner, a manner I secretly called his dead-life laugh.

Months later I received a telephone call from Tyrone, whose voice was utterly unrecognizable. "Hey, it's great to hear from you," I shouted into the phone, my delight drowned by trepidation. "How's it going, Tyrone? You got a cold or something?"

"Cut the crap, Thomas Cottle," came the desperate response, "and get me somebody. Cracking time is here. Got no time left, and neither do you. Cat's out of the bag, my man, and has done run away from home. You got that, my man? Cat ain't home no more. It's the morning of the dead-life. You hear? Now, you play that back like I told it to you."

I began repeating his words, but he cut me off in mid-sentence:

"Cat's out of the bag. Blackness pouring out of my eyes and my ears. My two eyes and my two ears and my two *lives*. You got it, my man? Got blackness pouring out of me, all the junk in the world's go-

ing in and going out. Gonna need the army to clean me up, and you
the guy's gonna order it. Army *and* the navy *and* the marines *and* the
pilots. Now, you play it back to me."

Again I tried to repeat his words and quickly assure him I would
care for him. But once again he cut me off: "Get the army and the
blackness birgade [*sic*]. You know the number. Tell them *Tyrone* is
waiting; the one with the crack and the secrets popping out. He's got
a rubber band, my man." He was practically singing the words. "He's
got the biggest rubber band this world or *any* world has ever seen,
and you know right where he's got it?"

"He's got it tied around his arm, doesn't he, Tyrone?" I asked.
The picture was obvious, and terrifying, and exasperating.

"Got it tied around both his arms, my man, and both his *lives*.
Now, don't you forget. Prove you can remember what I told you.
Nobody who doesn't remember would know the old black cat when
it runs in front of him, my man. You come over now and get the kid
with the biggest rubber band the world's ever seen. This world, that
world, inside world, outside world . . . hold that phone tight as you
can, otherwise you're going to *fly* away. Fly away, fly away, fly away
with the pilot. Now, then, how 'bout you telling your old friend
Tyrone one big juicy secret."

"Tell me where you are and I'll tell you a secret." Wise or not,
that was my response.

"I'm in *heaven*, my man. That's what you call a secret? You have
failed me, my man. That ain't no secret, that's a whisper. A nothing
old whisper. Ain't you got no imagination? Hell no, you don't. No
soldiers or sailors got no imagination."

"*Where are you?*" I screamed into the phone.

"In the middle of the world where I shouldn't be, 'cause children
aren't allowed here. Wanna hear a secret? The secret is ain't nobody
nowhere got secrets no more. The secrets are all gone. *That's* the secret. You want to play that back for me, my man, the part about the
. . . the . . . what you call them again?"

"Secrets."

"There you go, my man. That's the word I been looking for. Hey,
you been one helluva help, you know that. Don't need those sailors
no more. My man, I am going up to eighty million feet where there's
so much light you couldn't see nothing. . . ."

At this point he dropped the phone. I heard a clanging sound, but
the phone did not go dead.

Two friends of Tyrone's found him walking the streets near his
school. He had not attended classes that morning. It was the first

time in years he had been absent. He was taken to an emergency
room of a nearby hospital. Later that day I asked a young psychiatrist, Peter Swindin, to take charge of his case. For four weeks
Tyrone uttered nothing coherent to anyone. Still, the psychiatrist,
and some of the rest of us, stuck it out with him. We visited him
constantly, wholly prepared for an hour of complete silence or jib-
berish. And then, as we had hoped, the old Tyrone Morgan began to
reappear. One could tell by his look that he was improving. The
storm had passed. We spoke on and off for several weeks, although
technically he was under the care of Dr. Swindin, a wonderfully patient and sensitive physician. Tyrone good-naturedly called him his
skull doctor. At the end of one of our visits, Tyrone asked, "You
keep deep dark secrets, Thomas Cottle?"

"A few, I suppose." My response was meek. I feared that he might
fall back into it again, whatever "it" was. Moreover, I had grown to
despise that word, "secret."

"Me, too," Tyrone was saying, recognizing my nervousness. "I got
'em. Everybody's got 'em, you know. You *got* to have some. You
'member our conversation that one time?"

"Very well."

"You remember good. So do I. I think too good. Too much stuff
was coming in and staying in. I'm ready to start making up some
Christmas presents now."

I found his metaphor perfect. "For Dr. Swindin?" I asked.

"I think he looks like he could use some nice presents, don't you
think so?"

I obviously looked very pleased.

"Makes you feel good, don't it?" Tyrone said. His face was expres-
sionless. "I got a secret for you, Thomas Cottle," he said quietly, his
eyes scanning the floor. "Bad as she was, with all her secrets and her
badness, I wish I had my old lady with me now. I'd take her as a present, you know. What the hell, I been through this thing with the
rest of you guys. I could use a little Christmas present myself!"

NINE

Breakdown, Hospitalization, and Suicide

We open this chapter by reiterating a point. We are not attempting to suggest that the cases and accounts presented in this book may readily be generalized to the majority of all people. No one is intimating that accounts of this type could be selected randomly from a sample of families or young people. In particular, no one is suggesting that incest, drug taking, physical abuse, even marital separation is common practice. Indeed we are not seeking to determine how frequently these various behavioral patterns emerge. Instead, our focus is on a sample of children's secrets, their content, and importantly, the ramifications of preserving secrets for the young person. It is in this context that whatever generalizations we may make must be considered.

More precisely, what *is* commonplace is the holding of secrets. What *is* a common occurrence is the struggle within a young person to understand what certain forms of behavior and feelings may mean when, for various reasons, children are no longer free to explore these experiences and feelings with other people. At one time or another, all of us deal with the sort of psychological twistings and untwistings we discussed in the preceding chapter. All of us wonder about our individual development, our day-by-day experience, our changing moods and attitudes. It is a continual process, moreover, this wondering and self-reflecting. It is a quiet process, too, in that we share relatively little of it with others, even when we engage in forms of psychotherapy. That which we choose to tell of our personal secrets is not only quantitatively meager, it is also qualitatively distinguished from the material we keep from others as secrets. This is the point we have advanced explicitly and implicitly throughout our exploration: namely, a great deal of our ruminations about ourselves go on in our inner world consciously, deliberately, even systematically. They are themselves preserved and protected by the fact that no one can coerce us into revealing them. At times, it would appear that we are desirous of divulging some of these inner renderings, our problems and our temporary solutions. At least we may share snatches of the problems and solutions if only to learn whether others resemble us in engaging in these twistings and untwistings. But in the main, much of what we concern ourselves with in terms of keeping secrets has to do with our involvement in our own inner workings.

The children presented in this book, however, face an additional burden, one that adds extra weight to the normal acts of self-discovery and personal wonderment. Manifestly, this additional burden is the obligation to keep secret the personal problem of a family member. The obligation is usually couched in terms of (potential) family shame, outright disgrace, or even personal ruination. But notice that we use the word "manifestly," for there is a latent and more telling aspect, perhaps, to the matter of keeping family secrets. This would be that the secret kept by the child ramifies in the child's own personal ruminations, his or her psychological twistings and untwistings, or more generally in the child's work of determining what he or she is all about.

We may summarize the last few sentences by noting that family secrets ramify in the child's private or inner workshop, that part of the mind, if the reader will tolerate yet another metaphor, where the child "crafts" his or her identity. Clearly, the concept and actuality of identity, as Erik Erikson has so brilliantly revealed, is central to the continuous emergence of the person, no matter what that person's age. We are constantly changing while simultaneously preserving bits of ourselves. Thus, when we seek to determine who we are, we reach the inevitable conclusion that we are partly what we seem now, partly what we believe and feel we were, and partly what we believe and feel we will be in the future, as we imagine and project this future to be. All of this appears to be an existential given; the processes of personality development, identity, evolution could not be completed or shaped in the first few moments or years of life. But again, the matter of *who* I am is not precisely the point we wish to make. More exactly, let us suggest that much of the process of keeping secrets has to do with the issue of *what* I am. Our culture and our age, the cult and apotheosis of the individual, individuation, and individualism, only naturally conditions not merely psychologists and psychoanalysts but each of us to be concerned if not obsessed with the question of who am I. Even more, a philosophy of individualism would influence our decision to judge who we are at conscious or even unconscious levels, and to base our determinations partly on the "who-ness" of other individuals. Only naturally, then, do we (individually) become personifications of imitation and personal repetition as we strive to advance our reflections on our "who-ness."

David Riesman anticipated these deeply psychological processes in his books *Individualism Reconsidered* and *The Lonely Crowd*, especially in the latter where he wrote, in the late 1940s, of the "other-directed" individual, the person armed with exquisitely honed social antennae scanning the world to pick up information to be used in shaping or evaluating his or her own life. Needless to say, the other-directed person, the individual who relies, almost paradoxically, on other people's lives to determine his or her own *private, internal, psychological* individuality, hardly could be called free, much less liberated—that overworked term. If Freud's classical description of the neurotic revealed a person tortured by the conflict of forces extant within his or her own mind, the other-directed spirit seems to us tortured by the forces consciously brought into the mind (internalized) through these overworked antennae which day and night sweep the social environment gathering clues on how to lead one's life and find one's salvation.

We notice in other-directedness, however, that whereas the process seemed sociological in nature, that is, the antennae were aimed at social facts and values, public customs, and life-styles, the actual incorporation of the information as well as the personal *use* to which the information was put proceeded at a psychological level; the internal twistings and untwistings were all aimed, observers contended, at figuring out who we are. In time, "who-ness" came to be associated with humanness. We aren't *whats*, we protested, we're *whos*. Thus, any influence of a sociological, anthropological, even theological nature had to be transformed into the stuff of psychological who-ness. One dealt with one's God, one's religion, one's labor union, in terms of what these "things" meant for the shaping of one's personal identity, one's glorious who-ness. Here again we find the key term: the interest in *self* and, not surprisingly, *self-interest*. For surely American culture is undyingly committed to economic and social growth, which in personal terms means devotion to self-interest. Furthermore, or is it in consequence, corporations, industries, religious groups, universities, everyone has become involved with his or her personal identity, his or her who-ness. Much of the last decade's work in America could be viewed as people turning inward, at personal as well as collective levels, hoping to determine their identities. Sadly, many groups and individuals settle for *image*, or *persona*, and label their *product* identity. Yet whatever they do, and irrespective of how they do it, their personal work is defined as "who-ness"; "who-ness" enterprises tend to counteract, we are told, the alienation, bureaucratization, dehumanization of contemporary culture.

In fact, the enormous concern with who-ness, and the acts associated with determining who-ness, which only naturally become industrialized and bureaucratized, were overwhelming people and turning people into the very things they tried so hard not to be: namely, things. For in the end, the process of who-ness, no matter how eloquently the few lofty theorists wrote about it, was not a matter of who-ness at all: It was really a social phenomenon, an industry, a gigantic cultural process which overwhelmed people in public schools, offices, churches, hospitals, law courts, stadiums, airplanes, everywhere. The source of the psychological twistings and untwistings was the outside world, the public world of everyone else, and hence the final product—and when industrialization and bureaucratization take hold even of delicate psychological processes there must be a product —will then be presented back into the public world.

There is an old joke about a tin of sardines that becomes the unit of bartering, one buyer to the next. Bought by one man at three dollars, it sells to the next at four. This man then sells at five dollars to the next man, who makes a special deal with his friend and sells at six. On and on it goes until one man, having purchased the tin at twelve dollars, prepares to eat the sardines, which by now, of course, are rancid and wholly inedible. Infuriated, he calls the man who sold him the tin and complains angrily. The seller, however, replies, "Idiot! Those sardines aren't for eating, they're for selling!"

The same point could be made about the public use or display of what appears to be genuinely personal and individual experience. One performs an action or undertakes a project not merely for the intrinsic gratification offered by that action or project but because of some final and greater reward, namely, the public utility of it. One travels to Europe not for the experience of the journey, but so that others may hear of one's travels. It is not necessarily the need for social status that one necessarily craves, in this case the public recognition of financial success that allows one to travel abroad. It may be this feature of public who-ness that remains salient to the individual, but something of a more general nature should be noted. The desire to travel so that one may tell of one's adventures implies that the experience of traveling remains insufficient, or lacking. Furthermore, the public communications following the trip indicate that the trip must have some public reverberations. It must be put back into the public context; it must act as *product*.

The living of the single life has become another public industry; all humanity, seemingly, is part of some worldwide stock exchange. Our very identities represent our shares in a public corporation. Eventually our manifestly individual, idiosyncratic efforts and actions must find their way back into this public trust (the trust in the public), which they do through our revelations, divulgences, communications. If the individual is distrusted and made the object of scorn, as he or she is in institutions running on the current of publicness, then the quiet or shy person is also the object of ridicule. The quiet person must be deemed anomalous, deviant, even pathological, because he or she stands as a danger to the public trust, the worldwide industry of personal identity formation. The quiet person keeps secrets, and secrets are the basis of social and personal revolution. Hold a secret in our society and one is called a conspirator or is seen as treasonous. The one with secrets, in other words, does not *buy* into the public corporation. He or she does not prescribe to the notion that all experiences contain an ultimate value, and hence mean something to the individual strictly in terms of serving as means to some greater end. Secret keepers are takers; they take from the corporation of culture and give back nothing in return. They neither pay their dues nor present enough of themselves so that others may collect information on them. And we need information on people in order to categorize and ultimately neutralize them. How can we control a person whose major revelation to us is that there is much he or she will *not* reveal? How can we know if our punishment is taking hold if a child refuses to cry? How do we know if a change in a child's behavior, a change made in accordance with *our* demands and rituals, has come about as a genuine act of the will, or has been enacted merely to please us? For that matter, how do we know whether any action of a secret keeper is genuine!

At this point in our discussion, the world of adolescents becomes particularly relevant. The adolescent could be said to live on the edge of fixing his or her identity to the structure and form of both

the inner and outer worlds. That is, adolescence *appears* to be a period when a person may choose which path in life to pursue: the one
set down by the inner and private world or the one set down by the
outer and public world. And do not adolescents speak in just these
terms? Do they not attribute genuineness, authenticity, personal control, and self-determination to the inner world, and inauthenticity,
habit, boredom, loss of self to the outer world? Many adolescents
labor hard at trying to decide whether or not buying shares in that
public trust is worth it, even though they also appear to have accepted membership in the public trust of adolescence the moment it
was offered to them. Adolescence is a period when people struggle
mightily with psychological twistings and untwistings, and attempt
to understand and feel the press of the twistings of the public world:
their culture, society, and community. Parenthetically, the preoccupation with that word "community" may imply a size and magnitude of society beyond which people refuse to become committed.

Granted, adolescents, as we have repeatedly noted, are forever involved with public transactions. Much of what adults would call the
form of intimate behavior is passed on to others when one is young.
But that we rarely deal with young people's interior worlds, except in
psychotherapy, hardly means that adolescents are not "at work"
within their interior selves. It also does not mean that adolescents refuse to work at the vital problem of *what* they are, not only *who*
they are relative to "significant others," as George Herbert Mead
called them. I use the phrase "*what* they are," or personal "what-
ness," to remind us of that aspect of self-reflection and personal de-
termination involving the individual alone. That is, the conglomeration of personal information and feeling that the individual em-
ploys in attempting to work out the meaning of being alive and
being dead, being sane and insane, being the agent of action or the
object of another's action, being a person or a thing. These are the
fundamental features of what-ness, the questions with which philosophers and theologians, but only rarely social scientists, present us.
The struggle over human what-ness is precisely the philosophical
struggle in which all human beings engage. *Who* we are, in great
measure, is that part of ourselves we not only derive from the exterior world but, importantly, present back to the exterior world. *What*
we are may be derived from our dealings as public as well as private
persons, but what-ness is not necessarily poured back into the public
trust. What we are we keep for ourselves; it is our mystery, our
unexpressed or unannounced or inchoate definitions of ourselves, our
secret. It is also the unstated results of our self-observations. Not so

strangely, our what-ness often stands opposed to our who-ness. But again, the point to stress is the degree to which we hold the matter of what we are to ourselves, as secrets, as messages that might well be sent out into the public world but never are.

Another way of illustrating the distinction between who we are and what we are is to raise the familiar distinction between appearance and reality. We are constantly alert to those things that actually are, and those things that only appear to be. When we become preoccupied with appearance or images, we remind ourselves that we are suspending reality. We say, "Amazing, the things I do to try to convince myself I'm happy." The expression means that while we work hard at something, we recognize we are tricking ourselves. At some point, in other words, we have made a pact with ourselves to suspend reality. We *know* that if we lead our lives in a certain fashion we won't have to reflect on our finitude. Our work, life-style, or ambition will block out our fear of dying, or even the fact that we will die. So we suspend reality and carry on *as if* the inevitable were not inevitable. If we do not lie to ourselves, then we establish schemes by which reality becomes transformed into mere images of reality. The recognition and genuine confrontation of the pact with ourselves to suspend reality is part of our what-ness; it represents one of those self-observational products, one of those pieces of datum we collect during our "watch on ourselves." It is one of our living secrets, as well as one of the underlying reasons we become fascinated by as well as implicated in myths.

What we have seen in most of the accounts presented thus far are children trapped, in a manner of speaking, by personal and family myths. Utterly real in their content and impact, the myth illustrates the type of pact with oneself that children and adults alike must underwrite. The parent tells the child, "Don't breathe a word of this to anyone." In consequence, the child leads his or her life *as if* the information did not exist, *as if* the parent were telling the truth, *as if* things were as they seem. The deceit, however, as we now have heard in numerous accounts, along with the guilt, remorse, or confusion, remains inside and becomes part of the child's what-ness. The child must deal with this new twist of reality, the secret, as part of his or her philosophical contemplations. While the pain connected with the secret, or the actual events one has experienced, may be repressed, ushered into realms of the unconscious so that the child can recall neither the event nor the pain, at some (philosophical) level, the child must realize that a "decision" to repress something has been made. The action of the repression or forgetting must be recorded so that the child recognizes that to some degree, a piece of reality has been suspended. Something, then, about the way the child leads his or her life must seem inauthentic. The inauthenticity, furthermore, becomes part of the mythification of events and experiences, but typically a part the child keeps secret.

Another aspect of the mythification of events is noted in the distinction between what a person *feels* himself or herself to be, and what he or she actually *presents* to others. By definition, social behavior is an act; people act in concert so that a minimal degree of social order may be maintained. There is only minimal communication when two people speak at once. When one person wishes to speak but waits to hear another person, one, in a sense, is acting. The acting makes listening and hence communication possible. (Some people communicate the fact they are acting by showing they do not listen. In a sense, this is a redundant gesture: acting to show one is acting.) The recognition of public acting is also part of the mythification of human interaction. People contemplate their own and others' acting because they are struck by the differentiation between appearance and reality. We know when we present a false self to another. The children in this book stand out, we might say, in special relief precisely because they recognize the distinction between appearance and reality. It is for this reason, moreover, that we categorize the issues treated in this volume in terms of myths.

To repeat, as adolescents "study" the demands and properties of their inner world and the public corporation known as society, they become keenly aware, possibly for the first time in their lives, of the distinctions between appearance and reality, yet treat the distinctions as if they applied directly to them. In this regard, we note that adolescents typically condemn the use of compromise. A person must not *sell* out; people must be true *only* to themselves. Adolescents despise adults who lie, parents who demand honesty but cheat on their income-tax returns. Granted, adolescence is a time when the idealization of adults formed during childhood begins to crack, or gives way altogether. Most of these idealizations are connected with parents. The very concept of idealization derives from the child's relationship with his or her parents. During adolescence, however, the child begins to recognize that much of life is a sham. Too many dreams and fantasies, the child learns, will not become reality; appearance and reality are often in conflict, and compromise is inevitable. For these reasons, myth is hardly a stranger to the adolescent mind. Myths about a host of things occur to children and adolescents as they deal with the twistings and untwistings of their inner and outer world experiences.

Yet some children, particularly those we have dealt with in this study, encounter myths in discreet and explicit fashion. Act *as if* you believe this, they are instructed. Or *pretend* you didn't see this or don't know that. Live as if you were living in a myth; live as a myth, which brings us to the crucial point. The children whose words we have recounted have been asked to exist in a mythic realm. Because of the demand for secrecy, their very contemplations of reality and fantasy, their intellectual and affective involvements with myth, are being clouded by the mythic state of their own existence. In a sense, these children have become mythic beings contemplating their "mythic-ness." Granted, "mythic-ness" is hardly a poetic word; still it captures the sense of inauthenticity evident in many of the young people's accounts.

We mentioned earlier that one aspect of the process of contemplating one's what-ness involves the self acting as observer. In the process of keeping aspects of family life secret, children give the impression of watching themselves watching themselves. Their recognition, moreover, of the mythic nature of their social (family) and personal worlds results in the "establishment" of still another observer of the self. This is the observer who stands guard on the observer. Irrespective of how this double watch on themselves affects their actual behavior or the substance of their personal reflections, the fact is that children recognize how removed they are from living reality. Again and again they allude to the disingenuous nature of living, the phoniness, the acting quality of their lives, all of which suggests that the myths they are obliged to uphold influence their every action and thought. In the case of the children presented in this and the previous chapter, living as if one were caught up in the process of mythification must cause them to doubt their sanity. The facts, after all, that they must keep secret fall directly in the center of the myth of normalcy.

The account of the young woman that follows illustrates some of these points. But before turning to it, one final comment might be offered.

In the past few pages, I have repeatedly used the word "recognize" to emphasize the notion that adolescents engage in philosophical contemplations about themselves, their what-ness. The act of safeguarding secrets, living within a mythic shroud, underscores the self-reflective nature of adolescence. The terms "self-awareness" and "personal observation" also are highlighted by the concept of recognition. At some level, adolescents remain *aware* of their observations. Granted, adolescence remains a time of self-preoccupation, but part of the preoccupation is nothing short of research. The adolescent wants to know *what* he or she is. What is he or she composed of, what makes him or her tick, as the expression goes, an expression, incidentally, suggesting the imagined clocklike nature of the human apparatus. But no, it is not the clocklike nature of the human apparatus but human life that intrigues and dazzles the adolescent, and often consumes his or her thoughts.

Human life means contemplating one's being, one's "what-ness," and remaining aware of the processes that constitute self-preoccupation. If the accounts reported in this book provide us some clues to the reactions of children obliged to live in the so-called mythic state of secret keeping, they also reveal the degree to which young people *recognize* the properties of this mythic state, and the manner in which they cope, intellectually and emotionally, with it. When we allege that the accounts demonstrate a high degree of self-awareness, we base this allegation not only on our examination of the contents of the accounts but on our examination of the quality of *contemplation* and personal *reflection* that the accounts imply. Furthermore, while the substance of the accounts may not overlap with our own experiences, the self-observational and reflective nature noted in the accounts is something we do recognize. Each of us engages in these philosophical contemplations about ourselves, as well as the nature of our being, real and imagined, literal and mythic. We, too, recognize the tension experienced in attempting to tell *our* stories when these stories incorporate items we have consciously chosen to keep secret. We also recognize an existential tension resulting from a need to keep various portions of our life story to ourselves for fear that in telling these stories, we may destroy genuine aspects of our human nature. That is, we recognize that in recounting our stories, we make public what we may prefer to keep secret, and thereby produce myth from reality, reality from myth.

In telling our stories, especially ones involving our secrets (and secret lives), we recognize the density and richness of our inner world and how this density and richness are reduced when we impart some measure of them. We recognize, too, that in revealing mere portions of our inner selves, we become less true to ourselves. The entirety of our inner selves can never be revealed—no matter how intense our desire for revelation—and hence, revelation only perpetuates aspects of the myth of being, the mythic state of secret keeping about which our secret contemplations are focused.

In a word, our response to the children's accounts necessarily evokes in us our own encounters not only with secrets but with the secretive nature of human contemplations of living and dying, being and non-being, sanity and insanity, the private and the public, the real and unreal. I suspect, moreover, that my own response to the children is not unique. Surely I am not alone in wanting to tell them some secrets I, too, have safeguarded, while feeling simultaneously that I was holding more tightly to other secrets than I ever had before in my life. The desire to tell our stories strains against its opposite desire, namely, to safeguard these very same stories (and secrets) and thereby keep to (and for) ourselves that which we recognize as our unique self, the part we never offer up for display, advertisement, observation, or, heaven forbid, comparison.

ANGELA MARSH

The story of Angela Marsh, a beautiful sixteen-year-old girl from a well-to-do East Coast family, unraveled in quite a surprising manner. Harold Marsh had died before I met the family, leaving two beautiful daughters and a grief-stricken wife. A successful corporation executive, Mr. Marsh had died suddenly after a brief illness I assumed to be a heart attack. He was forty-six years old. His wife, Marlene, was five years younger, and, as an attractive, intelligent person, there seemed little doubt that she would remarry. Her friends encouraged her in this direction, and as time passed, her daughters, too, saw the value of a second marriage. Marlene, however, was in no hurry. Whereas she recognized only too well that her husband was dead, his life with her had not yet seemed to completely pass away.

Fortunately, the Marshes felt only a slight financial tremor when Harold died. His insurance policies and various investments combined to yield a sizable income. Marlene and the children had heard him say, "You won't have to worry," so many times they had grown numb to the message. Now with his passing, they discovered that in economic terms, in fact they did not have to worry. Essentially they would carry on as before. Marlene kept the house and her own car but sold her husband's car. She met with her husband's accountant to arrange all business affairs, and convinced there would be more than ample funds to put both girls through college, she began looking about for part-time employment. Once content to lead the life of a suburban housewife, she now felt the role empty, though not odious. She made certain to be at home when her daughters returned from school, and let them know she was more than eager to do things with them. The girls had to understand, she said, that they had lost only one parent.

In the beginning of my friendship with "the ladies," Marlene's term for the family, my conversations dwelled on a host of topics, none of them, however, generating much interest. Two or three minutes and we would move on to something else. The pattern held for the daughters as well. Even without mentioning it, all of us knew why we danced about together: The point was to avoid mention of a dead father and husband. Reminders of him were ubiquitous in the form of photographs, his favorite books and framed prints on the walls, his easy chair near the window, even a quilt that had been passed down to him by his mother. Yet just as the physical objects almost screamed his name, I found myself swept up in "the ladies'" technique of speaking only obliquely about him. Then again, I argued with myself trying to quell my own impatience and curiosity, who is to say how one best handles mourning? Who is to say that the "proper" thing to do is talk about the deceased? Who is to define what constitutes "normal" reactions to the loss of a father or husband? Some people simply don't put memories and feelings aside so readily. Besides, our culture might do better thinking of mourners in terms of their sensitivity and vulnerability rather than their psychopathology and obsessions. As I say, I argued with myself, but I remained impatient and curious. I did not believe secret information was being withheld from me. Nor did I have any reason to assume anything of a complicated or mysterious nature hovered about Harold Marsh's death. Imagine my surprise, therefore, when Angela, claiming she could no longer contain her secret, practically exploded one day with the news that her father wasn't dead at all:

"You didn't go to the funeral, did you? You never saw his body, right? You didn't even talk to anybody who saw him dead. In fact, *you* were the one who told me you were sort of surprised my sister and my mother and me talked so little about him. So you don't even know what we *did* see or hear, or *what* happened. I thought that since you keep coming here to listen to us talk about nothing most of the time, you deserved the truth. I really don't think I would have told you this if you asked, but you never asked, and you must have wanted to. You *must* have."

"Oh, I did," I laughingly conceded.

"I know. So here's the thing. My father *left* about a year and a half ago. He didn't die. One night, well, it really wasn't in the night, it was like early in the morning when it was still dark, I was awakened by some noise. I didn't know what it was, but it seemed like it was coming from the attic, which was strange because there's not too much going on up there. It's hard to get there, and in the winter, this was February, near his birthday, it's so cold, no one would be stupid enough to go up there, especially at five o'clock in the morning. So I thought, I'm going crazy 'cause there can't be anyone in the attic. Then the noise came again like some furniture falling down, which also meant I was going crazy since there isn't any furniture up there. All the stuff we keep in storage is in a closet in the basement. You have to work to get up to the attic; you have to go up these narrow stairs and everything. So I thought, Angela, you are definitely going crazy now.

"Then I thought, what if it's a burglar? Maybe he's up there . . . Angela, you're going out of your mind again. How could a burglar get up there without waking everybody up? And second of all, why would anyone even *want* to go up there? If you wanted to steal something, you'd steal stuff on the first floor. And third of all—you can see how my mind works—you'd have to be somebody who knows the house well to know where the stairs to the attic are. So what did brave Angela do? She got out of bed and went downstairs to get her ski parka. Then I went back upstairs to the attic closet. It was so dark I practically killed myself—not really, but you know what I mean. I mean, I didn't even hurt myself; you think you're going to bump into everything but you don't. When I got to the attic stairs, I decided I'd listen a little more and find out what was happening. So I crouched down and listened. It was pitch-dark. Whoever was up there not only didn't turn on the light, he didn't even have a flashlight. Then, and don't ask me why I did this, I called up: 'Daddy, is that you?' And it was. He wanted to know if he woke me up. I was so relieved I began to laugh. That was the first time I realized I'd been so scared I actually started to sweat. I asked him what he was doing and he said he couldn't sleep so he thought he'd sort of work around up there. He said he hadn't been up there in ages so he was looking around. I asked him if he was dressed and he said he was, otherwise he'd have frozen up there a long time ago. Then he said I should go back to sleep 'cause he was coming down. He'd just found a few old things, like some old stool and some rope and an old laundry basket, which was practically rotten. 'Haven't found any money.' I remember him saying that. He promised if he found money he'd give it to me; told me he'd put it under my pillow. I was supposed to go back to sleep and look under my pillow in the morning and see if it was there, like with the tooth fairy, which I actually believed in until I was eight years old. I must have been a slightly crazy child, too.

"That's all there was to it, at least the part with the attic. The next morning I looked under my pillow and sure enough there was a couple of dollars. They were crumpled up to make them look old. I knew he didn't really find them in the attic. He only wanted to make me think he did. I remember I went to his room to see him but he was gone. It seemed a little early to go to work, but I thought, maybe because he'd been up all night he wanted to get an early start. Later that night my mother told me and my sister he'd gone away and probably wouldn't come back. That's why he'd left so early. He might have even left in the middle of the night, she said. I didn't say anything about the attic. I thought maybe she'd be mad at me if I did. She kept saying you'll have nice memories of him; didn't he kiss you good night? I said yes, but I still didn't want her to know I talked with him. I also didn't say anything about the money. This is a while ago so I don't remember exactly. I mean, I *know* the part about the attic is perfect. I'll never forget that part because I was so scared in the beginning and then felt so relieved I started to laugh. I never understood too well about why he went away, but my mother made us feel we shouldn't ask questions about it, and for sure we weren't supposed to talk about it to anyone, and I mean *anyone!* *That* part she made very clear. In fact, that's where the big lie, like I call it, started.

"I remember her saying, we have a right to be sad about him leaving, but we also had to remember it reflects on us. That's what she kept saying: It reflects on us. People will wonder about *us*. *We* must have made him unhappy and that's why he went away. That's what she said. It reflected on us and we weren't supposed to tell. Only that he died. It was very sudden and only the family would go to the funeral. That way nobody would know what happened. It's like I told you: *You* never saw the body. Nobody ever saw him dead because he *wasn't* dead. It *seems* like he's dead because he's not here, but the phone could ring anytime, or a letter could come and there he'd be. We all know it isn't likely, but it *could* happen. Listen, after that craziness with the attic, *anything* could happen. Nothing in the history of the world could have been *that* crazy. I'll tell you more about it sometime, but you have to promise you won't tell anybody what I said, especially my mother and sister. My mother's own mother doesn't even know the truth. She thinks he's dead, too. She's still mad she wasn't invited to the funeral. My mother didn't even tell her he wasn't here anymore, I mean that he was dead—wink, wink—until a couple of days after. That's how much she worried about how it *reflected* on all of us. She keeps saying it's going to reflect on us the rest of our lives if people find out. It's even worse now because now people would not only find out the truth, they'd realize we'd been lying all these years. Well, not really lying, just sort of keeping our secret from everybody. Crazy, isn't it? It *must* sound crazy to you!"

My response to Angela Marsh was one of utter belief and credulity. Of course I denied to the rafters her references to craziness. Unusual happenings like fathers routing around in cold attics at five in the morning only naturally would make one believe craziness was near at hand, if indeed the world wasn't coming to an end. And of course I would keep her secret. It would make my relationship with Mrs. Marsh and Angela's older sister, Julia, a trifle cumbersome, but it wasn't the first time, as this book clearly documents, that I've kept a few rather precious secrets myself from family members good enough to submit to my interviewing. But even this wasn't the pressing matter. Far more serious was my lingering impression of this one conversation. For one of the few times in my work, I totally disbelieved Angela's story. Not a shred of it seemed genuine, although given my own promise of secrecy, it would be difficult to prove or disprove any of it. I dared not ask anyone about the matter. If two people in the family said he was dead, and one claimed he disappeared one morning after doing heaven knows what the previous night in a freezing attic, who was I to question anyone! Still, everything about Angela's account seemed false, as well as bizarre. Most disconcerting about the account was the utterly casual, almost jovial manner in which this presumably tragic event was recounted. It was not a burglar, it was her father. It *was* crazy, just as Angela said. As I thought of it, she used that word too frequently. By the end of the account, she seemed to be daring me to call *her* crazy. Was there, I wondered, a secret message embedded in the secret: Was she wishing me to say, "Angela, I love you and doubt every single word I've just heard? So now suppose you tell me the real truth!"

Apart from her casual tone, the timing of the events, as she recounted them, also seemed out of line with the chronology I had reconstructed. To listen to Angela was to believe that her father's death, or abandonment, had taken place not a year and a half before, but years before. Then there was the concentration on peculiar, almost incongruous details, which came across with special vividness and truth. The objects her father located in the attic, the old stool, laundry basket, and rope, surely they were objects one finds in most attics, but why had Angela remembered them? Or the episode of putting on her ski parka: a white ski parka as I now remember it. Was this an innocuous memory or a significant one? Other aspects of the story, too, disturbed me, but let me mention only one.

When I think back on that late afternoon conversation with Angela at the dining room table, where we sat separated by a half-completed jigsaw puzzle of seemingly a billion pieces, I recall several references not only to her craziness but to her mind figuring out something. Not only was she eager for me to believe her story, visualize the event in vivid detail, but she wanted in addition for me to derive some sense of the way her mind operated. She wished, in other words, to lay out for me the step-by-step processes that were her thoughts, impressions, and interpretations. I had to be able to *see* everything in her mind. Granted, this is not uncommon behavior among young people telling a treasured secret. Once the secret material is broached, children often feel compelled to cleanse themselves of it, which means they first reveal the secret and then attempt to display the secret recesses of the mind where the secret has been safeguarded all these years. So the vividness and the public demonstration of thought processes made sense in this one context.

In contrast, her account also had the ring of the person in the witness booth proceeding so cautiously and meticulously that everybody recognizes the witness is lying, however eloquently, between his or her teeth. It is utterly obvious, in other words, that the witness has fabricated a story which he or she believes in with such intensity that one is afraid to call the revelation an act, much less a sham.

But why share these personal ruminations with the reader? I do it not to elucidate the action I took upon hearing Angela's response. Instead, I offer the remarks first, to demonstrate the complexity of the relationship one establishes with families in the process of undertaking certain research work, and second, to outline the paths one is obliged to follow when family secrets and myths begin to assume prominence. The reader must remember that my role with these families is not one of a psychotherapist. Essentially I try to remain a history taker, a chronicler of facts and stories, myths, and secrets. Nothing that transpires in these interview-conversations, however, precludes the possibility of the researcher serving in some advocacy capacity. Surely the family is to be protected, helped if help is required. Few of us would stand idly by at the sight of children in turmoil or outright pain. But what, precisely, does one do in the face of conflicting accounts about the most serious matter confronting a family when one has been sworn to secrecy? The research itself provokes vexing ethical questions, but most of these arise out of real human contexts, not out of the safe confines of abstract or hypothetical argument. Proper or improper, I decided to hunt down the grave of Harold Clogins Marsh, if in fact there was one. I did this, moreover, without revealing my intentions to anyone. At the same time I decided that if my discoveries were worth sharing, only Angela would learn of them.

As it happens, tracing down deaths, funerals, burial sites turns out to be one of life's more distasteful but uncomplicated adventures, as journalists and detectives well know. Within a month of hardly intensive investigation, I found the death notification and burial plot of Mr. Marsh. The grave was well attended; the headstone, made of smooth granite, had recently been polished. There was no mistake; Angela Marsh's father was dead, and had been dead for *seven* years, which meant that Angela was nine when he died. My information also indicated that he died from natural causes, a familiar term as we know, but a particularly sad one when the deceased is four years short of his fiftieth birthday.

It was now three months since my talk with Angela Marsh, who by now, I might mention, seemed more relaxed in my presence than ever before. She even began to look forward to my visits, possibly because she believed she had nothing else to hide from me. If I had become a detective in my eyes, I must have seemed a peripatetic minister in hers. But if she was at peace with my questions and small talk, I was growing increasingly frustrated with our chats, not that I was surprised that she never again mentioned the story of her father and the attic. By this point in my work I was becoming a trifle more sophisticated about the behavior of secret tellers. Young people would recount their secrets, and then, after somehow righting themselves from the impact of their own revelations, they would confront me in subsequent visits with an air of innocence and naïveté as though nothing had *ever* transpired between us. It's not surprising that I would often associate this behavior to the action of lovers meeting on the street the morning after a tryst discussing the price of toothpaste as though they hardly knew one another. Indeed, the clear-cut quality of intimacy, despite all verbal protestations or behavioral nonchalance, becomes one of the major reasons a researcher is loath to comment on the genuineness of the intimate scene, the secret in this case. With Angela Marsh, however, I could no longer contain myself.

Five months after our fateful conversation, I shocked her, probably intentionally, with a simple request. "Angela," I began innocently,
"let's pay a visit to the attic."

It is not an exaggeration to say that Angela looked as if she had
been shot. Her body shook, and her limbs seemed to become rigid.
Color drained from her face and hands. She bolted up out of her
chair, fury in her eyes. She didn't speak to me, she screamed:

"You didn't believe me. I told you the truth and you didn't believe me. You *never* believed me. You sat there listening and I
believed you. You're a liar, a liar, and I despise you. I hate and despise you because you listened and made me think you believed me
and you didn't." Again and again she repeated the words, or words to
this effect. What would she do, I wondered, if she knew that I had
undertaken those little investigations and learned the truth of her father's death? I dreaded to find out her reaction. I waited, now
stricken myself, for her to throw me out of the house, but she never
did. She just kept on about how she thought I had believed her.

Suddenly the rigidity in her body vanished and she slumped back
into the chair and wept like a baby. Her shoulders shook, her face
was flushed, and the sobs came on, uncontrollable paroxysms. When
I put my arm around her, she seemed comforted, although it was
minutes before she could regain her composure. When at last she
lifted her head, I could see her face and sleeves drenched in tears.
Her eyes seemed smaller, and sadder.

Neither of us spoke. I stared at her, she looked forward, her eyes
moving not at all, into that chasm people must see at moments of
grief and despair. Then, without warning, Angela rose and beckoned
me to follow her. She mumbled the one word, "Okay," in a tone of
resignation that meant, all right, I'll confess everything. We as-
cended the stairs, her legs pulling at each step as though she weren't
going to make it to the top. At the second-floor landing she pointed
to a barely noticeable door built to make people think it was part of
a tall cupboard. "In there," she whispered. I opened the door and
saw the stairs leading to the attic.

"Will you come?" I asked timidly, my shame so intense I no
longer knew what I was doing.

"All right" came her reply.

We must have made a humorous sight, the two of us sitting up in
that lugubrious attic surrounded by insulation, and barely able to see
one another. The scene made her grin. The attic was utterly bare. If
there had been old objects up here once, someone had taken them
away. I was impressed by both the length and height of the space. I

remember thinking how such a room could be converted into a splendid ballet studio, not that either of the Marsh girls was a dancer.

"You found out, didn't you?" Angela said. She was sitting on the floor cross-legged, a peculiar position I thought, given what she was forcing herself to tell.

"I know your father is dead, and that he died when you were quite young. Was it nine?"

"Nine. It could have been yesterday. I found him dead. Did you learn that, too?"

"No."

"I heard a voice, like I told you. Up here. It was cold, and he was in the attic. All that was true. We didn't talk. I did, but he didn't. There was a noise, like furniture falling over. Remember that part? Remember the ski parka, too? They were true. Like the rope and the stool and the laundry basket. The noise *was* furniture falling over. My father hung himself. He stood on a stool and hung himself. Before he did he put his pajamas in the laundry basket. I went up and saw him. I don't know what happened to me. I sort of freaked out. I came back down and started talking to him. I knew he wouldn't answer. I knew he was dead. I *knew* it, but I didn't want to know it. I mean, I didn't want to know that I knew. Then I thought, and it was like the first time I thought it, he doesn't have any clothes on. He took his clothes off, his pajamas really, and put them in an old laundry basket in the attic. He even folded them very neatly, although I could never figure out why he did *that!* Anyway, I was downstairs on the steps talking to my father, who I knew was dead, and naked. That was sort of the crazy part of it. I guess I was so busy thinking about why he was naked, I didn't think about why he did it, killed himself, I mean.

"It was very cold that night, like I told you. I kept asking him if he was cold. Of course he didn't answer me. Finally, I decided he must be very cold so I went downstairs and got my ski parka. First I thought, maybe *I* better put it on because I didn't want to catch a cold. Then I thought, maybe I should go upstairs and put it on him. I told you the whole thing was crazy, or *I'm* crazy. Anyway, I decided I'd put the parka on my father. So I went upstairs talking to him all the time, because I was getting scared, although I don't know for sure what about. I tried to get his arm in one of the sleeves. I remember it was so heavy I could barely lift it and hold the parka at the same time. So I gave up. I told him something like, it wouldn't fit him anyway so I'd just put it over his shoulders. Then I went back downstairs and talked to him some more. I kept pretending he could hear me and that he was talking back to me. I'd say, 'Oh, that's nice, Daddy, because I'm enjoying talking to you, too.' Or I'd say, 'Well, if you aren't going back to bed I'm not going back either. I'll go to bed as soon as you come down.'

"Finally I pretended that he was going to come down. He told me, I mean I pretended this, that he was going to put his pajamas on and that I shouldn't worry because he'd take my parka downstairs and stick it in the hall closet. I told him it was all right, I'd do it since I was the one who got it for him, but he said no, he'd do it. My father always got angry at us for not keeping the house neat or not hanging up our clothes. He said it was because we didn't care about our belongings. So I wanted to do something I knew he'd like. I wanted him to like me, maybe even more than he liked my sister. It *is* all crazy when you think about it. I thought I was his favorite that night. I had a special talk with him. We didn't wake my sister up, or my mother. I was the only one with him, and I sort of wanted it to go on like that for all night. I didn't like the idea I had to go back to bed but I went anyway. When I got back in bed I found a note he'd written. It just said he loved me. That's all. It said, 'I love you, love, Daddy!' Then I went to sleep, and I'd just as soon not have to think about the next morning and the days after with the police and my mother screaming and this one reporter who kept coming back and coming back to our house. Lawyers came, too, and my father's boss and his wife. It seemed like everybody was there. People would call us, like weeks later, late at night. They'd wake us up and say how sorry they were. Can you imagine? That's when my mother told us not to tell people about what happened, because it would reflect on us. She didn't want people feeling sorry for us. Maybe they'd think we were bad people and that's why he did it. So I never said anything to anyone. I only told my mother once that I heard my father, but I was afraid to tell her I talked to him. I thought maybe she'd think I could have stopped him, or maybe I should have called her. But there wasn't any reason to call her. I saw him, and while part of me pretended to talk to him—I really didn't talk out loud 'cause I knew I'd wake people up—a part of me knew that he was dead. I mean, if you saw the way his head was you'd know he was dead. I never saw my white ski parka after that. My mother wouldn't let it stay in the house. She insisted it be taken out and burned. She had my uncle burn it. The pajamas, too, and the laundry basket, everything. That's why nothing's up here anymore. I think she wanted to burn the whole house down, maybe with me in it.

"My mother doesn't blame me for what happened, but you can tell she'd like to be able to blame someone. Maybe that's because she thinks it's partly her fault. Even after all these years, she doesn't forget about it, even though we never *ever* talk about it. I think about it almost every night, not that I'm afraid it's going to happen again; I mean I *know* it can't happen again. But her not letting us talk about it makes me think like, in some magical way, maybe it could happen again. Maybe it could happen again and again in our heads since it's still supposed to be the big mystery. Even you didn't know at first when he died. We all pretend. Pretend and pretend, like we're living in a fairy tale. But I wouldn't ever dare go up to my mother and tell her it would be better if we did talk about it. I don't know *what* she's pretending. Maybe she really thinks he's alive. Maybe the whole story I told you is what she'd like to say, or maybe would say if you ever talked to her about it. I lied for her sake *and* my sake. I've lied a lot, in fact. Maybe when I lie it's really *her* lie, or it's all our lie, even though I'm the one who found out about it first. Probably that's why I keep thinking one of these days everything that happened and the way we don't talk about it is going to make me crazy. All of us might go crazy, for that matter. I probably should have woken her up. I don't know why I didn't. I probably should still wake her up. We're all walking around this house dreaming. It really is like that. We're three sleepwalkers. Three sleepwalkers afraid to even look up at the ceiling because we're afraid to think about this attic.

"You know what? I think I'm going to cry a little bit in bed tonight. You think I should look under my pillow to see if there's a note there?"

CHICO ADRIAN

The story of Jack Adrian, a machinist with an automotive firm, a man who seemed to have more personalities than money, as his mother-in-law said over and over again, is not altogether unfamiliar to psychiatrists, psychologists, and social workers. The son of a carpenter's assistant who never seemed able to pull together enough money to buy a home, Jack Adrian, as they say, came up the hard way. He lived through difficult times, fell in and out of friendships, usually because people were unable to put up with his mercurial ways one day and his abject moodiness the next. "To know old Jack," his brother once told me, "is to know a half dozen guys, a hundred, for all I can count." The mood swings also never stood him in good stead at school. Teachers were either having to reprimand him for his verbal or physical outbreaks or asking his parents about Jack's sudden quiet ways and shyness. The family was perplexed. What the boy made of his own moods is something nobody ever discerned. Either he was too angry to talk about it or he withdrew into himself.

"The guy's nuts!" That's what they would say. The teachers, principals, friends, relatives, everybody. Nuttier than a fruitcake. Here today, gone tomorrow, a natural for the loony bin. Perhaps he was a "natural" because of the daily scenes he encountered at home. His parents, apparently, were constantly fighting, at least they did when they weren't drinking. His brothers and sisters had not the slightest interest in caring for him, even though as the youngest child, he was placed in their care a part of every day. Said simply, although one hesitates to reduce a man's problems to one single issue, Jack Adrian grew up believing not only that he was unlovable but that his very being engendered distrust if not open hatred. It wasn't that people had given up on him, for that would be to suggest they once did believe in him. If the accounts of friends and relatives are correct, Jack Adrian just grew up yearning for love, but distrusting anyone who might have wanted to show him the slightest morsel of it.

The years between his sixteenth and twenty-first birthdays were shaky ones. He had quit school at fifteen. His father died when he was eighteen, leaving his mother, physically weak and exhausted from years of heavy drinking, with debts she would never be able to pay. On the trip home from the funeral she harangued against her dead husband, blaming him for the world's evils and making certain that her son Jack knew that if he failed in business as miserably as his father, he had better not show his face in her house again. When he turned to his brothers riding with them in the car, their looks indicated they felt exactly as their mother did, even though neither of them was what anybody would call successful.

A long and complex story is shortened by noting that on his twenty-first birthday, Jack Adrian took it upon himself to throw a party. He invited as many people as he believed could fit into his mother's apartment, where he lived at the time. Most of the guests never showed up, but one who did, Sally Fuerst, more than made up for the absent ones. She was the first person to take a genuine interest in Jack Adrian; the first person, as it turned out, who showed him love, no matter what he gave her in return. It wasn't pity, she assured him repeatedly, it was merely old-fashioned love. It took him a while to get adjusted to this sort of treatment, but gradually his personality seemed to change, and he was the first to attribute what he called "the cure" to Sally. They were twenty-four years old when they got married, and the fact that Jack's mother was too drunk and one of his brothers too busy to attend the wedding didn't seem to faze him. It was more important, he told his wife, that *her* parents come, which they did.

Sally Fuerst Adrian never conceived of the relationship with her husband in terms of psychological rehabilitation. She never used words like that, nor thought in those terms. She didn't fall madly in love with Jack at the birthday party. Her most powerful recollection of that evening was that he seemed sad. She never believed, moreover, that he was an angry or depressed man. Somewhere among all the changing personalities was a decent man, not to mention a man who had been hurt often in his life and had never felt the warmth of simple kindness. "Don't make anything dramatic out of it," she told me when I first heard about the Adrians' courtship. "I liked him at first. No, at first I was a little afraid of him. Then I liked him, then I couldn't tell, then I decided just because *he* was afraid to love me or anybody, *I* didn't have to be afraid. It's not a plot for the movies. You don't really change people, at least I don't think so. You just bring out the good stuff in them, and try to keep them from being so overinvolved with their bad stuff, the stuff they like the least in themselves. And don't kid yourself, Jack did a lot for me, too. I'm not his nurse!"

Now I jump ahead, way ahead, in the story of Jack and Sally Adrian. I jump, in fact, over twenty years to the time when I met the family, knowing, of course, nothing of their personal histories. In retrospect, if I were to characterize those first few years of my friendship with the Adrians, I would say it was remarkable that their respective histories almost never cropped up in conversation. I knew that Jack's parents were dead, that he had little to do with his brothers and sisters, and that both the Adrians had always been closer to Sally's side of the family. I knew, too, that Jack reached a level of success that far exceeded his parents' expectations. The home, the car, the two-week vacations were hardly a part of his own childhood. But of his mood swings, the battles with his parents, his rather pessimistic outlook of two decades earlier, I knew nothing. Neither of the Adrians seemed to be secretive people. They were loving with their four children, though uncompromising when it came to discipline. They tended to judge themselves, moreover, strictly in terms of how well their children were faring. What I could not quite piece together was their concern that one of their children might begin to show the dreaded mood shifts that dominated Jack Adrian's early years.

While the Adrians never spoke to me of it, they clearly kept close watches on their children, fearing that Jack's mental illness might have been inherited by them. Again, I could understand their concern, although no one who knew the four Adrian children would have imagined they might be heading for psychological problems. They were lovely, talkative children with energy to spare. They adored the "right" foods, television shows, football and baseball teams, and rock songs. They fought with each other, and looked after one another, like all children. They didn't even seem to change that much when their father, wholly unexpectedly, grew increasingly depressed during his fifty-fifth year. Sally worried, but if the children were upset, they revealed it to no one, not that their parents asked them to verbalize their reactions. No one talked much about "it" even when Jack found himself making little or no progress in psychotherapy. Then a series of drugs were prescribed, some of which seemed to bring him back to an even keel. With the drugs, however, the children began to take increasingly more notice of their father. Part of their concern, naturally, were the side effects. First he was awake and alert. Then he would be quiet and lethargic for several days, to the point where he would stay in bed. Occasionally the children found him weeping.

To say the least, Jack Adrian's psychological state was not helping his position at the automotive firm. In the beginning absences were overlooked, but being out of work for weeks at a time was not tolerated. The more his employers questioned his behavior, the more angry and nervous he became. Eventually the Adrians decided not to answer their telephone during the daytime. Given Jack's condition, Sally grew conflicted around the issue of whether she should retain her own job as a secretary or stay home and nurse her husband, although she would never have used that term. She despaired seeing him unhappy and unconsolable, yet the family's financial problems would hardly be resolved with both of them sitting home. She made the obvious choice and kept working. She also discussed the possibility of hospitalizing Jack, although he fought the idea tooth and nail. He'd get better, he kept saying. He had been in the depths before, not that he and Sally spoke much about connections between present problems and his early history.

Whatever their decisions, the Adrians appeared to be dealing with their problems as sensibly and, if you will, nobly as anyone would dare expect. Privately, I took exception to one of their decisions: namely, their attempt to keep "the problem" from their children. Once again I was encountering what had now become a familiar family irony, the concealing of the unconcealable. How could people believe they could mask the mental illness of a father when the man was missing increasingly more days of work, staying in bed increasingly more hours a day, and showing himself to be increasingly more incapable of handling the normal responsibilities of everyday life? But of course this wasn't the predicament facing Mr. and Mrs. Adrian. Their problem was to keep neighbors as well as Jack's *and* Sally's employers from hearing of Jack's illness. This meant stopping any leaks, which in turn meant keeping the truth, the obvious, from their children. This part of the story I understood only too well. Often it seems as though people's reactions to a mentally ill person are more severe than the patient's condition itself. Furthermore, the stigmatization of patients, as if they required further evidence of their lack of self-worth, turns back upon them and probably perpetuates the illness. Could Jack Adrian's employment status be jeopardized if people learned of his condition? In Jack Adrian's world, and the world of people who shared his fate, situations most definitely are damaged by mere gossip. So these people are not acting strictly in *paranoid* fashion—that overworked term—when they express a need to keep their problems inside the family and away from their children.

As it happened, three of the Adrian children were adjusting fairly well to their father's troubles. They acted, in other words, as if simultaneously they knew and knew nothing of the matter. Thus, they were behaving exactly as their mother had instructed. It was a case of the Emperor's new clothes. If the parents said things were normal, then things were normal. But William Adrian, aged fifteen, the third oldest, a boy who since early childhood had been called Chico, found himself unable to abide by the family's charade. He became, in a sense, the little boy who cries fraud in "The Emperor's New Clothes," except that his proclamation was made in private, to me. Chico Adrian wouldn't buy the story. The earlier phrase about not swallowing the lie more accurately describes his feelings. After several months of watching his father sit in a chair for hours without uttering a sound and suddenly beginning to cry, Chico decided to stop eating. And it wasn't just liver, cottage cheese, and Jell-O that went off his list. The boy practically had to be forced to drink water. Occasionally when he consented to go with me on walks or car rides I got him to at least sip at a chocolate milk shake. I even worked out a foolish little game wherein the winner or loser had to munch pieces of a candy bar. "You're a fraud," he'd say. "All you're trying to do is get me to eat."

"I'm no fraud," I'd tell him. "There's nothing mysterious about me at all. If I could I'd shove it down you. I can't stand to see you like this."

If only to please me he would nibble at a sandwich or drink the milk shake. His older brother Ronald had a bit of luck with him as well, but his mother and two sisters had absolutely none. Not only did he refuse to take food from them, he complied with none of their demands. Still, given what the Adrians were going through, I felt that if only one child was (visibly) suffering, the family was coming out better than I imagined it would. Moreover, if we could keep Chico's problem under control, then surely everyone was ahead of the game.

Ahead of the game or not, the family went on this way for months. Sally Adrian was pleased that I spent time with Chico, but irritated by my desire to visit with Jack. In time she discouraged me from coming to the house, except to pick up Chico. Thus, I didn't know Jack Adrian had been admitted to a mental hospital until weeks after the decision had been made. I had a clue that something was worse than usual when I learned from Ronald that Chico had revealed a new symptom. This one consisted of him beating up on small children at school for no apparent reason. At first the teachers were surprised; aggression was not a quality Chico Adrian had ever demonstrated. But surprised or not, school officials could not condone it. The family was apprised of the situation, then warned that if the boy continued to act as he had, a suspension would ensue.

I learned all of this third hand. I learned of the actual suspension third hand as well. Chico told me nothing, until one afternoon when apparently he could hold his feelings no longer. As it turned out, he had heard the night before that his father would not be coming out of the hospital the following weekend as the children had been led to believe. Well, the words are not quite accurate. Chico had been told by his mother that his father would not be "coming home from his long trip." There still had been no talk of hospitalization. Sally Adrian had not altered her original edict: Mental illness and Jack's placement in a state hospital were not matters one discussed in front of the children. In response to his mother's edict, Chico had vowed he would never talk to her about his own suffering. In fact, he vowed he would never speak to *anyone*, but the feelings burst through all the same:

"My mother's crazy. I believed her stuff about why you couldn't tell anybody. But she's treating us like babies. That's what she wants us to be, her babies, or a bunch of puppies. What's she so afraid of? *I'm* the one who should be afraid. I'm becoming a murderer almost. I hit a kid a couple of weeks ago. He didn't even do anything and I hit him. Hard, too. You should have seen the way he looked at me. I could tell what he and his friend were thinking, too. They were thinking: Adrian, you are weird, man. You must have pretty weird parents, too, if you come out weird like that. I don't know what to do. I don't know what to do."

Chico Adrian's eyes were filled with tears, which he fought back bravely. I had seen him sad before, but until this moment he had always been able to keep his eyes (deceptively) clear.

"She's got to face it, and *he's* got to face it. Everybody, you know, grows up wondering if they're, like, all right in their mind. You got to wonder about that. No one talks about it, but they'll make fun of it, so you know they're thinking about it. My father did, my mother did. My sisters wouldn't admit it but they do, too. You gotta! You know how many days we had to tiptoe around the house pretending there was nothing wrong with him when you could *see* he was crazy. He wasn't my father, he was this crazy man, sitting in that chair staring at like nothing. He'd look at me and I'd think, he knows me, he doesn't know me. He knows me, he doesn't know me. You couldn't tell. I mean, I really couldn't tell if he even knew *he* was sitting there. And my mother, what does she say? 'Oh, Dad's a little under the weather,' or something unbelievable like that. Under the weather? I couldn't even have told you if the man could see or was he blind! That's when I decided I don't give a damn no more. I might just as well die. He doesn't know me, she's pretending like all he has is an upset stomach; maybe what he needs is a Dristan and he'll know his own son again. What kind of crazy shit is that? I'd go right up to him and say, 'Dad, you know me?' He didn't even move. Or he'd turn his head away like someone was shining a light in his eyes. And his eyes were dead. I can't explain it better. If he knew me it was only because I *pretended* he did. I was pretending my own father knew his son. I was afraid to ask him my name. I didn't even want to hear what he'd say.

"So I decided I'm not going to live to have this hanging on my head. Someone in this house is crazy. It's him, her, or me, but one of us is way around the corner. I'm no doctor, so I don't understand what's happening. No one's ever sat down to explain it. I told my mother, 'Okay, look, since you don't want to tell me what's going on, let Tom Cottle tell me.' She got so mad you wouldn't even believe it. My father was sitting there. That was one of the nights when he'd like, stare without blinking for a hundred hours. She told me, 'You are not now or *ever* to talk to Tom Cottle about this, your father, me, *anything!*' 'So why do I see him?' I goes. She goes, 'He likes talking to you and buying you food, that's fine, but he doesn't have to know all our family's secrets.' And she was really mad then. My father didn't even move. She was yelling and her face was turning red and he wasn't even moving. So I goes, 'He isn't supposed to hear no family secrets? Then all right, why doesn't someone tell *me* the family secrets. Is he going to die?' That's what I wanted to know. I mean, no one ever told me nothing so I didn't know. He could have been dying. If anyone saw him like that, they'd think he was dying. If you don't know, how you going to be able to tell?

"You should have seen her yelling. I practically could see the smoke coming out of her head. 'Don't you dare say that. Your father isn't dying. He's going to be absolutely fine.' 'When?' That's what I asked her. '*When?*' 'When he's ready.' I goes, 'Is that what the doctor said?' She goes, 'What doctor?' 'Well, if you know so much you must have seen a doctor.' I scared her. I could see I did, too, 'cause then I knew a little something. She doesn't want no doctor seeing my father. She wants to take care of him herself. When I asked her that question, she got scared 'cause she thought maybe a doctor did come and see him once when she was at work which would have meant someone in the family told someone not in the family how my old man was sitting all day in his chair looking through people. Now why'd I go and call him my old man? I hate the word. He ain't that; he's my father.

"I used to kiss my father. Lots of boys don't but I did. He'd say, come kiss me good night, something like that, and I would. I did it a little when he got sick. I call it sick no matter what she calls it or wants me to call it. I'd see him sitting all by himself, 'cause even if one of us was home we wouldn't talk to him 'cause she said there was nothing to be talked about, so she wanted to pretend, we pretended. If your father wants to sit all day staring into space, you pretend *everybody's* father's sitting home all day staring into space. She said pretend but it was more like she really meant for us to ignore him. In the beginning I'd talk a little with him, and maybe when I'd go to bed I'd kiss him. Sometime he'd move his head, like there was a bright light there or something. I don't know. But then I stopped.

I'd think, one of us in this house is crazy. Either he's dead and I'm kissing a corpse, or something really strange is happening.

"No one had to tell us something was wrong. We aren't children. And we aren't blind. I got to thinking that worse than he was was the way she was making us live with it; everybody was lying about it one way or another. I didn't want to eat. I figured out it wasn't really 'cause I wanted to starve myself to death. I just remembered my father telling us how his father would say, 'You don't deserve to eat if you haven't told the truth that day.' It was like even if you were the only person who knew you'd lied, you had to punish yourself. Maybe that's what I did. People like you making me eat only made it worse because it was like you were saying, you don't have to punish yourself, which means you really aren't lying. But I was, and so was she. And if you want to know the truth, I thought *he* was the biggest liar of them all. Like, I'd see him sitting there, or lying down, and I'd think, he's putting us on; this is a fake. Something's *really* crazy; my father's pretending to be nuts, which made me angry, until I realized he couldn't control himself. But I really did think he was faking the whole thing. I thought the two of them together were putting on some show for the rest of us and it was supposed to do something for us. Then I began to look around and I said to myself, how come, Adrian, you're the only one in the family that seems to be taking things bad? You aren't the oldest or the youngest, but you sure are the only one not eating. So then I figured, not only is it some kind of weird act, but I mean really weird, but I'm the only one who isn't on to it. You know what I mean? It's like the whole family was in on some secret except for me. Like they were testing me.

"So then I thought, if it *is* a test, what's it a test *for*? Has to be a test to see if I'm crazy? I mean, there's a mess of craziness going on in the house, I'm the queer one 'cause no one else seems much bothered by it, so that means I'm *it*. So I thought, okay, I got to either show them I'm not crazy, or I am. So I decided, I might just as well show them I am, or make them think I am so they'll stop the test and tell me the big secret. So I stopped eating, at least they thought I did. You did, too. But I was eating when nobody knew about it. At first anyway. Later, when I really got scared, I *did* stop eating. That's when I remembered that saying of my father's about how liars shouldn't eat. I really did think I was going to be crazy like him, except I was always afraid to think about him going crazy. I couldn't even say the words to myself. My father *isn't* crazy, I'd tell myself. He's *not*, not, not, not, not crazy.

"If I was bad off then, I thought I'd go out the window when I

came home one day from school and found out he wasn't there. I
went past his room expecting him to be there like always—and nobody. The place was empty. You know the first thing I did? I went
to all the windows to see if maybe he jumped out; I didn't know if
that's what people like him did. That night I asked my mother, she
said he was on a trip. You think I said anything? 'Where'd he go?'
'Well, we're not sure but he said he's for sure coming back.' One
minute he can barely move his eyes, and he didn't know who I was
before I gave up sticking my face up in front of him like a dummy.
Then the next minute he's on a long trip. I thought he died. I didn't
even think he was in a mental hospital. I thought he died and my
mother was going on pretending. I figured she got his body out as
fast as she could and made up her wonderful story about him taking
a trip. Later that night my sister told me he was in the hospital in
the northern part of the city or somewhere and now I could see how
it was even more important that I didn't talk to anyone about it,
even you. So I said okay, sure, fine. I can keep a secret, which I did,
only I hit the first kid I saw the next morning at school. I told myself
that's what I'm going to do. The first little kid, I'm going to pound
him. If he survives he'll think I'm crazy, but I've already been working on that one.

   "Then after that, I kept hitting kids. I couldn't control myself. I
didn't want to even if I could have. I wanted to kill people really.
They thought I was hurting them, but they should have felt what I
felt. They were lucky I didn't kill them. I kept thinking of these guys
you see on television who go *real* crazy and start shooting people for
no reason. Jeez, once I thought those people were, like, from the
moon. Now I could be one of them. Cops coming to shoot me like
some wild animal after I'd killed a bunch of little kids or something.
All I wanted to do was see my father. I told her take me there. 'Let
me see him.' 'No. It's not for children.' 'I'm no child, Ma.' That's
what I kept telling her. 'I'm no child. Stop calling me a child.'
'You're a child.' That's her standard answer: 'You're a child. Children don't have to know about this.' 'But *nobody* knows.' Oh man,
we can scream at one another like two mental patients ourselves. I
told her a couple of weeks ago, 'cause we really had a fight to beat all
fights after I got suspended, I told her they locked up the wrong person. She hit me. She did. Foom, like I hit those kids. Maybe the
reason I hit little kids is because she keeps treating me like *I* was a
little kid. I don't know, maybe that doesn't make sense. Anyway I
told her, 'You can hit me all you want, but they *did* lock up the
wrong person. I'd rather have him here than you, even though he

doesn't even know who we are half the time.' 'Yes, he does know,' she goes. She's always got to fight back, keep all the secrets going. I told her, 'Hey, man, I'm not going to break your big secret. Who'd I tell anyhow? No one's going to know, so don't worry.' 'You're not to talk about it,' that's all she says.

"I don't really know if I do or don't want to see my father in a mental hospital. It's hard for me to think about it. It's like everything else going on around here; I don't know anything. I always have to imagine it, and usually when you imagine things it's worse than they really are, so I don't know. I think I'd like to be there with him. Maybe he talks with people out there. Maybe if I was there he'd know he could trust me so he'd tell me something, like what he thinks about, *anything!* It's like another test: Prove you're crazy like him and he can speak his special language to you instead of turning his head away like he does. It's kind of like he doesn't want to know his own secret either. I'd start talking and he'd move away. I probably should have told him, 'Dad, you're crazy. Why not face it. You're crazy even if she won't let you think about it. You got to be thinking about *something.*' Maybe she took his mind away from him by making it all a big secret. Maybe when you keep that stuff in your mind, you go nuts. It happened with him, it sure looks to me like it could be happening with her, too. I don't know.

"She should tell us what it's like in the hospital. She should tell us what he's like there. Does he sit in a chair and stare? Does he cry? Does he talk to anyone? For all I know they got him in a padded cell. Maybe he's in there this minute, banging his fists on the wall like those people do. He could kill himself in there and she'd probably tell us he decided to take a longer trip than he thought he would. I tell you, she's got this business of not letting anyone know; that man could die and she wouldn't say nothing. He could be dead now but if she thought it wouldn't look good to someone to have him die, she'd say 'Oh, I hear from him all the time, he's doing fine.' She'd be hearing from him, all right, from the damn grave. It'd be better to have him dead than have someone in the neighborhood know her husband's a mental patient.

"I'll give her one thing: She kept all her secrets. Nobody I know knows anything about it. They're probably asking questions but I've never heard anybody even come close to guessing where he is. Kids in school don't talk about their fathers, so she got everything she wanted. I guess my brother and sisters did, too, 'cause I never heard them complain about anything. Everybody seems well adjusted around here except for Chico. We don't talk about it, none of us, so there I go again not knowing what anybody thinks. But I'm not going to stay with it like this. I'll give it a month till I reach my sixteenth birthday. I told her too, I told her, 'You got till I turn sixteen. If he ain't back here then, then I go, too.' 'You got school,' she goes. 'You can take school and everybody in it,' I goes, 'and put it in the ocean. Put it in his mental hospital, why don't you.' She went to hit me, but I didn't let her touch me. I had to dance around the kitchen to get away from her, but I made out. 'Stick in the loony bin. You get him here for my birthday, or I'm gone.' 'Go ahead,' she goes. 'Run away. Run away from all your problems.' '*My* problems? How come they're *my* problems.' I didn't even know till yesterday where he was and she calls them *my* problems. I'm telling you, she really is crazy.

"I know where he is. I called the place and found out how you get there. I told them my father's there and my mother's dead and I want to know how you get there. They told me. I'm going to go visit him. I'll check the place out first. She can keep all her secrets but she can't lock me up. She's done enough to my mind. We're living in a family of psychological warfare. How do I know what she did to him all these years? You don't know what she said to him. I'm going to find him; I'll ask him. I'll go there every day and ask him. He'll tell me. He'll tell me all the secrets. It'll be like me saving him and him saving me."

Chico Adrian's announcement that he had learned the whereabouts of his father placed me in a difficult position. I couldn't very well visit Jack without Sally's permission. Nor could I raise the matter with her for that would be to break my word of confidentiality to Chico. So there I was, sucked into the family's web of secrets exactly as Chico had described it. When I asked Sally about Jack, she told me the same story she had told her son: Jack was on a trip. I said nothing, but I made every facial gesture I knew, hoping to communicate my doubt. She saw my twitching but kept still. If I didn't buy her story, that was my business. Before leaving I let her know, without equivocation, that I would continue to visit Chico. That was fine with her. Would she make special plans for his birthday? She wasn't certain. Would Jack be back from his trip (and my words here virtually stank with sarcasm)? She wasn't certain of this either.

I hated Sally Adrian in those moments, and I felt pity for her and compassion and anger and every other emotion her son felt as well. Her situation was wretched, and probably she had made it worse. Probably, too, she realized she had not improved things, but she was a proud woman and she would not back down. Stymied, I found no way to properly intervene. My attachment with the Adrians was precarious enough. Whenever I wondered about them, I would recall a friend saying to me, if you can't force people to see a dentist when their teeth are falling out, how can you get a person to seek counsel for an overwhelming family predicament!

Chico was my concern. In fact, he was gradually becoming an obsession. The thought of him committing suicide was not outlandish. He had seemed utterly inflexible in his ultimatum: a significant change by his sixteenth birthday or he would leave. His mother, I know, heard this firmness. 'He's not a boy no more,' she whispered, but she wasn't home the night of Chico's birthday. She left a beautifully wrapped package for him, but she had to be somewhere. I took Chico, Ronald, and one of the girls, Patsy, for steaks, french fries, and hot apple pie. They seemed to enjoy the restaurant, although Chico wore a peculiar grin that evening.

Ronald told me a week later that Chico had carefully opened the present from his mother to see what it was, then wrapped it again so that she would think he had no interest in it. He didn't know that Ronald had spied on him, or that Ronald had told me about the unwrapping. The secrets pile had grown still higher. Then Chico threw out his own secret: He ran away, telling no one of his destination or plans. Ronald received a note in the mail but it held no clue to his whereabouts.

Learning of his disappearance, I telephoned the mental hospital. I was certain Chico would go there, if not immediately, then surely within a couple of weeks. Sally said he would return home when he cooled down. I tended to agree with her, but doubt remained. The doubt grew when three months passed with no word from him. Ronald, who now had become my closest ally in the family, was deeply upset. All three children, for that matter, were convinced Chico was dead. Interestingly, both daughters acted much like their mother when it came to befriending me. It was like they had convinced themselves never to change. From the beginning they had kept me at arm's length, and they would not waver from this position now, even though they expressed a need for me.

We contacted police, army recruitment offices, Chico's friends, but nothing turned up. Sally began going to church and taking the girls with her. Ronald refused on the grounds that it was hypocritical, and merely represented a way to ease her guilt. God knows how Jack Adrian was faring, although I did learn that he had been moved to another hospital, not that this signified improvement. Six months and still no word from Chico. Then eight, ten, and eleven months. No word, no hint, nothing. How tragically ironic that the final secret of this family was the whereabouts of their youngest son. Once again that same old motley collection of feelings welled up when I even thought of the Adrian name. Guilt, hate, anger, shame, fright, compassion, pity, helplessness. I was even growing angry at Chico, whose disappearance had the effect on all of us of a suicide. We were the survivors consumed by "survivor feelings." I swore if I ever saw him again I would tell him his "trick" was unfair; his leaving was too much to ask of us. The mind hardly works in rational ways during such times.

Then one night, dinnertime, a phone call. Our daughter answered. For me. Food in my mouth, irritation at being interrupted in my voice, "Hello." A strange voice, female, bad connection. Administrator at a mental hospital. Jack's first hospital. A boy had been admitted and she had found a card (from eleven months before) indicating I was to be called. Chico Adrian had committed himself.

The story is almost complete. Its ending, however, is far from satisfactory. Chico Adrian had traveled, seemingly, all over America. Looking for nothing, heading for nowhere, his mission merely was to keep moving. It went on this way for eight months, by which time he had reached the Pacific Coast, three thousand miles from his home. He worked at this or that, stayed with people, did what he had to in order to keep going. As he told it, his spirits were good. While he felt like a fugitive and imagined himself to be the star of a television show, he was not without energy and confidence. Finally the coast, new friends, new life-styles, new ideas and perspectives, some talk, although he kept his promise never to reveal his true name and address, and a great deal of alcohol and drugs. A weekly habit became a daily one, then a daily and nightly one. After a couple of months he was taking any drug anyone would offer. The cheaper they were, the more he liked them, no matter what their effect. Hospitalized on two occasions for overdosing, he was becoming known to certain medical authorities who tried their best to rehabilitate him, always without success. As one report on him noted, "He seems unable to limit much less quell his drug habit. He seems determined to become a full-fledged mental patient with the rights and privileges thereof."

The observation was perfectly apt. While drugs "solved" some of Chico's problems, or at least reduced some of the pain, they had become a means by which he could accomplish his true goal: namely, to be placed in the same mental hospital as his father. He later would admit it was the only way he could "break into" the place and find out the truth of his father. Exhibiting a fair amount of ingenuity, he worked his way back across the country, and using drugs and alcohol to achieve his psychotic state, he managed to be admitted to the hospital where originally his father had been placed. He was not aware that Jack had been transferred nine months before. By this point, Chico's intentions had become painfully transparent. Upon being admitted to the hospital he gave his name as Jack Adrian, and presented his parents' home address and telephone number. He also said he was the father of four children, two boys and two girls, although one of the boys, Chico, had died from strangulation. Apparently the boy had divulged too many family secrets so his mother choked him to death.

The hospital admitting officers needed little more from the young man to confirm their diagnosis: "paranoid schizophrenic, symptoms exacerbated by addiction to alcohol and hard drugs. He also reveals suicidal and homicidal tendencies." During his first several days in the hospital, Chico Adrian was placed in solitary confinement. This was done, it was said, "for his own good." At the end of a month he was able and willing to talk to me and a young social worker who expressed willingness to work with him. Chico was quiet, sullen, recalcitrant at first, but the social worker won him over with kindness. It was clear I would have to remove myself from the scene; I was too deeply associated with the past, the confusing, torturous, and evil past. I was also implicated in the secrets. I bowed out, just as Chico requested, leaving the door open for him to contact me at any time, for any reason. He shook hands when I left him at the hospital the last time. Moments before he had been laughing, somewhat ingenuously, over his "breaking in" escapades. It was utterly humorous to him to find that his father had been transferred. "How come you didn't say nothing about that?" he asked me flatly.

"You didn't ask," I joked.

"Hey," he responded, and here his response was as sharp and alert as I had observed it since his hospitalization, "I found out a long time ago you don't get nothing from asking. You can't even find out simple little things from your own mother. She kept me away from my father. She kept the truth out of my head. Now they got a whole lot of people wanting the truth out of my head. Why don't they ever ask me about all those people who shoved lies into my head in the first place? That's why I had to clean myself out. All those secrets everybody had, they were just air; air and shit. That's why I had to pump them out of my system. And find my father. I'm dedicated to it now. I'll find him. I'll track him down. There can't be all that many mental bins or graveyards in this country. I'll go from one to the other. I'll find him. Don't worry none, I'll let you know when I run across him. Him seeing me is going to cure him, you know. And me seeing him ain't going to do me no harm neither. I don't care what the hell my mother does about all this. She can float in the ocean for all I care. I haven't given up yet. They wrote I got suicidal tendencies. That's supposed to mean I want to kill myself. Can you imagine doctors being so wrong! I don't want to kill nobody. I wouldn't touch a fly. All I want is a little get-together with some special people where we talk about the old days. How's that sound, the old days! A little get-together, a little talk, and a secret pledge to have no more secrets. That ain't all that much, is it? You call that much? Wouldn't cost the state a penny!"

I couldn't keep myself from taking these almost parting words as a challenge to me. I chose to interpret the sentiment, moreover, in a sentimental manner: Send me my mother and father, which is what I did. First his mother visited him, then his parents came together, for Jack was making sufficient progress, and finally, three months after my last conversation with Chico, Jack Adrian came alone to Ward 11-H to see his youngest son. A nurse described the meeting as the most moving scene she had ever witnessed. Whatever feelings both had about the other, and the past as well, were concealed during the meeting when Sally was present. Alone, they wept and embraced and spoke for hours without respite. Jack Adrian, the nurse reported, spoke with animation, and his son smiled and laughed. And both men seemed younger and younger with each passing minute.

The substance of that first of many conversations between father and son is known only to them. It remains, until now, their secret.

Part VI

CONCLUDING
REMARKS

TEN

Children's Secrets,
Family Myths

Just as there is no easy way to draw together the myriad themes of an individual life study, so is there no ultimately successful way to draw together the strands of the life studies taken as a whole. So many queries remain open to explore that even as we pursue one, we ignore too many others. In this final chapter, we touch on a few familiar points and offer some new ones.

The two key words of this study have been repeated far too often: secret and myth. In certain significant ways, moreover, these two words are intimately related. When a child is obliged to keep a piece of experience secret, he or she is automatically obliged, at a conscious level, not only to make sense of the experience as it exists externally but to make sense of the internal reaction to the secret. This means that the child must undergo the psychological twistings and untwistings in order to decode the experience, the reaction to it, and finally, the nature of secrets themselves. We spoke in Chapter Nine of children beginning to observe themselves as part of the process of intellectually and emotionally decoding the secrets they are meant to keep. We have not stressed fully enough, however, the notion that the twistings and untwistings, what Claude Levi-Strauss might call "thought experiments," are themselves part of the secret children keep, and in time become part of the myths they subsequently hold about themselves, their families, and their cultures.

When children keep the sort of secret we have been examining in these pages, they come to believe in the mythic nature of their own existence only partly because they know a lie must be preserved. The lie, literally the inability to tell someone the truth, not only affects the perception of the world as being corrupt or counterfeit but colors children's own sense of themselves. So secretly, children view themselves as corrupt or counterfeit. The notion, then, that not telling others one's father, say, is a homosexual somehow preserves the myth of one's family as being straight, does not tell the complete story of mythification. For the child who keeps the secret, is himself or herself becoming "mythified." The mythification is part of an argument with oneself, part of a thought experiment or psychological twisting, the function of which is, first, to make sense, codify (public and private, that is shared and unshared) experience, as well as resolve the emotional responses to experience. As we have seen vividly in the various life studies, experiences must constantly be juggled in order to decodify them, or allow the person to make better intellectual and emotional sense of them. The young people discussed in the previous chapters are doing just this. Like anthropologists or philosophers, they are at work attempting to make public and private sense of experience. Their work, juggling, twisting, is itself a process of perpetual intellectual and emotional transformation. First one solution or resolution is formed, then another supplants it, then another, and on and on. Each transformation reveals something about the person, the experience, myth and secret, as well as secret keeping and myth making generally.

The work of secret keeping, moreover, as the life studies reveal, · retains a dramatic or dramaturgic quality. People become larger than life. Experience seems larger than life, mythic perhaps, because the child has no intellectual or emotional receptacle in which a particular experience might fit. Thus, the adolescent continues to work on the same problem and react to the temporary solutions as well as to the process of problem solving itself. Furthermore, just as the actual experience held as secret provides its structure (of and for experience) and plot, so do the mental acts of psychological twisting and untwisting provide their structure and plot for the adolescent. No myth is without structure or plot. Myths often make captivating stories partly because we are compelled by the underlying intellectual and emotional transformations we (consciously) recognize or unconsciously resonate to in the myth's transformations. Little wonder, then, that writers have grown fond of the terms psychological or social "scripts," implying as they do not only patterns for individuals to follow privately and publicly but mental and social acts for people to perform.

Now, what are some of these transformations? We cannot elucidate them in the detail they warrant, but we can note that myths often provide resolutions to the very sorts of antinomic feelings and concepts with which adolescents struggle. These include such issues as the private and public, individualism and collectivism, sanity and insanity, possibility and impossibility, finitude and infinitude, past and future, life and death. Antinomies, moreover, are not unlikely forms for myths; transformations in myths reduce the manifest conflict of antinomic concepts and attitudes. In classical myths, for example, the dead become alive, the sane insane; the future turns into the past, the private world becomes public, small becomes large, sad events become happy ones. Cowardice, furthermore, is transformed into courage, finitude into infinitude. Once again, our argument states that the normal act of secret keeping is itself akin to exploring myths, and particularly myths that deal with the sorts of issues with which adolescents work. Adolescence, we suggested earlier, is a time when people commence their thought experiments on just these topics, and gain from their psychological twistings and untwistings a new understanding of the nature of personal (or private) and public (or shared) experiences. Note that when we use the term *shared* experience, we mean an experience one either *performs* with another person or *tells* another person.

We need not be self-conscious about speaking of adolescents as philosophers. Levi-Strauss refers to the cognitive processes involved in tangling and untangling myths as *scientific thought* merely expressed in another idiom. In a sense, the secret, propelling the child into the realm of myth, could be viewed as the basis of a special cognitive and emotional idiom. Few of us could articulate precisely what this idiom would be, but the relevant point remains that when adolescents become involved in secret keeping (or myth making), they recognize this involvement with their private and public worlds in terms of a new idiom or medium. The meanings to an adolescent of thought and feeling are transformed just as the myth is transformed, just as the secret is coded (or codified), decoded (or decodified), then coded all over again. And coding does seem an appropriate term. To safeguard a message others are not meant to learn requires that the adolescent put the message through some psychological scrambling device which makes it understandable only to those capable of unscrambling it. But here again, the acts of (intellectually and emotionally) scrambling and unscrambling are precisely what the mythic sense is all about. "Let me turn it around in my head," we say. The phrase is a loaded one. It means, manifestly, let me work on that idea in order to make sense of it. More significantly it implies, let me play with the various meanings, find new interconnections of the various parts of the idea, as well as new *connections* to other ideas, other aspects of reality, other aspects of myself, other aspects of my *sense* of self. These processes and dynamics, too, are part of what we mean by the intellectual and emotional transformations inherent in myth making. For the adolescent, however, each bit of myth making, each instant of secret keeping, each psychological twist or untwist will necessarily have some implication for his or her sense of self as private and public being. It will also have an implication for the script adolescents create, the language they employ, the moods they develop. The thought experiments inherent in or demanded by secret keeping represent simultaneously adolescents' (emotional) psychologizing, their scientific investigating, their ordering of social events, and their spiritual trial.

To follow the path of a secret is to learn the logic not merely of the mind of the secret keeper. It is to discern the structure of the reality, private and public, that the secret keeper transforms into myth. In various interpretive passages, we have attempted to explore what secret-keeping experiences meant to individual boys and girls. Our focus, in other words, always stayed on the main character, the secret keeper. Yet the focus might also have been placed on the myth preserved by the act of secret keeping. The meanings, therefore, of individual or family harmony, stability, the meaning of affluence and traditional sexual behavior, also could be explored by examining the child's thought transformations, the so-called thought experiments. Any psychological exploration offers the possibility of an examination of the individual involved, or the historical or sociological contexts and realities in which the person exists. Any psychological exploration always provides one the opportunity to examine the mental acts of an individual and hence the mythifying enacted by that individual as he or she reacts to external or internal cues. We belong to myths in the same way that we create them. We hold them as secrets in the same way that we share them, make certain that others know of them or know the opportunity of embellishing them. The child keeps the family secret, which thereby activates an ongoing set of processes we have called mythification. The child keeps the family secret, which thereby perpetuates for the public a second myth, namely, the untruth the family wishes perpetuated. Both myths, underwritten by secrets, become codified, twisted, and untwisted by the child. Little wonder that so many of the children whose accounts we have considered would have so little time or energy to do much more than work at their myths and secrets. One might add that the normal process of adolescent development demands this sort of work. As we have already suggested, adolescence is a time for these scientific and social psychological cogitations to take place, cogitations that rarely become public or publicized. The results of adolescent thought experiments, like the thought experiments themselves, typically remain secret. It all makes for a great deal of work, it makes for a difficult time, it makes for a seemingly totally self-preoccupied soul.

Having offered these remarks about the conceptual connections between secret keeping and myth making, let me now point to the obvious linkage between these two processes, namely, the edict of silence that causes a message or communication to be called a secret. Psychological twistings and untwistings, thought experiments, psychological codifying and decodifying aside, the blatant feature of the secret is that the keeper cannot reveal the message or the experience, or even what he or she makes of the nature of secret keeping.

We have argued that the acts of secret keeping and myth making imply, indeed reveal, structures. The personality, like the secret, the myth, and life itself, has structure. Adolescence, we have suggested, is a period when people for the first time in their lives confront these structures in order to determine their form and content. The facts that we die, that the future is not limitless, that our possibilities and opportunities remain highly circumscribed, are systematically confronted for the first time during adolescence. Thought experiments are conducted on these rather troubling issues, just as thought experiments are conducted on all the antinomies striking the adolescent mind: sanity and insanity, privacy and publicness, reality and fantasy, etc. But all of these matters, irrespective of the idiosyncratic nature of their substance—for fantasy, dying, or privacy means something slightly different to each person—teach the adolescent something about the nature of the *structure* of these matters. There *is* a structure to the future and its relationship to the past and present. This temporal structure relates, moreover, to the structure defined by (realistic) finitude and (fantasized or wished for) infinitude. So the secret-keeping adolescent learns much about the structure of language, thought, and action almost as a by-product of his or her thought experiments and psychological twistings and untwistings.

Furthermore, adolescents learn that the very things they are (thought) experimenting on, provide certain structure themselves. To determine whether or not one is sane or insane, happy or sad, optimistic or pessimistic, requires that one engage in the structure of sanity and insanity, optimism and pessimism, etc. Said differently, a person must work out definitions of sanity and insanity, but in addition, must come to see that the way these definitions are worked out, or the forms of thought leading to the (forms of) definitions at which one ultimately arrives, are themselves aspects of the structure of sanity in which one is now engaged. The adolescent asks, "I wonder whether I'm crazy? Even more, I wonder whether asking this question proves that I'm crazy or not crazy?" This observation of the self, watching oneself watching oneself, attests to the fact that people remain fully aware of the structural aspects of thought and language, along with the substantive aspects of thought and language. It suggests, too, that people will often reach personal conclusions about themselves as much through inferences drawn from the *structure* of thought, language, myth, secret keeping, as from the *substance* of thought, language, myth, secret keeping. Furthermore, although the phrase seems tautological, one relies on the structure of thought, language, and action in order to make sense of thought, language, and action. Certainly adolescents are aware of this fact. Indeed, they regularly flirt with ways to change structure, "destructure" thought and language, as David Cooper has suggested.

Granted, destructuring often causes one to feel that he or she is going crazy, that there is nothing left to rely on, that nothing in the world remains calculable or predictable. We have noted this phenomenon in several of the life studies. The event the child has been asked to keep secret influences the child's fundamental perceptions of a particular structure. But again we must ask, where does secret keeping fit into this matter of structure or destructuring?

If the notion of restructuring thought, language, behavior, has merit, it suggests that people are constantly working out in their minds new and different meanings of thought, language, and action. We say, in light of what just happened, I now have to think about what that means to me, or how I feel about that thing (or myself). This is precisely what the children in this book are expressing in almost every account. In light of this or that event, I must change my feelings about my mother or father, or whatever. The change they feel they must make involves intellectual and emotional as well as behavioral matters. Several of the children have said that *everything* now is different in their families, and in their lives. These changes, moreover, are what we are calling restructuring. We use the term to suggest that the parameters and ingredients of thought and language begin to shift as one wrestles with a particular problem, as, for example, one's mother's infidelity. When we say, "It's like my whole world fell apart," we mean that many of the structural aspects of living, thought, feeling, language, behavior, have shifted, and hence each phase or activity of my life must now be redefined. Words and feelings do not mean exactly what they did prior to the event, i.e., discovering one's mother's infidelity.

Let us be clear on the matter that restructuring and destructuring, myth making even, need not be negative or frightening actions. Quite to the contrary; they may be productive, progressive steps. People wish to change, people seek to reorder or reshape aspects of their life, as well as those structures that allow them to think in new ways about their life. A trying event occurs and we counsel a friend, make the best of it, perhaps there is a blessing to be found (in the restructuring that you will be forced to undertake). Similarly, we regularly discover people working to alter the state of various thought, language, emotional, and behavioral structures in order to become (in part) something different from what they were. Altering the state of consciousness through drugs is an extreme form of restructuring, a form all too many adolescents attempt. Having, then, experienced different forms of consciousness may give people insight into the varying structures of consciousness. In general, an altered form of consciousness, just as an altered form of living, requires that old structures, in part, break down, or are juggled, thereby allowing the person to reshape, re-form, restructure his or her existence. At times the need to change is societally determined; at times it is personally or psychologically determined. Adolescence, however, remains a time of an externally as well as internally motivated need to change, or restructure.

The children heard in this book have been obliged to restructure their lives, as well as their thinking about themselves and their existence. Still, they cannot speak about the restructuring that their thought experiments yield, which in turn affects the quality of the restructuring. If their psychological twistings and untwistings represent an idiom of scientific thought, then their secret keeping prevents them from confirming the findings these thought experiments are meant to yield. Without confirmation, the children are encouraged to believe that their thinking or feeling is bizarre, even absurd. Put simply, the children are never quite certain what to make of their secret experiences. But note as well, that if their thinking about these matters, the myths they are constructing, seems to them absurd, then the reality in which they find themselves is equally absurd. It is not absurd to learn that one's father is psychotic, but it *is* absurd to discover that one's mother is denying this all too obvious fact. (The theme of the entire family already knowing the secret is also common to most of the children's accounts.) Thus, the act of secret keeping is often perceived as an absurd action; the absurdity of it reflects in turn on the child's assessments of himself or herself, assessments, to repeat, that go on in private as still another aspect of the secret.

If children's secrets are predicated partly on the recognition of external and internal absurdity, they are simultaneously constructed in great measure from shame. The secret, in other words, remains shameful; it symbolizes shame. It yields shame of the parent about whom the secret is being kept, shame of the family living with an absurd sense of itself, shame of self for keeping the secret in the first place, and hence shame of being. Restructuring, destructuring, thought experiments, myth making, psychological twistings and untwistings, require communication, even telegraphic, abbreviated communication. Secrets preclude communication. They require communication not because the final stage of a thought experiment is informing someone else of one's recent psychological findings, but because without expression the sense of (privately and publicly based) shame cannot be expiated, and reality cannot be confirmed. Shame festers without communication. When it festers, anger grows, but without the right to communicate, as the secret demands, the anger must be turned against the self. Telling an experience, in other words, does not literally mean reliving it. A report of a holiday journey abroad hardly represents an experiential replication of that journey. Yet in telling about it, we restructure or recontextualize the experience; we make sense of it. We also make further sense of our reactions to it. The telling of the experience, therefore, serves a public as well as a private value. The experience is "better integrated" when we tell it, because the telling "proves" that it is real. Telling is not the experiment; it is the "replication" of the experiment.

When we examine a potentially traumatized person, we inquire first, whether he or she is able to speak of the traumatizing event. Indeed, we strenuously encourage people to speak of the event, for we hope to keep it from receding forever into the unconscious, where it festers, ultimately to affect perceptions, emotions, possibly even thought and behavior. We would like to think that the potentially damaging experience is one a person *prefers* not to speak about rather than one the person is *unable* to speak about. If the person can tell of the experience, the chances of it becoming the agent of trauma are significantly diminished. Turning this thought around, we may advance the following argument: Demanding that a potentially serious event, like discovering one's mother's nymphomania, be kept secret causes the event to be dealt with, by the secret keeper, as a potentially traumatic event. That is, if the experience does not cause sufficient psychological harm, then the demand for secrecy may produce it. There is no guarantee of this, naturally, but as we have seen from these albeit specially selected life studies, to demand that certain family issues be kept secret is tantamount, one might say, to traumatizing the child.

Let me present the argument in another way. In many of the cases we have examined, a child's entire life, entire sense of being actually, had to be recontextualized, rethought, restructured. No solution the child might have conceived could possibly have worked out satisfactorily, since the reality of the parents' and hence the family's circumstances remained intact. Indeed, almost all the solutions the children reached seemed unsatisfactory, if not utterly absurd, especially to them. No one needed to tell Peter Malone that his experiments with drugs hardly represented a productive way of "working through" (which in effect means restructuring) his problems. Similarly, no one needed to inform Chico Adrian of the futility (and absurdity) of his goal of landing himself in the mental hospital where he believed his father was incarcerated. But had anyone advised the children of the absurdity of their behavior, or for that matter of their emotional responses, the children's sense of shame would have increased that much more. Their level of anger, too, would have soared. One should not overlook this last point, for the life studies are replete with expressions of anger. Suicidal gestures, as absurd in their intent as in their content, run through the material. They emerge, however, in the expressions of the children in most pathetic tones. The children seem to be indicating that suicide or any form of self-destructive thinking or behavior would be foolish, ungratifying, absurd. The absurdity of the gestures and self-destructive reasoning only reaffirms for the child the sense of shame and the feeling of anger. Expiation of shame, like the release of some of the aggression, might be possible through the confession of the secret, but almost none of the thought experiments has yielded significant satisfaction.

To hold tightly to secrets, as the children in this book have done, convinces the child at some level that he or she is mad. If the shame and anger or the restructuring and psychological twistings and untwistings do not contribute to this belief, then the perceived absurdity of the external situation and one's internal thought processes must encourage a sense of madness. The inability to tell the secret only adds to the fear that one is mad. For cognitive as well as emotional reasons, the artist seems able to escape madness (during the process of making art, that is) by saying the unsayable, expressing the unexpressible. In saying the unsayable, the artist, paradoxically, recognizes, codifies, and ultimately tames or controls the madness. In the expressing of the madness lies the possibility of capturing madness, or at least containing it. Almost all radical restructuring processes, almost all cognitive and emotional jugglings, cause one to feel that madness is near. We noted in Chapters Eight and Nine how the experience of discovering some horrendous news about one's parents may cause one to believe one has been made crazy. Yet the restructuring of thought, language, feeling, and behavior made in response to the discovery can only enhance this belief, especially when one is unable to confess either the experience or the thought experiments made in response to it. Secrets, therefore, of the urgent type we have been considering remain deeply related to the sense of madness, which is itself a common theme in mythology. Through myths, people reveal their constantly changing comprehension of and response to madness and death. It is no coincidence, then, that several of the children should allude to demons possessing them or boogey people living inside them. Granted, demons may be the personification (the incubus) of impulses and emotions, just as physical symptoms may be somatic representations of impulses and emotions. But (believed) madness also may be personified by demons and boogey people. In the beginning the demons reside outside us, but then we bring them inside; or is it that they are born within us? Does the ultimate secret, therefore, have something to do with our sense of madness and normality, or at least our wonderings about madness and normality? And if it does, if secrets and madness are thus entwined, can we properly expect children not to feel the evocation of madness when their culture or family, or their very being, demands that they keep a portentous secret!

In looking back on the life studies, the reader will note many instances when the child's relationship to me seemed to suffer somewhat after a confession. Contrary to my original assumptions, telling me of the family ordeal did not bring me closer to some of the children. In several cases, the confession actually seemed to exacerbate the shame. Yet, expiation of the shame was made possible by my moving away from the child, almost as if I took a bit of the shame and anger away with me. The popular expression "Let me lay some of my burden on you" seems particularly relevant in this context. For there is a fantasy, a wish that the hearer of the confession will physically carry away the shame or burden of the secret, and bury it forever. One way to bury the secret, although hardly a satisfactory one for the researcher, is to disappear altogether. If secrets kept the children chained to their families, then telling the secrets often let them feel that if they were not liberated or released, then at least they had earned their parole. Yet even this point must be examined against the background of adolescents' normal ambivalence about being imprisoned within their families. Despite youthful belligerence and protestation, who is to say that total freedom from one's family is precisely what all adolescents covet? As we have remarked repeatedly, individual personalities, families, and cultures create and perpetuate the need for secrets; and all must bear responsibility for these secrets.

Given the themes and philosophy of this book, it seems appropriate that a child be granted final say. Accordingly, we conclude our work with one last life study, one last secret. In this instance, however, the secret is of a more hopeful kind. I seriously doubt that the following life study could be called typical of anything. Still, it contains a momentous secret, a secret of the type we rarely encounter. If nothing else, it is comforting to observe how one young woman overcame anger, shame, a sense of life's abject absurdity, and found the results of her thought experiments sufficiently gratifying that she would affirm nothing more, and nothing less, than her own being.

Patsy Sawyer is now twenty-six years old. She is a tall, strongly built woman with warm brown eyes and hair cut short, very short. She smiles easily, but rarely laughs. When something amuses her she merely nods, and perhaps taps her fingernails on a table. The small one-bedroom apartment she has rented for several years is crowded with books, pictures, record albums, all sorts of objects. And plants. The windows are covered with plants. They hang from the casings and ceilings. Any available space reveals a plant. Yet as crowded as the apartment surely is, it remains orderly. Objects have their place. When moved, they are put back. The orderliness is not excessive, but apparent. Patsy is all too aware of why it may be this way, why it probably has to be this way. She has told me: "It's part of my way of making the old mess feel more straightened out. I put it together nicely now, the way I want it; that helps me to keep the past from coming back and destroying everything, or most everything."

It is no secret to Patsy Sawyer's friends that her father spent a stretch in prison for attempted murder, and that her mother was convicted for prostitution and issued a suspended sentence only because her husband, though they were estranged, was serving time and nobody was around to look after their three children. In fact, there were never *any* secrets around the Sawyer home. By the age of five, Patsy, along with her older brother and younger sister, had watched their parents' marriage collapse. Arthur and Sally Sawyer were always fighting, never friendly, if Patsy's recollections are accurate. When Patsy was seven, she learned from her mother that her father had been sentenced to prison. Her mother told the news with relish; Arthur's criminal act publicly confirmed his reprehensible nature, and served to condone Sally taking in one lover after another, each of whom pranced through the Sawyer household practically advertising their illicit intentions.

At age ten, it became clear to Patsy Sawyer that her mother was a prostitute and that her older brother, Tim, was selling drugs. As it turned out, he was arrested six times for possession and sales but released from custody each time on the grounds that prison, as the judge claimed, would only serve to harden his criminal tendencies. Besides, the court-appointed lawyers always argued in his behalf, imprisonment would only add problems to an already beleaguered family. Patsy was relieved Tim was never put away, but her mother could never understand the judge's reasoning. How could a prison sentence possibly add to *her* burdens? It would mean one less person to worry about. It would rid her of the men in her family, and might just make a decent man out of a "sick mixed-up psycho," her pet description of Tim.

At thirteen, Patsy Sawyer had quit school and with one of her close friends had become a prostitute. A man named Donlevy pimped for the two girls who took in more money than Patsy ever imagined she would earn. In the beginning, she found the trade disgusting, and frightening. In a few months she felt herself to be a seasoned professional. She hustled five or six men a day and pocketed between one and two hundred dollars after Donlevy took his share. It wasn't a bad life. In fact, it was a good one if you didn't get arrested as no intelligent woman should. Only the irresponsible ones, like her mother, were arrested, and they deserved it. Getting arrested, Patsy told me, was no different from getting pregnant. If you took the precautions, there were no problems. If you lost your head, anything could happen. Her mother took chances and got caught. Patsy took no chances; the only policemen she ever met were the ones who came to her as customers.

Add one more fact to this brief view of a family's history—that Patsy's younger sister also became a prostitute—and one has what

Patsy Sawyer calls her family's vital statistics. She told me once: "Some people, it takes them weeks to spin out the story of their lives. Me, I'm lucky. I can do it in a few sentences. Mother convicted for prostitution but sentence suspended. Brother arrested six times, drugs, possession and selling, no convictions. Why, I'll never figure out. Father in jail. Deserves to be, although his life wasn't so great, even before he met my mother. Sister, a prostitute, school dropout, the whole business, no chance; no, I take that back. No chance for my brother, or that I can see, still a chance for my sister. Pretty moral family, huh? Maybe we should have gone to church. That might have had an effect, though they tell me you have to pick a religion before you go. Our poor family, they couldn't even get it together enough to *think* about religion much less pick one, much less spend a Sunday in church. But what am I getting so worked up about religion; I don't have one, and don't seem to be moving toward it. So I'm no better off. Anyway, there you have the Sawyers' wonderful vital statistics."

No one, of course, could adequately summarize his or her life in such a short passage. For that matter, no one could describe her life experiences in any number of words; experiences never stop, there are always more. For convenience sake, and psychological sake, and because of the natural constraints of space and time, we offer up abbreviated life histories and hope that we have presented the flavor of our lives, as we call it. And, as much as we may decry the use of those inevitable human classifications, I come from a typical middle class, or Greek, or affluent background, we find ourselves resorting to just these categories in our shorthand self-descriptions. Patsy Sawyer did. She saw her family in the context of their criminal activities and court judgments and pronouncements. Yet, while her early descriptions of her family were truncated, and sorely incomplete, they were also compelling. One isn't accustomed to hearing, even in shorthand versions, a family story where *nothing* seems to be turning out well. But let me not sit in judgment of the young woman I met when she was eighteen. Let me say only that it was she who consistently called her family amoral or immoral—she used the terms interchangeably— and found nothing of value in their behavior. The Sawyers had always known poor conditions, Patsy would agree, but that was hardly an excuse for attempted murder, drug selling, or prostitution. There were other routes all five Sawyers could have traveled. In Patsy's own words, life didn't have to "fall out" the way it had. People aren't mere victims of their circumstances.

I have known Patsy Sawyer for eight years. I've now met all the members of her family. I have spoken with them about their lives, and have heard their perceptions of Patsy's life. Each of the Sawyers views the family as a home of immorality, a seedbed of unhappiness, dishonesty, hardship. They see nothing good coming out of families like theirs. They have recollections of experiences where children lied, parents lied, children hit one another, parents beat one another and the children, family members stole money from one another. It also seems clear that incest was practiced on more than one occasion. "Put it together," Arthur Sawyer remarked to me from his prison's visiting room, "and you get a family heading for hell because they were already living in hell." But then one learns of the last seven years of Patsy Sawyer's life, seven years of the most remarkable turning around. At twenty-six, this young woman has, well, transcended the past. She cannot shed it, she cannot forget; too many experiences and regular contact with her family keep the past very much alive within her. But her own life has changed. She returned to high school, entered college, worked jobs, and presently contemplates the idea of attending graduate school. It is a very likely outcome given her strong academic record.

It is difficult to speak about this extraordinary shift in the trajectory of Patsy Sawyer's life without sounding patronizing. She knows I marvel at her accomplishments and constantly stand on the brink of congratulating her each time another one of the pieces of what she calls her master plan falls into place. She is more than sympathetic to such a response; she knows better than anyone the magnitude of the effort, and the result. What accounts for it all, however, is her personal secret:

"It wasn't really anything I planned to do. I just started feeling, sort of all of a sudden, my life was pretty terrible, even though I was earning pretty much money. I knew if I followed along the way I was going, I'd end up right alongside my mother, so I made a change. I made it on my own, didn't tell a soul, not even my brother. I took a job in a cleaning store that paid so much less than what I was getting with Donlevy it was a laugh, took a one-room apartment, worked my way through those evening high school courses, got into college, and that was that. I had to do it on my own because I *was* on my own. I mean, there was nothing in my life that had been set up proper for me. I was like a kid trying to get out of a room with the doors and windows boarded up. See what I mean? No way to get out. So, I disappeared. I started all over again. It was like I left behind everything I had, and I was; kept only some clothes and my name, 'cause I wasn't really ashamed about who or what I was, and started again.

"My philosophy, the little it is, says that people have to start with where they are right this minute, not just from what they've always been. I mean, you don't have to be a sociologist to see the odds of my reaching anything worthwhile were a million to one. Is hitting a child bad? I was hit. Is letting your kids go hungry bad? We went hungry, lots of times. Is incest supposed to do anybody any good? We all knew a little about that, too. Nothing was good; nothing was set up the way it was supposed to be. My mother always told us my kid sister was an unwanted pregnancy. Is that good to tell your children? But it didn't matter because my brother and me, we knew we weren't wanted either. She just had us, accident or not. But when you're small, you don't know what to think, or how to think about any of this stuff. So I said to myself, look, Sawyer, the start stinks, there's not much good to take out of it, so you got three choices: Go on like you're going and your mother and father will give you a pretty good idea of how that road turns out. Or, change, become what you become on a different road. Or, kill yourself.

"I'll tell you, for a long time I did think a whole lot about that last choice. Because I could only see down the one road. All I could know was what had been; I had to assume the future wouldn't be any different. Then I decided, now hold on, girl, there are lots of things going on in the world, and I don't have to keep going in the same direction. Dammit, I'm *not* going on in the same direction. So I changed. I took fifty steps backward, it sure looked like in the beginning, but then I saw how they were really fifty steps forward. As I look at it all over again, I see they were really fifty steps neither backward *nor* forward; they were just steps to the side. See what I mean? I was moving away from childhood; not back to it, not forward to anything, not yet anyway, just to the side. I told myself, Sawyer, you have to be a little bit like the schizophrenic kid, a little of this and a little of that. A little bit of life on the low side, you might say, a little bit on the high side. But there's going to be a difference, because the schizophrenic, he's walking both sides of those two lives at the same time. It was easier for me; I only had to give up one and take on the other. I suppose I had to see the high life wasn't really the one on the top, and the low life the one on the bottom; it was just on the side of the city. So I went sideways first.

"My parents were very bad with me. Maybe they couldn't do any better, maybe it was because they always needed money, maybe it was because their parents treated them lousy and they didn't have the strength or energy to turn it around for themselves. But they were bad. They didn't make mistakes with us; the whole *thing*, life, family, the works, was a mistake—okay? And maybe deep down where I love them, despite all the awfulness, I hate them, too, and *won't* or can't or won't—I was right the first time—forgive them. I don't know about this. But it struck me, looking at my life the way I was doing there, ending up in the direction where they had sent me was foolish. Talk about cutting off your nose. I thought to myself, part of me is formed, part of me isn't; it's just as simple as that. Now I can believe all of me is formed, which is what a lot of people think, I'm pretty sure, but how do I know? I don't know until I work hard on another road, a really different road, and see just how formed I am. And if I fail then, well, maybe I'll give it up for lost. Because I came to believe I wasn't all formed. Part of me, but not all. How much was left of me to be formed, no one could say. If *I* couldn't say, no one else could say either, let me tell you. So that's where the schizophrenic idea came in. I told myself, I'm not going to be a different person, or a new person like all these articles tell you you should be. I was going to try to tack a couple of different-looking lives together. Where one leaves off, the other starts up. No more complicated than that!

"I don't really think I did anything that special. I just decided, hey, people can lead a couple lives, ten lives for all I know. It helps to have money, but money isn't all there is to it. You have lots of people going on and on living the same life. They could change even easier than I did, too. But I said, I'm moving myself into a different life, and the trick is not to pretend you didn't have the old one. You don't forget. Not one thing, not one day, not one minute! It's always there. It may not be calling you back or, like, in my life telling me you sure don't want to come back to this, do you! But it's there. Because lots of people are there, in this city, in this neighborhood, living that life. It's there because my parents and brother and sister are there, going on in their little rotten jungles, and they know they're rotten, too, not just my father. People don't forget those things no matter how hard they try. I cry for those people. I can be sitting in the middle of having a conversation and I'll start crying because I don't even know I've been thinking about one of them, or something that happened to one of us. You believe, I don't have one single happy memory of all my childhood. I mean, the only good days I can remember, barely, is when it was calm, when the war wasn't going on in our house between someone and someone else. I cry for them, about them, to them. But I have to live my life, not their life.

I'm going to make it; I can see that now, I won't fall back. Couple of years ago I thought I would, but I won't. I honestly think I could go back to the streets, be an honest-to-God hooker, tomorrow, on the stroll, and I still wouldn't be back where I was. I'd be starting a whole new low life, I suppose, but it wouldn't be the same old one, not after all this other stuff has happened. I'd be the third me, although that's not about to happen. All I said it for was to show what I meant about stopping one thing and going on to something else. Sure, it's always me doing it; the little girl in me will never go away. But there's a lot of new experiences the little girl doesn't understand at all. It's like the big girl has to explain the new stuff to the little girl, then sort of tell her, but this new stuff isn't really for you. You see what I mean?

"There *is* a kicker in all this. I mean, I have a little sort of secret to confess. S-C-H-O-O-L. See what I'm getting to? A child grows up in what you could call two homes. Home where he's born, and home where he goes to school. One fails him, he's got the other. It can work either way. But if both fail, he can call the music to an end. I was up to calling my own music to an end several times there myself. Family didn't do too much good, and I wouldn't have thought the schools were going to be any different. But they did their job. I didn't think so at the time, but they were grinding away, all those evil little school machines; putting all those facts in my brain.

"Why do I call it a secret? 'Cause when you're a kid growing up like I did, you don't have all that much you want to brag about. Wasn't too much I could say about all the folks I was living with. Not too much to brag about school either. Then later on, I thought to myself, you know, Sawyer, there's a game going on here, and everybody's playing it. I'm playing it, too, 'cause there's no way nobody can't play it. Game goes like this: Tell everybody your old man and old lady is worse than their old man and old lady, and for God sakes don't tell *nobody* you like *any*thing about school. Even if one day, by some miracle or other, they're serving some kind of pie you like for lunch, don't tell nobody. You just eat it but make all your friends think you're ready to throw it up. Play it the same way with your subjects. Don't tell nobody you like what you're doing in the classes. Teacher comes up to you and says, 'Patsy, you're really smart, you look like you might be enjoying this, you could be somebody.' You just look at 'em tough and say, 'You got the wrong kid, Mrs. Thernstrum. I can't stand this work, I can't stand the work we do. Can't stand you neither.' You're playing the game, see. That's all you're doing. Playing out your life like everybody's telling you to. With the pie, with the books, with your old man and old lady, you got to make them think you're about ready to throw them all up. You certainly ain't going to let 'em think you're smart, 'cause that ain't playing fair.

"My secret was not so much liking everything we did in school—I certainly didn't like *all* the lunches—but I did like some of it, and a few of the teachers. Not a lot of them, but you don't need a lot of them. Fact is you only need a few. Maybe you don't need to like any of them if the principal is your friend, or the guidance counselor. Course, even if they are, you don't tell nobody. You play the game out till the end, which is supposed to be when you either quit school, throw the pie in their faces, or get yourself thrown out, which I guess is supposed to win you the big prize, 'cause now you've proved how horrible *everybody* in your life really is. Got to win the game now, don't I, gang? I'm the biggest failure you've seen, ain't I?

"Good teachers, they know the game. Hell, they play it, too. Some of them even teach it to us. But some of them, they have their ways of letting you know there's a couple other games you can play, and you can keep them a secret, too, if you want. I mentioned Mrs. Thernstrum. She was somebody who knew another game. She told me once, I was a freshman in high school, coming in and going out, like I used to do. She told me after English—kept me after class like she was going to punish me or something—don't be afraid to like some of the books. Don't feel ashamed to be sort of smart. She didn't tell nobody else in the class, she just, like, planted a little seed. I don't remember what I said. Probably told her to go to hell. None of her business how I wanted to feel about nothing. I was still playing the game. 'Nother teacher, couple years later, Miss Pellicote, hated her, least I thought I did. Never said two words to me. Didn't even know she knew who I was. She stops me in the hall one day, and she's treating me like I did something bad so's the other kids won't think I'm getting special attention. Woman takes my arm, almost slugged her, pulls me over to the side, tells me, Patsy, I expect you to be taking the exams for college. For college? You crazy? I want you to try, and for one lousy day, that's what she says, for one lousy day I want you to give it everything you got. But everything! Probably told her to go to hell, too, knowing the way I was, and how you had to play the game to the day you died. But I never forgot her saying that. 'Cause what they both were telling me was, okay, you want to make a secret out of it, that's cool. But we could either forget you and let you fall away like everybody else, or we can, like I say, plant a little seed in you.

"That's what both of them did, too, plant little seeds. Took a long, long time for those seeds to grow into something, but they did. I didn't speak much at all to Pellicote, but she got her message across. What they were telling me, see, was, you can play the game, but we want to tell you we'll support you playing a whole 'nother game if there ever comes a time you feel you might be ready. Maybe they were daring me. And the school, see, it stunk like it always stunk. Nothing changed. Wasn't like the day after they spoke with me everything was perfect again, and my mother was all good and my father flew out of prison. No magic. But the seeds. Two funny old ladies, two funny little seeds. So school didn't fail out like everything else. Didn't teach me all that much, but how the hell could it? Teachers knew they were in a losing battle right down the line. But like, what they did was plant those time capsules of theirs, kind of like they were saying, Hey, you might like to see what's inside you one of these days. Might like to find out there's more than one way to go in this world, game or no game. Fact, they never did say, think about it. Neither woman did. They just took a chance. Probably took it with lots of kids. Damn strange, school. Damn strange somebody seeing inside you to where you keep your secrets, where they *know* you keep your secrets. I had a secret, too, going with my school. Used to say to myself: School, get me a ticket out of this life. And baby, make it one way!

"I think a lot about my mother. Maybe when I'm *really* over all that happened to me I won't think of her as much, but maybe not. I'm sure I won't think of her when I'm sixty like I do now. But I can tell myself, look, my parents didn't need me, they didn't particularly want me, I'm not even sure what they think about me now. But they see me for what I am now, and they admire me. I know they do. They see me as a good person, a sort of moral person, even though I did all the things I did. They can sort of put some of the stuff where I'm concerned behind them. They never lost sight of the good life, the high life. They knew what they were doing was immoral, amoral, nonmoral, every kind of no-way moral. Somehow they must have taught that to me, taught me not to forget there was another way, not that they did a damn thing to make it easier for me to find that damn other way. But they put the thought inside me. Tell you something else that mattered, two things really. They never got a divorce. They fought and hated each other, and split up, but they never married another person, and they could have. Funny how I keep thinking about that, isn't it? They stayed together in their sort of separate way. For some reason that's always meant something. It was like they were saying, we made our choice, and we're living with it, not happily 'cause it didn't work out, but we won't complain. And they could change certain things in their life if they wanted to.

"The second thing they did was never send me to a foster home. That might have really done me in. They told each one of us a million times how it was the worst mistake of their lives to have us, but they kept us. Course it didn't affect my brother and sister too much, but I think about that, too. I just thought, maybe the way it worked out, I might have stayed the way I was if it hadn't been for my brother. He took the low-life road but good. So in a way, if I wanted to be special, or different, I had to take another path. It's all too complicated. But I think about those two things. I guess I think about those two people, too, more than I admit. But they won't drag me back there. But why'd I say that? They wouldn't want to. Only my thoughts would drag me back there. They want me up here. I know they do. They better. It is really complicated, isn't it? But *you're* the psychologist. *You're* the one who's supposed to know why I am like I am. Or maybe I should say, why I'm *not* like a lot of people would think I'm supposed to be."

BIBLIOGRAPHY

ALBIN, M., ed. *New Directions in Psychohistory: The Adelphi Papers in Honor of Erik H. Erikson*. Lexington, Mass.: D. C. Heath, 1979.

ATTEWELL, P. "Ethnomethodology Since Garfinkel." *Theory and Society*, 1974, 1, 179–210.

BAGLEY, C. "Incest Behavior and Incest Taboo." *Social Problems*, 1969, 16, 505–19.

BATES, ALAN P. "Privacy—A Useful Concept." *Social Forces*, May 1964, 42, 429–34.

BECK, A. *Cognitive Therapy and the Emotional Disorders*. New York: International Universities Press, 1976.

BERGER, P., and T. LUCKMANN. *The Social Construction of Reality: A Treatise in the Sociology of Knowledge*. Garden City, N.Y.: Doubleday, 1966.

BETTELHEIM, B. *The Uses of Enchantment: The Meaning and Importance of Fairy Tales*. New York: Alfred A. Knopf, 1976.

BOK, S. *Lying: Moral Choice in Public and Private Life*. New York: Pantheon, 1978.

BRONFENBRENNER, U. *Two Worlds of Childhood—U.S. and U.S.S.R.* New York: Russell Sage Foundation, 1973.

BRUNER, J. "Myth and Identity." *Myth and Mythmaking*, H. Murray, ed. New York: George Braziller, 1960.

CAMPBELL, J. *The Hero with a Thousand Faces*. Princeton, N.J.: Princeton University Press, 1968.

———. *The Masks of God: Creative Mythology*. Garden City, N.Y.: Doubleday, 1968.

CHILD, I. *Humanistic Psychology and the Research Tradition*. New York: John Wiley, 1973.

CICOUREL, A. *Method and Measurement in Sociology*. New York: Free Press, 1964.

CLAUSEN, J., and M. YARROW. "Paths to the Mental Hospital." *Journal of Social Issues*, 1955, 11, 25–32.

COOPER, D. *The Death of the Family*. New York: Pantheon, 1971.
———. *The Language of Madness*. London: Allen Lane, 1978.
COOPERSMITH, S. *The Antecedents of Self-esteem*. San Francisco: Freeman, 1967.
COTTLE, T. J. *A Family Album*. New York: Harper & Row, 1974.
———. *The Abandoners*. Boston: Little, Brown, 1972.
———. *Children in Jail*. Boston: Beacon Press, 1977.
DENZIN, N. K. "Symbolic Interaction and Ethnomethodology." *Understanding Everyday Life*, J. Douglas, ed. Chicago: Aldine, 1970.
DEVEREUX, E. C. *Social Contexts, Family Relationships and the Moral Development of Children: A Speculative Analysis*. Ithaca: Department of Human Development and Family Studies, Cornell University, 1972.
ELIADE, M. *Myths, Dreams and Mysteries*. P. Mairet, trans. New York: Harper & Row, 1967.
———. *Myth and Reality*. W. Trask, trans. New York: Harper & Row, 1963.
ELIOT, A. *Myths*. New York: McGraw-Hill, 1976.
ELKIND, D. "Growing up Faster." *Psychology Today*, February 1979, p. 38.
ELMER, E., et al. *Children in Jeopardy: A Study of Abused Minors and Their Families*. Pittsburgh: University of Pittsburgh Press, 1967.
ERIKSON, E. *Childhood and Society*, 2nd ed. New York: Norton, 1963.
———. "Identity and the Life Cycle." *Psychological Issues* 1, No. 1 (1959), 1–171.
FEINSTEIN, A. D. "Personal Mythology as Paradigm for a Holistic Public Psychology." *American Journal of Orthopsychiatry*, April 1979, 49, 198–217.
FINNEY, J. C. "Some Maternal Influences on Children's Personality and Character." *Genetic Psychology Monographs*, 63 (1961).
FLUGEL, J. C. *The Psychoanalytic Study of the Family*. London: Hogarth, 1957.
FREUD, A. "Adolescence." In A. Freud, et al., *The Psychoanalytic Study of the Child*. New York: International Universities Press, 1958.
FREUD, S. *Character and Culture*. New York: Collier Books, 1963.
———. *Civilization and Its Discontents*. London: Hogarth, 1953.
———. *Moses and Monotheism*. E. Jones, trans. New York: Random House, 1939.
FROMM, E. *The Forgotten Language: An Introduction to the Understanding of Dreams, Fairy Tales and Myths*. New York: Grove Press, 1951.
GARDNER, R. *Therapeutic Communication with Children: The Mutual Storytelling Technique*. New York: Science House, 1971.
GARFINKEL, H., and H. SACKS. "On Formal Structures of Practical Actions." *Theoretical Sociology: Perspectives and Developments*, J. C.

McKinney and E. A. Tiryakian, eds. New York: Appleton-Century-Crofts, 1970.

GERGEN, K. J. "Social Psychology as History." *Journal of Personality and Social Psychology*, 1973, 26, 309–20.

———. *The Concept of Self*. New York: Holt, 1971.

GIARRETTO, H. "Humanistic Treatment of Father-Daughter Incest." *Child Abuse and Neglect: The Family and the Community*, R. Kempe and H. Kempe, eds. Cambridge: Bollinger, 1976.

GLOBUS, G., ed. *Consciousness and the Brain: A Scientific and Philosophical Inquiry*. New York: Plenum, 1976.

GOTTMAN, E. *Asylums*. Garden City, N.Y.: Anchor Books, 1961.

GREENBLAT, C., et al. *The Family Game*. New York: Random House, 1974.

GROF, S., and J. HALIFAX. *The Human Encounter with Death*. New York: Dutton, 1977.

HANDEL, G., ed. *The Psychosocial Interior of the Family*. Chicago: Aldine, 1967.

HARTSHORNE, H., and M. A. May. *Studies in the Nature of Character, Studies in Deceit*. New York: Macmillan, 1928.

HEAP, J. L., and P. A. ROTH. "On Phenomenological Sociology." *American Sociological Review*, 1973, 38, 354–67.

HENDERSON, D. "Incest: A Synthesis of Data." *Journal of the Canadian Psychiatric Association*, 1972, 17, 299–313.

HOFFMAN, M. L. "Moral Development." *Carmichael's Manual of Child Psychology*, P. H. Mussen, ed., third ed., Vol. 2. New York: John Wiley, 1970.

JACOBS, J. *Adolescent Suicide*. New York: Wiley Interscience, 1971.

JAHODA, M. *Current Conceptions of Positive Mental Health*. New York: Basic Books, 1958.

JAMES, W. *The Varieties of Religious Experience*. New York: Crowell-Collier, 1961, original ed., 1901.

JUNG, C. "The Archetypes and the Collective Unconscious." *Collected Works*, 9. Princeton, N.J.: Princeton University Press, 1968.

———. "Psychological Types." *Collected Works*, 6. Princeton, N.J.: Princeton University Press, 1971.

———. "The Structure and Dynamics of the Psyche." *Collected Works*, 8. Princeton, N.J.: Princeton University Press, 1969.

KAGAN, J., and H. A. Moss. *Birth to Maturity*. New York: John Wiley, 1962.

KAUFMAN, I., A. PECK, and C. TAGIURI. "The Family Constellation and Overt Incestuous Relations Between Father and Daughter." *American Journal of Orthopsychiatry*, 1954, 24, 266–79.

KEEN, S. "Man and Myth: A Conversation with Joseph Campbell." *Psychology Today*, 1971, 5, 35–39.

KETT, J. *Rites of Passage*. New York: Basic Books, 1977.

KIRK, G. *Myth: Its Meaning and Function in Ancient and Other Cultures*. Berkeley: University of California Press, 1970.

KOHLBERG, L. "Moral Education." *International Encyclopedia of Social Sciences*, 1968.

KUBLER-ROSS, E. "Death Does Not Exist." *Journal of Holistic Health*, 1977, 1, 60–65.

KURDEK, L. "Perspective Taking as the Cognitive Basis of Children's Moral Development: A Review of the Literature." *Merrill Palmer Quarterly*, 1978, 24, 3–28.

LAING, R. D. *The Politics of Experience*. London: Penguin, 1967.

LANGER, S. *Philosophy in a New Key: A Study in the Symbolism of Reason, Rite and Art*. Cambridge: Harvard University Press, 1951.

LASCH, C. "The Narcissist Society." *The New York Review of Books*, September 30, 1976.

LeSHAN, L. *The Medium, the Mystic and the Physicist: Toward a General Theory of the Paranormal*. New York: Viking, 1973.

LEVI-STRAUSS, C. *Structural Anthropology*. New York: Basic Books, 1964.

LEWIS, J., et al. *No Single Thread: Psychological Health in Family Systems*. New York: Brunner/Mezel, 1976.

LOWRY, R. P. "Toward a Sociology of Secrecy and Security Systems." *Social Problems*, Spring 1972, 19, 437–50.

LUSTIG, N., et al. "Incest: A Family Group Survival Pattern." *Archives of General Psychiatry*, 1966, 14, 31–40.

McCLELLAND, D. C. *Power: The Inner Experience*. New York: Irvington, Halsted-Wiley, 1975.

McHUGH, P., and A. BLUM, eds. *Friends, Enemies and Strangers*. Norwood, N.J.: Ablex, 1979.

MAISCH, H. *Incest*. London: Deutsch Publishers, 1973.

MALINOWSKI, B. *Magic, Science and Religion and Other Essays*. Garden City, N.Y.: Doubleday, 1954.

MARIN, P. "The New Narcissism." *Harper's Magazine*, October 1975.

MASLOW, A. *The Farther Reaches of Human Nature*. New York: Viking, 1971.

———. *The Psychology of Science*. New York: Harper & Row, 1966.

MEISELMAN, K. C. *Incest*. San Francisco: Jossey-Bass, 1979.

MUSSEN, P., et al. "Honesty and Altruism Among Adolescents," *Developmental Psychology*, 1970, 3, 166–94.

NEUMANN, E. *The Origins and History of Consciousness*. R. Hull, trans. Princeton, N.J.: Princeton University Press, 1954.

OFFER, D., and J. OFFER. *From Teenage to Young Manhood*. New York: Basic Books, 1975.

PARKES, C. M. *Bereavement: Studies in Grief in Adult Life*. London: Tavistock Publications, 1972.

PEAL, A., D. GRANT, and E. WENK, eds. *The Value of Youth.* Davis, Cal.: Responsible Action, 1978.

PERRY, J. *Roots of Renewal in Myth and Madness: The Meaning of Psychotic Episodes.* San Francisco: Jossey-Bass, 1976.

PHILIP, A. F. *Family Failure.* London: Faber & Faber, 1963.

PIAGET, J. *The Moral Judgment of the Child.* New York: Harcourt, 1932.

———, and B. INHELDER. *The Psychology of the Child.* H. Weaver, trans. New York: Basic Books, 1969.

PINCUS, L. *Death and the Family.* New York: Pantheon, 1974.

———, and C. DAVE. *Secrets in the Family.* London: Tavistock, 1977.

PLATT, G. M. "Thoughts on a Theory of Collective Action: Language, Affect and Ideology in Revolution." *New Directions in Psychohistory: The Adelphi Papers in Honor of Erik H. Erikson,* M. Albin, ed. Lexington, Mass.: D. C. Heath, 1979.

———. "Twenty Lashes for Sociology." *Contemporary Sociology,* March 1979, 8, 179–87.

PSATHAS, G., ed. *Phenomenological Sociology, Issues and Applications.* New York: John Wiley, 1973.

QUAY, H. "Patterns of Aggression, Withdrawal and Immaturity." *Psychopathological Disorders in Childhood,* H. Quay and J. Werry, eds. New York: John Wiley, 1975.

RANK, O. "The Myth of the Birth of the Hero." *The Myth of the Birth of the Hero and Other Writings by Otto Rank,* P. Freund, ed. New York: Vintage Books, 1964.

RAPOPORT, R. "Normal Crisis, Family Structure and Mental Health." *Family Process* 2, No. 1 (March 1963).

———, and R. RAPOPORT. *Fathers, Mothers and Society.* New York: Basic Books, 1977.

RIEGEL, K. F. "The Dialectics of Human Development." *American Psychologist,* 1976, 31, 689–700.

RIESMAN, D. *Individualism Reconsidered.* Glencoe, Ill.: Free Press, 1954.

———. *The Lonely Crowd.* New Haven: Yale University Press, 1969.

ROBY, P., ed. *Child Care—Who Cares.* New York: Basic Books, 1973.

ROKEACH, M. *The Nature of Human Values.* New York: Free Press, 1973.

ROSENTHAL, M. *Drugs, Parents and Children.* Boston: Houghton Mifflin, 1972.

RUTTER, M. *Maternal Deprivation Reassessed.* Harmondsworth: Penguin, Original Publication, 1972.

RYLE, A. *Neurosis in the Ordinary Family.* London: Tavistock Publications, 1967.

SACKS, H. "On the Analysability of Stories by Children." *Directions in Sociolinguistics,* J. Gumperz and D. Hymes, eds. New York: Holt, Rinehart & Winston, 1972.

————. "Everybody Has to Lie." *Sociocultural Dimensions of Language*, M. Sanchez and B. Blount, eds. New York: Academic Press, 1975.

SAINSBURY, E. *Social Work with Families*. London: Routledge & Kegan Paul, 1975.

SAMPLES, B. *The Metaphoric Mind*. Reading, Mass.: Addison-Wesley, 1976.

SAMPSON, E. E. *Ego at the Threshold*. New York: Delta Books, 1975.

————. "Psychology and the American Ideal." *Journal of Personality and Social Psychology*, November 1977, 35, 767–82.

SCHAFFER, H. R., ed. *The Origins of Human Relations*. London: Academic Press.

SCHORR, A. L., ed. *Children and Decent People*. London: Allen & Unwin, 1975.

SCHULTZ, A. *The Phenomenology of the Social World*. Evanston: Northwestern University Press, 1967.

SHANAS, E., and G. STREIB, eds. *Social Structure and the Family*. Englewood Cliffs, N.J.: Prentice-Hall, 1965.

SHEIKH, A. "Mental Images: Ghosts of Sensations?" *Journal of Mental Imagery*, 1977, 1, 1–3.

SHILS, E. H. *The Torment of Secrecy*. New York: Free Press, 1956.

SHORTER, E. *The Making of the Modern Family*. New York: Basic Books, 1975.

SIMMEL, G. *Conflict and the Web of the Group-Affiliations*. Glencoe: Free Press, 1955.

SINGER, J. *Imagery and Daydream Methods in Psychotherapy and Behavior Modification*. New York: Academic Press, 1974.

SKOLNICK, A. *The Intimate Environment*. Boston: Little, Brown, 1973.

SLATER, P. *Footholds*. New York: Dutton, 1977.

SLATER, P. E. *The Glory of Hera*. Boston: Beacon Press, 1968.

SOBO, S. "Narcissism as a Function of Culture." *Psychoanalytic Study of the Child*, 32, 1977, 155–72.

————. "Narcissism and Social Disorder." *Yale Review*, 1975, 64, 527–43.

SOMMER, R. *Personal Space*. New York: Prentice-Hall, 1969.

SULLIVAN, H. S. *The Interpersonal Theory of Psychiatry*. New York: Norton, 1953.

SYMONDS, P. M. *From Adolescent to Adult*. New York: Columbia University Press, 1961.

SZASZ, T. *The Myth of Mental Illness: Foundations of a Theory of Personal Conduct*. New York: Dell, 1967.

TART, C., ed. *Transpersonal Psychologies*. New York: Harper & Row, 1975.

TRILLING, L. *Beyond Culture*. New York: Viking, 1965.

VAN KAAM, A. *Existential Foundations of Psychology*. Pittsburgh: Duquesne University Press.

WEINBERG, S. *Incest Behavior*. New York: Citadel Press, 1953.

WESTIN, A. F. *Privacy and Freedom*. New York: Atheneum, 1970.

WHITEHEAD, A. N. *Adventures of Ideas*. New York: Macmillan, 1933.

WILSON, T. P. "Conceptions of Interaction and Forms of Sociological Explanation." *American Sociological Review*, 1970, 35, 697–709.

YANKELOVICH, D. *The New Morality: A Profile of American Youth in the Seventies*. New York: McGraw-Hill, 1974.

YUILLE, J., and M. CATCHPOLE. "The Role of Imagery in Models of Cognition." *Journal of Mental Imagery*, 1977, 1, 171–80.

ZIMMERMAN, D. H., and C. WEST. "Sex Roles, Interruptions and Silences in Conversation." *Language and Sex: Difference and Dominance*, B. Thorne and N. Henley, eds. Rowley, Mass.: Newbury House, 1975.